DIVINE VARIATIONS

DIVINE VARIATIONS

HOW CHRISTIAN THOUGHT
BECAME
RACIAL SCIENCE

TERENCE KEEL

STANFORD UNIVERSITY PRESS • STANFORD, CALIFORNIA

Stanford University Press
Stanford, California

Printed in the United States of America on acid-free, archival-quality paper

Library of Congress Cataloging-in-Publication Data

Names: Keel, Terence, author.
Title: Divine variations : how Christian thought became racial science / Terence Keel.
Description: Stanford, California : Stanford University Press, 2018. | Includes bibliographical references and index.
Identifiers: LCCN 2017012164 | ISBN 9780804795401 (cloth) | ISBN 9781503610095 (paper) | ISBN 9781503604377 (epub)
Subjects: LCSH: Race—Religious aspects—Christianity. | Race—Historiography. | Religion and science—History. | Eurocentrism—History.
Classification: LCC BT734 .K44 2018 | DDC 305.8001—dc23
LC record available at https://lccn.loc.gov/2017012164]

Typeset by Bruce Lundquist in 10/15 Minion Pro

For Zemmie, Terry, and Terell

CONTENTS

ACKNOWLEDGMENTS

New thoughts come into the world by passing through the ideas of others. I am indebted to the support of many individuals and institutions that helped make this work possible.

I have many mentors to thank. I am grateful for Janet Browne, who encouraged me to bring together the connections I pursued over the course of this ambitious project. I am indebted to Evelyn Higginbotham's encyclopedic understanding of race and American history and her constant reminder not to lose sight of the politics of knowledge. I learned from Amy Hollywood the importance of being attentive to the multivalent expressions of religious thought—particularly in discourses about human difference. From Andrew Jewett I came to appreciate the virtue of sound historical argument and to see how we carry the past into the present. Noah Feldman's lively exchange and precise criticism pushed me to be a better scholar. I am grateful for Evelyn Hammonds and her commitment to my intellectual and professional success. Elizabeth Lunbeck, Emily Martin, and Duana Fullwiley were incredibly important during the very early stages of this work. I am also thankful for both Eddie Glaude and Wallace Best, whose important work inspired me to move my scholarship on race and religion in a new direction.

I am fortunate to have many dear colleagues and friends who read drafts, offered support, and provided feedback as I was researching and writing this book. I am grateful to Sherene Seikaly, Sears McGee, Gabriela Soto-Laveaga, Howard Winant, Kate McDonald, Paul Spickard, Jonathan Khan, Osagie Obasogie, Deborah Bolnick, Kathryn Lofton, Kelsey Moss, Laura Portwood-Stacer, and Eram Alam. I was fortunate to have had Thomas Franke and David McIntosh help me make final adjustments near the very end of the process. There were also many close friends who were simply there when I needed them. Special thanks go to my brother Terell Keel, who spent many hours help-ing me sharpen my writing during the early stages of the book. Finally, my family deserves recognition for being a constant foundation of support and inspiration, most especially Jaelen and Carter.

My research would not have been possible without numerous sources of financial and institutional support. Resources that allowed me to conduct re-search and write my dissertation came from the Social Science Research Council Dissertation Development Fellowship; the Charles Warren Center for American Studies at Harvard University; the Mark and Catherine Winkler Foundation; and the National Science Foundation Dissertation Improvement Grant Science, Technology and Society Division (SES-1027045). I am also grateful for the help provided by the staff at the American Philosophical Society, the Meharry Medi-cal College library, and Göttingen University. Generous institutional support to share and develop my ideas came from the Harvard University North American Religion Colloquium; the Incubator Series in the Department of the History of Science at Harvard University; the Modern Sciences Working Group at Harvard University; and the Center for Science, Technology, Medicine, and Society at University of California (UC), Berkeley; UC President's Faculty Fellows in the Humanities; and my colleagues in the History and Black Studies Departments at UC Santa Barbara.

DIVINE VARIATIONS

INTRODUCTION

> The so-called universal ideas that Europeans produced in the period from the
> Renaissance to the Enlightenment and that have since influenced projects of
> modernity and modernization all over the world, could never be completely
> universal and pure concepts. . . . For the very language and the circumstance
> of their formulation must have imported into them intimations of pre-
> existing histories that were singular and unique, histories that belonged to the
> multiple pasts of Europe. Irreducible elements of those parochial histories must
> have lingered into concepts that otherwise seemed to be meant for all.
>
> Dipesh Chakrabarty, *Provincializing Europe*

IN 2002 the American geneticist and anthropologist Spencer Wells published *The Journey of Man: A Genetic Odyssey*.[1] Therein Wells detailed an account of the origin and dispersal of the first humans out of Africa and into Eurasia, Australia, and the Americas. He made his case based on the then-recent technological innovations that allowed geneticists to analyze thirteen genetic markers on the Y chromosome and in the process recover the hidden history of early humans.[2] The Y chromosome is passed on from father to son, so it does not become diffuse during the genetic recombination process when each parent contributes 50 percent of a child's DNA. What makes DNA on the Y chromosome useful for reconstructing the ancient past is that it remains relatively stable while being inherited through successive generations. When changes occur, most often through random mutations, they leave a trail of genetic markers that biologists can use to retrace the steps of human evolution. Using this method of genetic analysis, Wells claimed that all humans can trace their ancestry back to a few courageous humans who took advantage of changing climate conditions and migrated out of Africa in two major waves. The earliest wave, according to Wells, happened sixty thousand years ago as our ancestors moved along the shores of the Indian Ocean through the Arabian Peninsula, the Middle East, and India and eventually arrived in Australia. In the second wave, humans left Africa roughly forty-five thousand years ago, settling in the Middle East and eventually branching off into smaller groups with an eastward migration into India, central Asia, and Europe. Wells believes that cold temperatures and geographic isolation made these populations significantly paler and shorter than the humans they left behind in Africa. Eventually, some twenty thousand years ago, a small number of central Asians migrated north into Siberia and the Arctic Circle. After about five thousand years, a group of these central Asians followed reindeer across the Bering Strait land bridge into North America, thus setting the course for the rise of indigenous populations of North and South America.

The Journey of Man was turned into a widely popular PBS documentary film in 2003. It features Wells—strawberry-red complexion and blue eyed—committed to sharing the good word of his genetic discovery, explaining that despite our physical differences we are all essentially African. The film captures the steady conscription of indigenous people into a biogenetic narrative about the evolutionary steps taken by our assumed collective ancestors. *The Journey of Man* is as much a scientific documentary as it is an artifact of missionary conversion.[3] Indeed, the film puts on display a set of inherited conceptual problems that inform the core argument of this book: Universal narratives of human becoming created by modern science are derived from Christian European traditions of thought and belief that conceal their parochial foundations.

One of these patrimonial dilemmas reveals itself during Wells's visit to western New South Wales with the Mungo people, descendants of the first Australians who arrived approximately forty-five thousand years ago. With no evidence of a land journey Wells has a difficult time convincing Greg Inibia Goobye Singh, an aboriginal artist from Queensland, that genetic evidence places the beginning of all human life in Africa. In their exchange Greg says,

> If our stories aren't correct, you know, if they are a myth—the way that you guys might believe they are and we know they're not—why isn't it possible that the Africans actually come from us, you know?[4]

In a remarkable moment of candor Wells responds:

> In a way, what I'd like you to think about the DNA stories we're telling is that
> they are that; they are DNA stories. That's our version, as Europeans, of how
> the world was populated and where we all trace back to. That's our song line.
> We use science to tell us about [our origins] because we don't have this sense
> of direct continuity. *Our ancestors didn't pass down our stories.* We've lost them,
> and we have to go out and find them, and *we use science, which is a European
> way of looking at the world*, to do that. You guys don't need that. You've got your
> own stories.[5]

By "song line" Wells was referring to the oral tradition of the Mungo, who have
transmitted a creation narrative that places the beginning of humanity in Australia. Greg replies, "We know where we come from. We know about creation.
We know we come from here. We didn't come from nowhere else." The challenge of Greg's aborigine creation story is removed almost seamlessly as Wells,
who serves as both subject and narrator in the documentary, explains with detached confidence:

> Tradition rarely sits well with cutting-edge science. The aborigine song lines say
> that mankind originated here in Australia—no stories about journeys. *But the
> blood of aborigines tells me* that they've inherited a very ancient marker from
> Africa—it's around fifty thousand years old—while Africans have no trace of
> aboriginal markers in their blood. The human traffic was strictly one way, from
> Africa to Australia.[6]

There is a second scene in the documentary that lays bare how contemporary genetic science constructs a universal narrative that conceals its parochial
European traditions. Near the end of the film, Wells has an encounter with
three members of the Navajo tribe in Canyon de Chelly in Arizona as he explains that their direct ancestors came from central Asia. One of them, Phil
Bluehouse, insists,

> We believe that we were created here in the four sacred mountains area. There
> is where we came up from the ground. In other words, we were birthed into this
> place just like we are all birthed by our mother.[7]

Wells responds,

> I also have my own sense of what that story might be, using science. I'm a genet-
> icist, and everybody around the world is very closely related to each other. We're
> all part of one big family. In fact, we're all related to people who lived in Africa
> as recently as fifty thousand years ago. That's only about two thousand genera-
> tions. So you have distant relatives living all over the world who are essentially
> African. And you yourselves are essentially African. So am I.[8]

The conversation moves to Wells describing his pursuit of the genetic trail of
humankind out of Africa into Australia and then the other continents. A discussion ensues about the diversity of social life in Australia, as Wells explains,
"There are lots of different populations in Australia, speaking very different languages. They have different cultures, different myths." As the other two Navajo
grapple with what Wells has said, Phil retorts,

> Why do you call something that a people will tell you a myth, as opposed to an
> experience that they had and they relive it over and over? Rather than calling it
> a myth, would you be able to call it something else, because I have a real strong
> feeling about that—that, you know, if you call something a myth, it's a substan-
> dard event that does not have any relevance. . . . Because they are real as we
> understand them. They're not myths, you know? That's important.[9]

On camera Wells gets the last word: "That's a very good point. And *my bias as
a scientist is that I like to see evidence for things.*"[10]

Perhaps more than the text itself the documentary *Journey of Man* reveals
how genetic science produces racial narratives that are assumed to be universally applicable, seek a singular explanation for our beginnings, and disclose
primordial truths hidden in our biology. Leaving the workbench and encoun-
tering his subjects in the field, Wells goes in search of the signs—inscribed on
the bodies of the indigenous—that confirm his evolutionary story. Interviews
with natives support Wells's ideas; their seemingly static creation stories facilitate the belief and perception that genetics supplants superstition and myth. As
a scientist Wells contends that his starting point is not prefigured by tradition,
cultural knowledge, or religious belief. Instead, his point of departure begins
with an intellectual deficit.[11] As Wells explains, "Our ancestors didn't pass down

our stories." Thus, "we use science to tell us about [our origins] because we don't have this sense of direct continuity." The "we" implied here is clear, for Wells believes that "science is a European way of looking at the world." But what makes the scientific study of race European? Were we to accept the preconditions of his evolutionary story, are we also to believe that all of Europe's ancestors failed to transmit this vital knowledge about human origins? If so, what enabled this catastrophic loss of cultural and social memory? What purpose does this assumption of intellectual deficit serve?

In *Divine Variations* I show that the ancestors of Europe did in fact pass down stories about the origins of human life that continue to inform modern science. These narratives do not have a pure secular origin. Instead, they draw from Christian patterns of reasoning about the abrupt solemnity of creation, human difference, and the universal applicability of a Christian worldview. Collectively, these concepts enable the belief that human races descend from a common ancestor (monogenism) and that modern science must tell a story about the origin of all people.

Despite the evolutionary concerns that this belief in common ancestry might settle, there remain unresolved questions: Why does a void in European understanding about human origins come to be seen as global ignorance about human creation? What were the conditions under which Euro-American scientists came to be certain that their account of human racial beginnings was universally applicable? How did the modern study of race gain the epistemic authority to adjudicate between scientific and nonscientific human origin narratives? If we can provide an answer to these questions, might we also explain the history of the imagined intellectual deficit in the Western scientific imagination on the question of human origins?

Divine Variations is a provincializing project of sorts and reveals how the formation of the race concept in the minds of Western European and American scientists grew out of Christian intellectual history.[12] This was a unique social and religious history that colored European intellectual life and bled into German, British, and North American scientific constructions of race. I challenge prevailing assumptions about the progressive transformation of Western accounts of human origins into a distinctly modern secular activity, freed of all traces of Christian theology. The history of racial science, I argue, does not fit into a tidy narrative of linear secularism as was assumed by a generation of historians and anthropologists who penned seminal works in the field after the Second World War. "Religion" was not subtracted from "science" during the development of modern theories of human biodiversity. Far from being left with an intellectual deficit, Euro-American scientists inherited from their ancestors a series of ideas and reasoning strategies about race that have their origin in Christianity and continue to shape contemporary thought. Wells's assertion that he has no social or cultural inheritance from which to build his vision of race is a myth that obscures the epistemic privileges modern science enjoys precisely because of the Christian legacy it has subsumed into its own view of human biodiversity. This book makes facets of this religious heritage explicit and, in the process, provincializes the scientific study of human variation.

The Religious Prefiguring of Race and Science

This work reexamines paratheological texts and biblical commentaries from the seventeenth and eighteenth centuries, writings from early Christian natural philosophy, seminal studies in ethnology and early nineteenth-century social science, debates among twentieth-century public health researchers, and recent genetic analysis of ancient human DNA. The narrative I propose does not attempt to provide a comprehensive account of the history of modern scientific theories of human origins. Neither are my intentions to retell the entire cultural-religious history of Euro-American ideas about race. Other scholars have done these things well.[13] *Divine Variations* focuses on four different historical moments that reveal how religious and scientific epistemologies have converged on the question of race. Thus, I trace the formation of racial science out of Germany in the eighteenth century, follow its transformation among nineteenth-century American ethnologists, move through the biomedical theories of the Progressive Era, and finally arrive at present-day genetic research on the Neanderthal genome.

For the purposes of this study what is meant by "religion" and its relationship to Christianity, science, and race warrants further reflection. The category "religion" is a precarious heuristic created by scholars in the West to describe a range of human activities that are constantly in flux and not easily separated from other forms of life.[14] This book shows how Christian intellectual history produced a series of ideas and beliefs that would have consequences beyond the walls of the church. Therefore, this work is not bound by attention to conventionally defined religious institutions or figures; it focuses instead on ideas drawn from Christian thinking about a creator God, Judaism, nature, time, and human ancestry that influenced scientific ideas about race. By retracing this history, I do not intend to argue that modern scientists are somehow "Christian" by virtue of this intellectual inheritance; I have no stake in demarcating the boundaries of religious membership. This book reveals the ideas that scientists appropriated from Christian intellectual history in their effort to construct theories about human variation that were consistent with the standards of scientific truth presumed for their time.

Recognizing this intellectual history involves coming to terms with Christianity's investment in discourses and practices that draw divisions between social groups. This religious prehistory is the fertile soil out of which modern scientific views of race emerge. Yet it is widely believed by Christians and those who share its cultural heritage that to be a member of the body of Christ is to transcend racial differences and ascend into a universally inclusive community. There are biblical warrants routinely cited to reinforce this perception: "For [God] has made of one blood all the nations of the world to dwell on the face of the earth" (Acts 17:26); "There is neither Jew nor Greek, neither slave nor free, male and female: for you are all one in Christ Jesus" (Galatians 3:28). Moreover, the perception of Christianity as a community open to all and therefore beyond race has also been supported by the theological claim—widely defended across the history of Christian thought—that the races share a common ancestor with Adam (monogenism), whose original sin has been passed along to all nations. This inherited sin, therefore, set the stage for the redemptive significance of Christ, believed to be the redeemer of all.

While Christians have long claimed to be universal and inclusive, scholars have recently shown how central race reasoning has been to Christian thought and intellectual history.[15] Denise Kimber Buell has noted that the early followers of Jesus understood their community in ways that were consistent with the ethno-social thought of their ancient contemporaries. She notes, "Many Christian texts explicitly guide readers to understand their entrance into these emerging communities as a transformation from one descent group, tribe, people, or citizenship to a new and better one."[16] Buell argues that early Christians possessed an understanding of peoplehood that functioned conceptually like an ethno-racial group and at the same time understood themselves to be superior to other forms of social membership by virtue of their claims to have knowledge about the destiny of all of humanity. Indeed, we will see that this knowledge of salvation, which implicated all people, would leave a lasting impression on future Euro-American notions of universal human species and race.

Claims of Christian truth being superior to other ethno-religious knowledge had specific consequences for the relationship between Christianity and Judaism. We can see this in Jeremiah 31:31–32:

> The days are surely coming, says the Lord, when I will make a new covenant with the house of Israel and the house of Judah. It will not be like the covenant that I made with their ancestors when I took them by the hand to bring them out of the land of Egypt—a covenant that they broke, though I was their husband, says the Lord.

This biblical passage often became the inspiration for a theological position known as Christian supersessionism. According to the logic of supersessionism the truth of Christianity supplants the law given to the ancient Israelites. In the minds of the early church fathers Christians were a unique social-spiritual community who possessed a more perfect understanding of the purpose and destiny of humankind. Justin Martyr (100–163 CE), for example, wrote in his *Dialogue with Trypho*, "For the true spirit of Israel . . . are we who have been led to God through his crucified Christ."[17] If the early church was established to be God's new chosen people, what did this mean for God's previous covenant with the Israelites?

J. Kameron Carter has argued that the effort of Christians to answer this question produced patterns of reasoning about race that would become deeply embedded not merely in Catholic and Protestant theology but also in modern Euro-American beliefs about human diversity. According to Carter, "Modernity's racial imagination has its genesis in the theological problem of Christianity's quest to sever itself from its Jewish roots."[18] The consequence of this severance, Carter argues, is that Jews were cast as a distinct ethno-spiritual group, and this racialization would later create a wedge between the Euro-American Occident and the assumed Orientalism of the Jews.

During the medieval and early modern period Christian racial thinking regarding Jews had a profound influence over Europe's own self-understanding as well as its perception of native populations in the New World. Jonathan Boyarin, in his study of the religious and racial diversity that marked Spain before and after Europe's colonial encounter with the New World, argues that "the troubling instability of Jewish difference shaped both Christian Europeans' self-image and their reactions to those they encountered in the course of exploration and conquest beyond what became Europe's borders."[19] Boyarin notes that the persistence of Jewish otherness throughout the medieval period consolidated what it meant to be Christian and European and revealed the limits of Christian universalism and the failed efforts of the Catholic Church to unite all under Christ. Herein lies a paradox as the universal significance of the church could not be realized if the Jews remained Jews. Yet Jewish otherness helped clarify the borders between Christian and non-Christian identity. Boyarin has shown that Europe's self-understanding as a collective Christian unity did not emerge with the colonial encounter, as is commonly misunderstood, but was an extension of the patterns of racial reasoning constructed in the face of the Jew well before 1492.[20] Boyarin, much like Carter, argues that modern Christian European identity is the result of a sustained intellectual rejection of its Jewish origins.

What we must draw from this history is that Christian thought has been sustained by a long tradition of racial reasoning. Recognition of this tradition exposes the fallacy of viewing Christianity as a belief system that transcends race. Instead, we must see Christianity as a tradition equipped with an expansive set of concepts and reasoning strategies forged initially in opposition to Jews, Greeks, and Romans and then subsequently against racial and religious others (e.g., Muslims, Native Americans, Africans, Asians, Catholics). We would be mistaken to assume that the spirit of Christianity is expressed merely in its inclusiveness. Rather, we must see that Christian universalism entails a series of conceptual negotiations with racial difference, negotiations that simultaneously "other" specific populations and shore up the boundaries of Christian European identity.[21]

Recognizing the deep linkages between Christianity, practices of ethno-racial reasoning, and science, *Divine Variations* reconfigures our understanding of the modern study of race in the following ways. First, modern racial science is indebted to a religious intellectual history that it has attempted to deny and supersede, which I call the "modern scientific appropriation of Christian supersessionism." As we saw earlier, this theological idea had antecedent forms in early church attitudes toward Jews. During the seventeenth and eighteenth centuries Christian supersessionism shaped disputes over the antiquity of human history. During this time the Bible was an intellectual authority in European social life. Increased commercial and archeological exchange between Europe, Asia, and the Levant brought to light a wealth of historical records possessed by the Chinese, Egyptians, and Babylonians that described accounts of human history that predated scripture.[22] Human history became a contested site where Christianity's truth was at stake, as was the intellectual superiority of European social life as the paragon of civilization. English, French, and German historians would reject the antiquity of the human-origin narratives of non-European populations, claiming that the history detailed by scripture was sacred and superseded all other "fabulous" historical records.[23] For example, the great English scholar Matthew Hale dismissed the records of "primitive" people while leaving intact the historical framework demarcated by the Bible. In *The Primitive Origination of Mankind* Hale wrote,

> Notwithstanding these great pretensions of Antiquity, yet upon a true examination, their great pretended Antiquity is fabulous; and the Origination of their Monarchies began some Ages after the general Deluge; and so the truth of the Holy History concerning the Inception of Mankind, the Inception of all the Monarchies in the World . . . is not at all weakened by those Fabulous Antiquities of the Babylonians, Egyptians, or Grecians.[24]

The great Sir Isaac Newton expressed similar sentiments: "The Egyptians anciently boasted of a very great and lasting Empire. . . . Out of vanity [they] have made this monarchy some thousands of years older than the world."[25] European historians cast aside the records of non-Europeans on the grounds that the Bible provided a proper representation of human history and accounted for the origin of all humankind—any record beyond the parameters of scripture was nothing more than myth and fantasy.

Modern scientific ideas about race appropriated this supersessionist view of history—one step removed from its theological expression as an anti-Jewish disposition—by claiming to possess an account of human origins that was intellectually superior to all other creation narratives, was universally applicable, and overcame the errors and partiality of previous religious traditions. By the nineteenth century, we begin to see American ethnologists develop a scientific account of race that explicitly disavows and replaces the Christian account of human origins that preceded it. This represents what I call "Christian supersessionism" turned upon itself. Ethnologists in the nineteenth century helped seed what scientists would harvest in the twentieth century following the spread of Darwinian evolution and the professionalization of modern science: A critique of Christianity that would further remove explicit reference to religion in any scientific study of human variation and lay the groundwork for present-day myths about the intellectual deficit and secularity of modern biological theories of race. This is the unacknowledged intellectual prehistory at work in Spencer Wells's pursuit of genetic markers in indigenous populations that corroborate an evolutionary narrative believed to be universally applicable and factually antecedent to non-European creation myths.

Second, I argue that despite the decline of the Bible as a cultural authority in the Western Euro-American imagination, the concept of the creator God described in the Genesis narrative would continue to facilitate the formation of scientific ideas about race. Throughout the modern study of human diversity we find what I call "secular creationism" being used by scientists to help explain the origin and dispositions of the human races. In this secular creationism, scientists project onto nature the attributes and power of the creator God described in scripture—a God who gave shape to an earth that "was without form and void" (Genesis 1:2) and "created mankind in his own image" (1:27). In the eighteenth century we find German physicians and early biologists claiming that a teleological force embedded within nature gave rise to and shaped the formation of the human races. American ethnologists in the nineteenth century spoke openly of nature's capacity to create human types within specific

IMAGE 1. God, as architect and creator of the world, with a compass. Mid-thirteenth century, cover colors on parchment. Source: Bible moralisée, Österreichische Nationalbibliothek, Vienna, Picture Archive, Cod. 1179, fol. Iv.

environments and locations. By the twentieth and twenty-first centuries secular creationism manifests itself in the idea that biology or genetics determines the destiny and life chances of the races.

My observations about modern science giving nature the attributes of God to explain the origins of race parallels Michael Allen Gillespie's claim in *The Theological Origins of Modernity* that Christian commitments continue to inform the structures of modern life. Gillespie argues that the rise of nominalism during the fourteenth and fifteenth centuries dealt a devastating blow to the scholastic worldview of the medieval period, which posited that all life was governed by universal axioms. Nominalists believed that human universals were mere fictions, and this called into question the intelligibility of God's existence. Gillespie explains that in the wake of the revolution of thought provoked by the nominalists, modern thinkers were forced to build a coherent worldview out of the rubble of a collapsed medieval system. However, we were inconsistent in our understanding of whether humans, nature, or God should be given explanatory preference when accounting for phenomena in the world.[26] Gillespie explains:

> What actually occurs in the course of modernity is thus not simply the erasure or disappearance of God but the transference of his attributes, essential powers, and capacities to other entities or realms of being. . . . To put the matter more starkly, in the face of the long drawn out death of God, science can provide a coherent account of the whole only by making man or nature or both in some sense divine.[27]

The conclusion Gillespie wants us to draw is that presumably secular modern thinkers in the West continue to create meaning in their world either by assuming that they are God themselves or by implicitly transposing the power of God onto nature, society, or history. In *Divine Variations*, I argue that modern scientists construct race and explain the origins of human variation by transferring the creative power of God onto nature, biology, and genetics. This means that the modern scientific study of race is not merely shaped by Christian intellectual history but is engaged in a secular form of theology, a secular creationism.

Unmasking the Secularity of Racial Science

To suggest that racial science is a product of Christian intellectual history is of course a claim that sits at odds with the progressive secularism that generally filters how historians have perceived the development of modern racial science after the Enlightenment. Indeed, were one to scan scholarly literature across the history of biology, intellectual history, anthropology, and religious studies, one would find that Max Weber's account of secularization—understood as a modern disenchantment with the Christian worldview and a division of labor between religious and nonreligious institutions—has implicitly shaped how the history of racial science has been told. John C. Greene's seminal 1959 study, *The Death of Adam: Evolution and Its Impact on Western Thought*, figures prominently in this literature. According to Greene the gradual emergence of an evolutionary worldview, beginning around the time of the scientific revolution, marked the declining significance of Christian thought for scientific perceptions of race and human origins. The disenchantment of the natural world precipitated by the Enlightenment resulted in the replacement of Christianity with evolutionary theory as the prominent paradigm for understanding humanity's place in nature.[28]

Versions of this account of secularization—as religious decline—are common among historical accounts of evolutionary biology.[29] For example, David Hull's *Science as a Process: An Evolutionary Account of the Social and Conceptual Development of Science* represents scholarly work that endorses what we might call a "strong" secular take on the history of modern science.[30] Unlike Greene, Hull provides no connection between Christian intellectual history and modern theories of race and human diversity. Hull posits instead the influence of Platonic essentialism and Aristotelian notions of natural kinds as the driving force behind post-Enlightenment visions of human types that were later overcome by Charles Darwin.[31] The "decline thesis" centers on two reinforcing assumptions about secularization: Christian and scientific epistemology are incommensurable, and modernity naturally entails the erosion of religious influence over the structures of knowledge that govern social life. These beliefs foreclose the possibility of recognizing the persistence of Christian rational forms in scientific research on race.

A new story can be told about the relationship between Christianity and modern science if we think of secularization not in terms of a rupture from the past but instead as a transference of religious forms into nonreligious spaces of thought and practice.[32] This broadening would involve shifting our attention to the questions that scientific thinkers inherit and the tools used to answer them. We can then assess how biologists interested in race have been either constrained or freed to theorize about human diversity through an elaborate wealth of ideas, beliefs, and questions drawn from the Christian roots of Western intellectual history.

My understanding of secularization being linked to inherited questions borrows from the thought of the late philosopher Hans Blumenberg. In his work *The Legitimacy of the Modern Age* Blumenberg argues that ideas that appear to be secularized aspects of Christian thought are instead "the reoccupation of answer positions that had become vacant and whose corresponding questions could not be eliminated."[33] By this he means that modern thinkers have fashioned new concepts and ideas to answer questions inherited from Christian intellectual history. Yet, rather than assess if these questions can be answered under the conditions of belief and intelligibility that mark the present, Blumenberg notes the tendency of modern thinkers to overreach and occupy intellectual spaces that ought to be left unresolved. This he calls the inheritance of a "cultural debt."[34] The trouble is that the questions of a previous generation or era can be rendered intelligible, and this legibility often brings with it the misguided sentiment that those questions can be answered. For Blumenberg the inheritance of problems from the past "obliges the heir . . . to know again what was known once before."[35] At the center of Blumenberg's critique is the hope that we might reevaluate the importance of uncertainty and thus generate more open-ended forms of thought and existence that are freed from pursuing questions that cannot be resolved in our own era.

Blumenberg's observations are valuable for rethinking the history of the race concept in modern science. In *Divine Variations*, for example, we will see how concepts like "nature's formative force," or biological determinism, have reoccupied the conceptual space once filled by the concept of God that previously resolved the problem of explaining how the organic world was given shape and form. In *Divine Variations* we will also see that racial science reoccupies the epistemic authority on the question of race and human origins that was once enjoyed explicitly by Christian theology and the biblical tradition. In both these instances, and the many others explored throughout this work, modern scientists use race to produce answers about the origin and meaning of human variation. These explanations, however, are often accompanied by latent beliefs about God/nature that regularly transgress the rational limits that modern science has set for itself and thus reproduce Christian assumptions it claims to have overcome.

If we view the scientific study of race as the reoccupation of Christian intellectual history—rather than assume racial science marks a radical break from the past—the following becomes clear: Our scientific ideas about race are not purely scientific. Modern ideas about human biodiversity in science, then, are a hybrid creation built on what I call a "mongrel epistemology." By this I mean that the race concept in science is the brainchild of scientific and religious ways of knowing. Yet even this must be understood provisionally. Much like biological mongrels, we can never know in its entirety the complete intellectual heritage found within racial science; we cannot expect to fully resolve the question of where we have inherited our ideas and beliefs about race because whatever religious and scientific progenitors we identify are themselves not pure. "Christianity" is an amalgamation of Greek, Jewish, and other ancient Near Eastern traditions.[36] "Science" in the West has an equally mixed intellectual heritage and is the product of political, economic, and nationalist influences whose contributions and effects are multivalent and not fully recoverable in the sense of our ability to disclose permanent ideal substances over time. We must view ideas about race in science as a type of mongrel creation, with only part of its intellectual heritage knowable. This then means that we cannot look to race, or science for that matter, to resolve the existentially troubling question of what this living entity we call the human is in all its apparent variations. Indeed, the desire to resolve this question using race is itself a symptom of our Christian intellectual heritage.

Our desire to know with certainty where we come from has left us unwilling to recognize the Christian epistemology that has shaped modern racial science. *Divine Variations* reveals intellectual influences hitherto unacknowledged, thereby embracing the fact that we are mongrels in thought as much as we are in ancestry. Modern scientific positions on race did not take shape because of a traumatic rupture with the past, and they are not merely the reappropriation of Greek metaphysics. Contrary to Spencer Wells's belief, Euro-American scientists have inherited a continuous story about human origins that stems from Christian intellectual history. Indeed, this parochial history is in large part why modern racial science is a "European way of looking at the world."

Roadmap to the Religious Pursuit of Race

Divine Variations opens with the eighteenth-century ethnologist Johann F. Blumenbach, whose 1775 work, *On the Natural Variety of Mankind*, is often represented as precipitating the secular turn in the modern study of race.[37] Revising the human racial taxonomy of Carl Linnaeus, Blumenbach was the first ethnologist to divide the human species into five distinct types (African, Asian, Caucasian, American, Malayan). Blumenbach's racial theory became highly influential among American ethnologists during the nineteenth century.

The elimination of explicit theological concerns in post-Enlightenment explanations for human origins did not mean, however, abandoning habitual modes of apprehending nature within a framework shaped by Christian intellectual history. Blumenbach in fact deployed a form of secular creationism to explain the origin of human life. He also understood human history within the time line delimited by James Ussher, Johann Michaelis, and other biblical scholars. The persistence of these Christian patterns of thought discredits the idea that Blumenbach liberated modern science from theology.

Therefore, Chapter 1 offers an alternative account of the intellectual ancestry alive in Blumenbach's racial theories by recovering the Christian sources of his thinking. I explain how political and philosophical anti-Judaism prevalent in late eighteenth-century Germany, the transformation of the Protestant Reformer Martin Luther into an icon of German national identity, and the anti-Jewish writings of Johann David Michaelis in the emergent field of biblical geography at Göttingen University were all crucial political, cultural, and intellectual influences during the time Blumenbach developed his racial theories. Drawing on my notion that the epistemological origins of racial science are fundamentally mongrel, I argue that Blumenbach's racial theories were not an expression of pure, untainted, secular rationality. A wider view of the social and cultural setting in which he constructed his scientific theory shows that

Blumenbach's account of race was deeply shaped by reasoning strategies drawn from Christian intellectual history.

Blumenbach's account of common human origins was widely cited during the first half of the nineteenth century by American naturalists interested in defending as well as contesting common human ancestry (monogenism). In Chapter 2, I analyze the criticisms leveled against secular and religious articulations of common human descent beginning in the 1830s. I focus on the thought of Josiah C. Nott, a southern physician, early epidemiologist, and major figure of the so-called American School of Ethnology. Nott claimed that humanity's common origin, or monogenesis, was an unscientific belief and a mere carryover from the time when natural historians were indebted to Christian ideas about nature and human life. Nott attempted to establish an account of the history of human racial groups that moved beyond the constraints of the creation narrative recorded by Moses in the Bible. The polygenism of the nineteenth century marks what I consider the turn of Christian supersessionism against itself. Indeed, Nott and his fellow polygenists in the American School were the first nineteenth-century thinkers to argue systematically that the human chronology based on the Bible did not provide enough time for the various races to develop from a common white ancestor. Despite his aspirations, Nott ultimately failed to offer an account of race that stood independent of Christian thought. His alternative theory of polygenesis (multiple human origins) was also buttressed by Christian ideas about the supernatural origins of human life, the stable heredity of racial traits, and the inherent order of nature. This persistence occurred notwithstanding Nott's self-conscious effort to depart from the "ethnology of Moses."

The influence of polygenism on twentieth-century medicine and science has not figured prominently in historical accounts of the development of racial science. Yet assumptions during the turn of the twentieth century about separate human ancestry often structured debates across the United States about whether racial heredity was responsible for "innate dispositions" toward certain diseases. Chapter 3 explores how polygenist carryovers made their way into early twentieth-century medical and public health studies on the links between race and venereal disease during the American social hygiene movement (1910–40). This persistence further embedded ideas about race derived from Christian intellectual history into the methods and reasoning of modern scientists and public health researchers. At the start of the twentieth century, we find that the concept of biological determinism—the idea that the fixed biological makeup of a racial group determines the group's health, behavior, and intelligence—along with the notion of pure racial ancestors, reoccupies the epistemic space once filled explicitly by a theological view of nature. In other words, biodeterminism and polygenism were conceptual tools used to perform the same role once offered by the God concept.

This chapter also introduces the work of the African American physician, ethicist, and social hygienist Charles V. Roman, who departed from the racial logic of his time. Roman stressed instead that the idea of common human ancestry should push public health researchers to think more creatively and critically about the social and environmental factors shaping health outcomes and African Americans' susceptibility to diseases. If the polygenists of the nineteenth century marked the turn of Christian supersessionism against itself, Roman's use of Christian forms in his defense of shared racial susceptibility to disease represents an attempt to reverse this trend within the history of biomedical conceptions of race. Moreover, highlighting Roman's making a case for social causes of disease demonstrates how public health science is beset by what Gillespie has described as modernity's ambivalence concerning the prioritization of humans, nature, or the divine while attempting to explain events in the natural world. We will see that this ambivalence continues to shape contemporary biomedical disputes over whether society or racial ancestry plays a greater role in shaping health outcomes.

Despite several attempts to discredit race thinking in science, the last decade has witnessed a resurgence of what social scientists have called the return of racial typological thinking in genetics.[38] By looking at the most divergent qualities of the most geographically separated individuals, geneticists have been able to increase the likelihood of detecting differences between populations. Specifically, scientists have sought out genetic markers called single-nucleotide polymorphisms (SNPs): variations in the DNA nucleotide base-pair pattern of A (adenine), T (thymine), G (guanine), and C (cytosine). An SNP is thought to occur when a single nucleotide within one of these base pairs switches to another nucleotide. Population geneticists interested in human difference have used full genome-sequencing technology and statistical-modeling techniques to identify SNPs unique to the four major continental populations (Africa, Asia, Europe, and North America) from which contemporary humans are thought to have descended. In this most recent form of typological thinking, geneticists have used a catalogue of carefully selected SNPs to hypothesize the various ancestries (or genetic admixture) that an individual might possess.[39] The public has now grown familiar with this technology due to the popularity of various television documentaries on human genetic ancestry as well as the increased availability and affordability of direct-to-consumer DNA ancestry testing.[40]

Recently geneticists have made discoveries about ancient human ancestry that have further refined ideas about race drawn from Christian intellectual history and given renewed significance to the secular creationism that has underwritten biological views of race. In the final chapter I examine how this process has unfolded in the sequencing of the Neanderthal genome and the unanticipated discovery that mating occurred between this hominid group and modern humans around forty thousand years ago.[41] Geneticists from the Neanderthal Genome Project (NGP) claim that evidence of this encounter is found exclusively in the genomes of Europeans and Asians. Africans, however, are said not to possess Neanderthal genetic ancestry. This conclusion has given further evidence for the belief that race is biological. This chapter also traces the continuity in attempts between the nineteenth and twenty-first centuries to make sense of the relationship between humans and our ancient ancestors. I show how scientists in both centuries deployed notions of distinct continental groups and fixed racial traits to draw conclusions about human-Neanderthal relatedness. The perceptions of race at play in both centuries remain indebted to concepts and reasoning strategies about human ancestry drawn from biblical notions about human ancestry—and specifically the story of Noah's three sons, Shem, Ham, and Japheth—that have explicitly come to frame the algorithmic representations of human racial beginnings into three original groups.

ııı

Instead of a radical break between religion and modern biology on the question of human origins, *Divine Variations* argues that modern scientific theories of race are an extension of Christian intellectual history. We can see this continuation not merely in terms of the universal claims and intellectual authority that shape modern scientific thinking. It can also be seen in terms of the scientific appropriation of Christian ideas about non-Christian others, inherited beliefs about a creator God, and the relationship of human life to nature. These concepts would be translated into secular notions and put to use by German, British, and American scientists as they constructed universally applicable ideas about the racial origins of humanity. Thus, to answer the question of what makes the scientific study of race European, to provincialize a scientific discourse that claims for itself universal applicability, we must turn to the Christian ancestors of modern scientists who have guided them in their efforts to reconstruct the world's ancestral beginnings and inform us about the hidden truth of our biology.

IMPURE THOUGHTS
Johann Blumenbach and the Birth of Racial Science

THE EIGHTEENTH-CENTURY German comparative anatomist Johann Friedrich Blumenbach is an unlikely character for making a case about the Christian valences of racial science. He was surely not a theologian and did not study nature for the sake of venerating God's creation as John Ray had done in the previous century.[1] Blumenbach's professional writings appear remarkably secular; he believed that observable laws and uniform forces, not God, governed nature. Blumenbach's thinking was a product of the Enlightenment. He studied medicine at Jena and earned his MD from Göttingen University in 1775, which at the time was one of Europe's most distinguished institutions for the study of natural history. Blumenbach's doctoral thesis, *On the Natural Variety of Mankind*, published in 1795, was a seminal text for post-Enlightenment European and American anthropology. He was the first ethnologist to divide the human species into five distinct types (African, Asian, Caucasian, American, Malayan). With Blumenbach's reconfiguration of the term "Caucasian"—a concept he adopted from a colleague at Göttingen University, Christoph Meiners, who initially associated Caucasian with Europeans in his *Outline of the History of Humanity* (1785)—he offered one of the first "scientific" explanations for white people as the progenitors of the human race.[2] Blumenbach's career as the first secular ethnologist extended well into the nineteenth century.[3]

Despite Blumenbach's seminal importance for inaugurating modern secular ethnology—or perhaps because of it—very little attention has been given to the Christian epistemic setting in Germany near the end of the eighteenth century under which he wrote and thought about race and human origins. It is true that there was a structural secularization happening in the German academy at this time, during which institutions like Göttingen University broke from confessional theology and took the lead over intellectual matters once primarily in the hands of the Lutheran Church.[4] Blumenbach was a part of this institutional division of labor between the religious and the secular. He founded the Department of Ethnology at Göttingen with the intention of freeing the study of human origins from the partisan concerns of the church, thereby allowing naturalistic explanations on the wide diversity of biological life to be debated among scholars and budding German Romantic intellectuals.[5]

New institutional spaces, however, do not necessarily engender revolutionary epistemologies. Although Blumenbach was inspired by the principles of Newtonian science and sought an empirically grounded account of our beginnings, his understanding of human origins and racial variation was consistent with a Christian cosmology—a *Weltanschauung* framed by a creationist view of nature and the belief that human life was the pinnacle of living things. Scholars have noted the teleology that marked Blumenbach's understanding of nature. Robert Richards has argued that Blumenbach followed other German Romantic biologists, known as *Naturphilosophen*, who understood nature to be goal driven, logically ordered, and self-producing, not merely inert matter or the passive result of God's design.[6] When Blumenbach's theory of the organic world and his racial science are viewed as complementary parts of a larger whole, however, he appears to be inspired as much by Christian creationism as he is by teleological reasoning. Creationism (the belief drawn from the Abrahamic faith traditions that God directly gave shape to the world and all living things) and teleological reasoning (from the Greek *telos*, signifying end or purpose) are not mutually exclusive, and both are operative in Blumenbach's philosophy of the natural world. Indeed, the explanatory mechanism Blumenbach used to account for species diversity—a mechanism he called *Bildungstrieb*—effectively reoccupies (to invoke Hans Blumenberg) the creative powers of the God in the Genesis narrative. This divinized conception of nature is threaded throughout

his account of the organic world and human racial diversity. The full consequences of these creationist commitments reveal themselves most brilliantly in
Blumenbach's claim that the white patriarch of humanity was a spontaneous,
naturally civilized, and unprecedented creation. Blumenbach's Caucasian was
a secular Adam.

To account for the religious concepts embedded in Blumenbach's thinking
about race and human origins, it is worth noting the wealth of ideas and reasoning strategies about otherness that have been a constitutive part of Christian intellectual history.[7] According to Denise Kimber Buell, signifying ethnic,
religious, and racial others has enabled Christian thinkers to shore up and police the boundaries of their seemingly inclusive community.[8] Similarly, Jonathan Boyarin argues that modern Christian European identity was the result
of a sustained intellectual othering and rejection of its Jewish origins.[9] Ronnie
Po-chia Hsia has also observed that Protestant Reformers in Germany believed
they "represented the true Israelites, the spiritual descendants of the Old Testament Israelites, as opposed to the Jews of their times."[10] This claim was built on
the notion that diasporic Jews were no longer racially pure and had become
"half breeds," which rendered them constitutionally different from the bloodline of Jesus.[11]

Ideas about difference were not merely at the periphery of Christian thought
but deeply entangled with central theological beliefs. For example, by the seventeenth century, naturalists used the creation narrative in Genesis to articulate
early biological theories about the origins of human life and the biospiritual
bond shared across the races. Original sin and Adam's Fall have sat at the center
of the Christian notion of common human ancestry and the redemption of
Christ since the time of the early church.[12] The fallout of Adam's transgression against God's will was imagined by Christian theologians to quite literally
be passed down ancestrally to all races. This theological idea functioned as a
background assumption for the biological theories of the seventeenth-century
Dutch insectologist Jan Swammerdam. He proposed an account of embryo formation that argued that the entire human race existed within the reproductive
organs of humankind's first parents: Adam and Eve.[13] In this view adults pre-
existed within the eggs found in a woman's womb. Swammerdam, who was a
follower of an early occult form of Christian ecumenism, believed his theory of

the preformation of humankind within Eve's womb accounted for how humans inherited original sin: all races were literally present within the loins of the first humans who fell from grace.[14] What this history reveals is that Christian thinkers have remained invested in giving meaning to ethnic or racial differences. Blumenbach inherited this tradition and used it to form the conceptual scaffolding for his scientific account of human variation. An account of this intellectual inheritance is largely missing within the scholarship on Blumenbach's work and the tradition of racial science he inspired.

Emerging from the recesses of Christian thought, modern racial science is a mongrel creation. That is, racial science is the synthesis of an unrecognized Christian intellectual history and the modern hope for a scientific account of our beginnings. Not only did Christian thinking carry with it consequences for science, but it also provided an epistemological ground for political discrimination against Jews during the time Blumenbach fashioned his theory of human origins. Latent Christian ideas would color both modern scientific and political reasoning about race in eighteenth-century Germany. It would be within the muddy stream of this Christian intellectual heritage where Blumenbach would father an allegedly secular ethnology whose subsequent forms remain with us today.

Blumenbach and the
Self-Legislating Power of Nature

In 1781 Blumenbach published the second edition of his dissertation thesis, *On the Natural Varieties of Mankind*. In this version Blumenbach had yet to give proper names to the ancestral human types. He did, however, introduce the explanatory mechanism that would later allow him to do so. This was the concept of the formative drive, *Bildungstrieb*, drawn from a work also published in 1781 titled *On the Formative Drive and the Process of Procreation (Uber den Bildungstrieb und das Zeugungsgeschaft)*, which made refinements to an essay written just the year before.[15] In both the essay and book Blumenbach attempted to account for how previously unorganized organic matter came together to create lasting varieties of species. He also tried to explain what appeared to be nature's ability to repair itself. Blumenbach surmised there had to be a force inherent in organic matter capable of this task. Thus, he developed the notion *Bildungstrieb*, a concept that would have a major influence on post-Enlightenment perceptions of nature and offer Blumenbach a theoretical tool to explain human racial descent.

In the time between the scientific revolution and the Enlightenment the field of embryology was closely tied to the study of human origins. A key issue for naturalists was whether the embryos of mammals were preformed within the reproductive organs of their progenitors (specifically among females) or if embryos came into being over time as organic matter was organized through some natural force (epigenism).

These varying approaches to embryology were accompanied by different ideas regarding God's role in nature. The defenders of preformation, such as Jan Swammerdam, mentioned before, maintained a more theocentric understanding of life's origin and development. As God had done for Adam, the defenders of preformationism claimed that God directly shaped all living humans that were to exist. God had buried adult "seeds" in Eve's womb that only needed to be conceived later under the conditions appropriate to each racial group.[16]

Epigenists believed that organic matter was capable of organizing and giving shape to new life-forms. The sixteenth-century English physician and early theorist of the human circulatory system William Harvey developed this theory based on his observations of caterpillars.[17] At the center of Harvey's model was the idea that embryos were not preformed but emerged out of a formless organic mass that gradually developed the structures and organs of specific species. The naturalists who followed him later in the seventeenth and eighteenth centuries put forward what was called a "vitalist" account of nature. Vitalists stressed nature's nearly intelligent capacity to mold organic material into complex structures under specific conditions, thus making preformation unnecessary.[18] This reconceptualization of nature as dynamic and life producing—rather than static and inert—annexed the power of creation from God and made it an attribute of nature.[19] Nature in effect was divinized. The vitalist conception of the organic world would reoccupy the explanatory void left open in the wake of rejecting a God who was intimately involved in the creation and destiny of living things. This repurposing of the attributes of God the creator was an especially prominent feature of Blumenbach's account of nature.

Blumenbach was initially partial to preformation theory in his earliest writings on the generation of natural species.[20] His ideas changed, however, toward the end of the 1770s after vacationing in the countryside and observing various animal and plant species. The regenerative capabilities of living organisms led Blumenbach to conclude that nature directed the reproduction, maintenance, and restoration of living things.[21] It was the *Bildungstrieb* that drove this process, ultimately nurturing and preserving life after fitting each organism with its species-specific form and constituent parts. He wrote, "If by chance [an organism] should be mutilated, [it] lies in [*Bildungstrieb's*] power to restore it by reproduction."[22] Nature's freedom to organize life out of formless matter explained why animals of the same species produced varying forms and how hybrids were possible. These phenomena could not exist if each organism were already preformed within the womb of its progenitor. There must be an intermediary step between organic material and fully formed species—a step that Blumenbach believed had to be guided by some force or power within nature. This gap was pregnant with the possibility for variation and the formation of novel species. According to Blumenbach it was the *Bildungstrieb* that facilitated the creative ingenuity discovered in the organic world. He argued that through its formative force nature could turn "aside from its determined direction and plan" to create changes within species and ultimately produce new life-forms. Blumenbach believed that climate, diet, mode of life, hybridity (the crossing of two different species), and the passing on of hereditary diseases were all factors that had "great influence in sensibly diverting the [*Bildungstrieb*] from its accustomed path." This deflection, he claimed, was "the most bountiful source of degeneration," which yielded nature's splendid diversity, including human racial varieties.[23]

Blumenbach's *Bildungstrieb* was a potent concept. With it he endowed nature with the capacity to determine the form and destiny of living things. Conceptually, Blumenbach's formative drive took on the same epistemological labor as that of God the creator found in Genesis. God may have been further removed from the processes of the organic world in Blumenbach's system, but living things existed in a logical and ultimately benevolent cosmos where omnipresent forces governed the form and destiny of species. Blumenbach's *Bildungstrieb* was not a revolutionary concept. It was a mongrel one: a hybrid of biblical creationism and a secular account of life's origins. The significance of this hybrid view of nature and the origin of species was perhaps no more apparent than in Blumenbach's use of *Bildungstrieb* to explain human racial descent.

In the Beginning Was the Caucasian

Blumenbach's explicit thoughts about each of the human varieties were fully elaborated in section 4 of the 1795 edition of the *Natural Varieties of Mankind*. Blumenbach argued that every racial type descended from an original human. Blumenbach believed this first "man" was an ideal form with beautiful features and physiological symmetry. Using beauty as his guide, Blumenbach sought out the Georgian population near Mount Caucasus, thought to produce "the most beautiful race of men" where "all physiological reasons converge," because in this region, "if anywhere, it seems we ought with the greatest probability to place the autochthones of mankind."[24] Contemporary Georgians functioned as "stand-ins" to represent this primeval form.[25]

Blumenbach claimed there were several reasons for positing the white Caucasian as the original human type:

> For in the first place, that stock displays, as we have seen, the most beautiful form of the skull, from which, as from a mean and primeval type, the others diverge by most easy gradations on both sides to the two ultimate extremes (that is, on the one side the Mongolian, on the other the Ethiopian).[26]

The perceived symmetry of the Georgian skull reinforced the belief that the first humans were aesthetically pleasing. Blumenbach also understood the white Caucasian to be the primeval human type because of skin color. He claimed that animals with dark skin were less resistant to degeneration and did not readily produce successive forms that were novel. Blumenbach reasoned that this must also be true for humans:

> It is the white in colour, which we may fairly assume to have been the primitive colour of mankind, since, as we have shown above, it is very easy for that to degenerate into brown, but very much more difficult for dark to become white, when the secretion and precipitation of this carbonaceous pigment has once deeply struck root.[27]

The white Caucasian was the original human form because the skulls of his or her living descendants (the Georgians) appeared to Blumenbach as the most aesthetically pleasing and symmetrical, with skin readily capable of degeneration into other colors. Nonwhite humans, therefore, were newly formed beings—novel variations whose dispositions and traits were guided by the *Bildungstrieb* first present in the Caucasian. According to Blumenbach the diversity of our species followed the solemnity of our pure beginnings.

Scholars have argued that Blumenbach was under the influence of Platonic idealism in his decision to use beauty as a determining factor for appointing whites as the first human type.[28] Consequently, he is perceived to have inaugurated a tradition of racial science that was indebted to Greek, rather than Christian, intellectual history. For example, the biological anthropologist Jonathan Marks writes that Blumenbach's "Platonic approach to biological diversity (in which natural variation is ignored in pursuit of a transcendent form) was the only approach available in the 18th century, and would not be superseded until a century later by Darwin."[29]

Marks's claim that a Platonic understanding of biodiversity was the only available strategy for conceptualizing race in the eighteenth century is an interpretation that forecloses the very possibility that race thinking was a theological problem, as though post-Enlightenment thinkers saw human diversity as merely a biological puzzle. This oversight is a symptom of long-standing beliefs within the history of science that modern biology is a product of the forces of secularization unleashed during the Enlightenment and brought to their maturity with the emergence of evolutionary theory during the nineteenth century. Being derived from Greek thought, racial science is seen as one of many secular activities that facilitated the collapse of a Christian worldview. Thus, the American intellectual historian Reginald Horsman could say,

> [Though] Enlightenment thinkers stressed the unity and general improvability of mankind, they also accelerated the process of secularization of thinking which had begun in the age of discovery and in the scientific advances of the sixteenth and seventeenth centuries. Enlightenment philosophers defended the unity of mankind on non-Christian grounds and often challenged the traditional churches. By separating science from theology they opened the way for science to reach entirely different answers from those of the orthodox.[30]

Horsman adds that Blumenbach was "influential in taking the study of mankind out of the realm of theologians and in making it a matter of physical comparison. . . . Blumenbach's five fold division formed the basis of the work of the most productive writers on race in the first half of the nineteenth century."[31]

Blumenbach, with his allegedly secular ethnology, is believed to have inaugurated the birth of our modern view of human ancestry.

This interpretation of Blumenbach's role in the development of modern racial science has succumbed to what Michel Foucault called "the myth of pure origins." Foucault argued that too often an idea is believed to take on its purest form at its inception, as though it "emerged dazzling from the hands of a creator or in the shadowless light of a first morning."[32] This is true of our perceptions of the emergence of racial science. Blumenbach, the architect of modern biological ideas about race, is believed to have transcended the religious prehistory that captivated the imagination of Christian theologians. It is as though racial science emerged in its greatest perfection, dazzling, from the hands of an enlightened creator who escaped the vestiges of history.

The Theology of Blumenbach's Racial Science

There is an alternative explanation for why Blumenbach used beauty as a guide for defining the first human. Rather than be inspired by Platonic idealism, Blumenbach's reasoning about human origins actually appears to be a secular translation of the biblical creation narrative—a narrative that claimed "God created mankind in his own image" (Genesis 1:27). The influence of biblical creationism on Blumenbach's thinking becomes apparent when one considers an often-overlooked paradox sitting at the heart of his ethnology: If human varieties were created through a process of degeneration from a primeval type, from what variety did the white Caucasian degenerate? The answer to this question involves careful consideration of how creationism and Christian theology provided the conceptual scaffolding for the connections Blumenbach made between the formation of the earth and the development of human life. Here again Blumenbach's *Bildungstrieb*—nature personified as God—played a key role.

According to Blumenbach the *Bildungstrieb* was busy at work during the development of the pre-Adamite world, or the period of time before the life of the first human.[33] By the end of the eighteenth century Christian geologists and biblical scholars had come to see that the history of the earth (natural history) was far more ancient than what Christian chronologists discerned during the previous century by using the Bible.[34] This was a position that eighteenth-century naturalists arrived at following the discovery of fossils deep within the layers of the earth's crust.[35] As a result, scholars began to view the creation narrative in the Bible as a metaphorical rather than literal account of the earth's creation. This gave naturalists more leeway to reconcile scripture with the new theories about the age and formation of the earth.[36] The most notable position developed as a result of this reconciliation was that the earth existed several millennia before the creation of Adam. Like most of his contemporaries Blumenbach held a progressive view of the earth's history but did not develop a theory of human development that challenged the James Ussher chronology for the length of time humans were believed to have lived on the earth—which was still understood to be less than six thousand years.[37] Blumenbach affirmed a division between earth history (based on geological evidence) and human history (based on scripture), which was widespread among European and American naturalists until the publication of Darwin's *Origin of Species*.[38]

He also endorsed what was known as catastrophism, a biblically inspired theory claiming that sudden and violent global events shaped the earth's surface and its crustal features.[39] Blumenbach claimed that during the first creation of the earth and its inhabitants, nature's formative force gave shape to life out of formless organic matter. Blumenbach argued that after the pre-Adamite world had come to a catastrophic end, "the Creator took care to allow general powers of nature to bring forth the new organic kingdoms, similar to those, which had fulfilled that object in the primitive world."[40] These general powers were the *Bildungstrieb*, which following the first global catastrophe, retained some sort of living memory of the original species and drew on these forms to create new varieties:

> The formative power of nature in these remodelings partly reproduces again creatures of a similar type to those of the old world, which however in by far the greatest number of instances have put on forms more applicable to others in the new order of things, so that in the new creatures the laws of the formative force have been somewhat modified.[41]

New species, in this theory, were derived from antecedent creations that provided a template for the creative powers of nature's formative force. All of the plants and animals thriving at the time of Adam's creation were essentially degenerations from the forms found in the pre-Adamite world. The white Caucasian marked the only exception.

We arrive here at a key tension within Blumenbach's theory. According to his reasoning, humans were not present during the first iterations of life on earth. Consequently, there was no template from the pre-Adamite world for nature to draw on in the creation of the first human. In fact, Blumenbach argued in *Contributions to Natural History* that the first human was a "naturally domesticated species."[42] He arrived at this position after his critical study of "Peter the wild." Peter was a mute and highly unsocialized child who gained attention among eighteenth-century naturalists across Europe because he was thought to resemble "man-in-nature."[43] Yet in Blumenbach's eyes, Peter was simply a mentally disabled individual who had been abused at a young age and not properly assimilated into the virtues of civilization.[44] Humans, Blumenbach asserted, possessed within their lineage no antecedent primitive form. The first human was a domesticated species in which "his Creator has therefore fortified him with the power of reason and invention, in order that he may accommodate himself" to the "variety of climate, soil and other circumstances" that shape the human form.[45] Natural domestication was the birthright of the first human being.

By eliminating the possibility that humans evolved or developed from a primitive into a civilized state, what evidence did Blumenbach draw on to account for the creation of the white Caucasian? Moreover, if humans did not evolve from the animal world but were naturally domesticated, how does Blumenbach explain human origination? Nowhere in the *Natural Varieties of Mankind* does Blumenbach provide an answer. The fact that present-day scholars have overlooked this omission is remarkable given the widespread perception that Blumenbach transformed the study of human life from a theological problem into a scientific one.

Instead of an explanation for how the first human came into existence, we find the "Caucasian variety" arbitrarily designated as the "autochthones of mankind"—the original human species. But positioning the white Caucasian as the first human is not an explanation for how this original form came to be. Doing so merely provides a marker for explaining how other races came to pass from this original form.[46] Although degeneration could explain ethnic variation within the European race (i.e., differences between the Germans and the French), this naturalistic theory—by virtue of its own assumptions about descent from antecedent forms—could not explain the birth of the original white

Caucasian. Blumenbach's *Bildungstrieb* was designed to explain the development of the racial differences that appeared following the origination of the
white Caucasian.

Thus, with no clear explanation for how the first human form originated, we
must look elsewhere for clues about Blumenbach's belief. One important place
to begin is Blumenbach's understanding of the inherent design of the natural
world, which helps clarify whether he believed the traits of the first human to
be mere coincidence or ordained directly by God, a claim that would transcend
the empirical boundaries of his project and surely cast doubt on the notion that
Blumenbach's ethnology was independent of Christian theology.

It is key to keep in mind Blumenbach's insistence that humans were naturally domesticated. In his *Contributions to Natural History*, Blumenbach reasoned that natural kinds and their unique characteristics were not a matter of
chance or mere utility. Rather, they were designed according to final purposes.
For Blumenbach, this was clear to "anyone who has ever had the opportunity
of comparing the interior structure of any animal" and observed the "pre-
established harmony, as it may easily be called, between the proposed structure
of creatures and their mode of life." Moreover, Blumenbach believed there to
be "hundredfold proofs which may be deduced from comparative anatomy" to
dispute the claims of those "who supposed that the animal structure was not ordained for its functions, but that the occupations of animals were only the mere
consequence of their organization."[47] His affirmation of a teleological view of
natural kinds and the hand of the creator inscribed on their specific traits puts
into sharp relief the theological influences that shaped his naturalistic theory of
race: Blumenbach was a man of science whose thinking still reflected Christian
assumptions about the place of human life in nature and human history.

The relationship between traditional Christian theology and Blumenbach's
racial theory can be better understood if we broaden our attention to the cultural influences shaping scientific work during his time. One must keep in mind
the central role that Göttingen University played in refashioning German racial
identity over the course of the eighteenth and early nineteenth centuries. The
modernization of Christian thought was a key component of this project of nationalization, which involved purging the "Jewish" elements of Christian faith
and turning the Bible into a German cultural artifact. Moreover, the positioning of biblical studies and theology within secular institutions like Göttingen

allowed these fields to stand free of orthodox concerns while remaining "practical" for modern issues of government, legislation, and bureaucratic matters.[48] Göttingen created an intellectual environment for the pollination of ideas across disciplines, where historians drew from biblical studies, and biblical scholars and theologians drew from the methods and insights of philology, classical studies, and the burgeoning field of ethnology.[49] Blumenbach forged his theory of human descent in this setting of German nationalization and interdisciplinary exchange among an enlightened faculty that sought to make anew the traditions of the past.

An often forgotten component of the cultural context in which Blumenbach wrote his theory of human beginnings was a surging interest among intellectuals in the Protestant Reformer Martin Luther. As the historian Jonathan Sheehan has argued, renewed appreciation for Luther's work also helped transform the cultural and racial identity of Germany during the Enlightenment.[50] By the end of the eighteenth century Friedrich Herder and Johann Gottfried Eichhorn helped turn Luther's commentaries and translation of the Bible into a piece of German national literature that was consumed and discussed among the reading clubs that had formed in major cities throughout Germany.[51] Jonathan Sheehan writes that "it was not so much that the intelligentsia 'were catching up with the people' in their appreciation of this standard text, but rather that the 'folk' aspects of the Luther Bible were valorized by a generation of poets and scholars questing for an authentic biblical treasury of the nation."[52]

Blumenbach's account of common human descent from the white Caucasian must be understood as part of a larger effort to solidify the cultural and racial identity of Lutheran Germany. This nexus of Christianity thought and racial reasoning should not strike us as new if we view Blumenbach's ethnology as an extension of, rather than a radical break from, Christian intellectual history. Keeping in mind Denise Buell's claim that Christianity is not a tradition that transcends race but one that defines its borders through racial reasoning, Christian discourse had much to offer Blumenbach, and it would be consistent with the intellectual climate of late eighteenth-century Germany if he was inspired by the cultural revival of Luther into a national icon.

Turning to Luther's commentaries on the Bible, one finds an uncanny formal symmetry shared between Luther and Blumenbach's reasoning about common human descent. Luther explains in Moses 2:7 that God created the first

Gottes wort
bleibt ewig.

Biblia/ das ist/ die
gantze Heilige Sch=
rifft Deudsch.
Mart. Luth.
Wittemberg.
Begnadet mit Kür=
furstlicher zu Sachsen
freiheit.
Gedruckt durch Hans Lufft.

M. D. XXXIIII.

IMAGE 2. Front cover of Luther's 1534 Bible. Source: Luther Bible, 1534 edition, Herzogin Anna Amalia Bibliothek, shelf mark vol. 1:CI:58b. Courtesy of Klassik Stiftung Weimar, Herzogin Anna Amalia Bibliothek.

man, Adam, out of "the dust of the ground, and blew the breath of life into his nostrils. And man became a living soul."[53] In the first creation narrative, Adam's origin comes only after many days of formation during which the world was given shape and inhabited by plant and animal species (1:1–26). God's image is reproduced in Adam: "And God said let us make man in our image" (1:26). The reproduction of the divine image onto the human is the unique birthright that distinguishes human life from all antecedent creatures that populated the pre-Adamite world (1:26–28). The Genesis narrative explains that the creator's intentions for Adam were twofold. Adam was to name and have free use of all living creatures on the earth (1:28). But most important, Adam, along with his female counterpart, was to live in the Garden of Eden, freed from the knowledge of good, evil, and death (2:8–9).

God's benevolent intentions for the first man and woman are diverted after Adam's wife eats from the forbidden tree of knowledge (2:1–7). In their tragic "fall" from grace the first man and woman are cast out of Eden and dealt two separate punishments. God first punishes Eve, claiming, "I will greatly multiply pain, if you are pregnant, you shall bear children with pain and thy desire shall be to thy husband, and he shall rule over thee" (2:16).[54] Eve was condemned to being subject to Adam's dominion, much as in the animal world, and charged with the burden of giving birth to Adam's offspring. Adam is forced to labor the ground of a barren earth for his subsistence and cursed to return to the dust out of which he was formed (3:19).[55] Only after the Fall does Adam call his wife Eve, whose namesake, according to Luther's translation, corresponds to her burden as "the mother of all living" (3:20).[56] Cain and Abel are the first sons of the human race, born shortly after Adam and Eve have been forced out of the Garden of Eden (4:1–2).[57]

Luther's account of the Christian creation story of the birth and fall of mankind is mirrored in the logic of Blumenbach's theory of human degeneration from the white Caucasian. Nature's latent formative force (*Bildungstrieb*) miraculously gave shape to the human form after populating the earth many times with plant and animal life. Europeans are the primeval human type, a naturally domesticated species. The Caucasian is a perfect form out of which all other humans have degenerated. Yet unlike the other races, no other human form precedes the white European. The Americans, Africans, Malayans, and Mongolians come into being after the Caucasian primeval human type deviates

IMAGE 3. A depiction of God as creator from Luther's 1534 Bible (also known as Weimar Bible of 1534). The cosmos emanates from God's mind; Adam and Eve are on earth in Paradise, surrounded by God's other creations. Note that God, along with the first humans, is depicted with European features: Eve is in fact blonde; Adam and God are brunettes. From Füssel, *The Luther Bible of 1534*, 63. Source: Luther Bible, 1534 edition, Herzogin Anna Amalia Bibliothek, shelf mark vol. 1:CI:58b. Courtesy of Klassik Stiftung Weimar, Herzogin Anna Amalia Bibliothek.

from the intended pathway of Blumenbach's omnipresent force. Blumenbach reasoned that "it is white in colour, which we may fairly assume to have been the primitive colour of mankind, since . . . it is very easy for that to degenerate into brown."[58] He went further to claim that it was nearly impossible for those non-Europeans farthest from the Caucasian primeval type—those farthest from God's image mirrored in man—to return to the physical form of their Caucasian forebears. Blumenbach believed that "the proximate cause of the [dark] or tawny colour of the external integuments of the skin is to be looked for in the abundance of the carbon in the human body." Blumenbach believed that once this "carbonaceous pigment has [deeply] struck root," it is "very much more difficult for dark to become white."[59] Blumenbach was so confident that black skin could not return to white that he wrote, "We must not be surprised if [Ethiopians] propagate unadulterated, even under another climate to succeeding generations, the same disposition which has spread such deep and perennial roots in their ancestors from the most distant antiquity." This disposition of dark skin appeared to Blumenbach as a fixed racial trait, thereby making it "a miracle" for present-day Europeans "to contract the Ethiopian habit of body."[60]

Blumenbach's idea of human deviation from the white Caucasian appears to be the secular counterpart to Luther's belief that humans lost the image of God following Adam's original sin. In his 1534 Bible Luther depicts God the creator along with Adam and Eve as Europeans. This was no mere accident and clearly reflected the racial reasoning that framed his account of human creation. In fact Stephan Füssel notes that Luther was directly involved in the illustrations of his 1534 Bible. Füssel cites Christoph Walther (ca. 1515–74), who worked as a typesetter in Hans Lufft's workshop where the 1534 Bible was produced. Walther, according to Füssel, claimed that Luther "would not tolerate that a superfluous and unnecessary thing be added, that would not serve the text."[61] We must conclude that the Europeanization of Adam and Eve was an intentional effort on Luther's part to center whites as the original humans. When Johann Blumenbach would do the same in the eighteenth century, we must realize he was reproducing the racial logic of his Christian ancestor.

In his commentaries on the book of Genesis, Luther wrote that God's original intentions for human life in Paradise, what he called "the glory of the divine image," were distorted by Adam's original transgression against the will of God. Luther reasoned that "through sin and that awful fall not only our flesh

is disfigured by the leprosy of sin, but everything we use in this life has become corrupt."⁶² In Blumenbach's thinking one finds parallel notions of physical change of the human form occurring after human deviation—indeed, "a
fall"—from the original human type. Blumenbach claimed, "A species may fall
off from its primeval conformation."⁶³ All colored races were deviations from
the original and most beautiful white Caucasian form.⁶⁴

The inheritance of universal sin was one of the major theological stakes
of the eighteenth-century debate between monogenists and polygenists.⁶⁵ If
human varieties were not all derived from Adam, this put into jeopardy the
truth of the Bible, the universal inheritance of Adam's original sin, and the
significance of Jesus Christ as the redeemer of all human beings. Eighteenth-
century skeptics, most notably Voltaire, asked how orthodox Christianity
could be the universal truth if all humans were not descendants of Adam and
therefore did not inherit his original sin.⁶⁶ Blumenbach, one of the century's
staunchest defenders of monogenesis, was no doubt aware that his theory of
formative force remained in step with the biblical anthropology and a Christian
vision of history. Indeed, one can hear Adam's calling Eve the "mother of all
living" (Genesis 3:20) reverberate in Blumenbach's claim that deviations from
nature's formative force were "the mother of varieties properly so called."⁶⁷ Only
after being cast out of Eden, God's intended home for humanity, does Eve "conceive and bare Cain" (4:1), the first of Adam's kin born in sin, the first biological
deviation from God's divine plan and self-image. It would seem only fitting
then that Blumenbach would understand "the mother of varieties properly so
called" to in fact be deviations from nature's intended design and destiny; his
allegedly secular description of biological diversity reoccupied a pattern of reasoning initially forged by the Christian narrative of creation and the Fall.

The notion of shared human inheritance was equally important for the
biblical anthropology detailed by Luther as it was for Blumenbach's account of
racial degeneration. Both men reasoned that present-day humans have only a
partial understanding of the features and qualities of the original human. According to Luther, not only has humankind's physical form been altered since
the Fall, but humans have also lost the "exceedingly important gifts" once possessed by Adam: "namely, a perfect knowledge of the nature of the animals, the
herbs, the fruits, the trees, and the remaining creatures." The consequences of
Adam's transgression were passed down to all of his descendants, who lived in

a "fallen state" of nature. Luther wrote that God's image in humankind "was so obscured and corrupted that we cannot grasp it even with our intellect."[68] Blumenbach wrote in *Contributions to Natural History* that "no one knows the exact original wild condition of man." He offered no reasons for this claim, only an unsubstantiated belief that "mankind was a naturally domesticated species."[69] He is noticeably silent on the question of how humans came to be but vocal regarding our distinction from the animal world. Blumenbach saw that this distinction lay in the fact that "nature has limited him no wise, but has created him for every climate, and every sort of aliment and has set before him the whole world as his own and given him both organic kingdoms for his aliment."[70] There is an analogous sentiment in Luther's biblical commentaries on the creation story. For Luther, mankind's distinction from the animal world lay in the fact that Adam was endowed with the "image of God." According to Luther this image was

> [assigned] to the most beautiful creature, who knows God and is the image of God, in whom the similitude of the divine nature shines forth through his enlightened reason, through his justice and wisdom. Adam and Eve become the rulers of the earth, the sea, and the air. But this dominion is given to them not only by way of advice but also by express command. Here we should first carefully ponder the exclusiveness in this: no beast is told to exercise dominion.[71]

According to Luther, "God's image" was a mark of distinction possessed by "the most beautiful creature," humankind. For Blumenbach it was humanity's natural domestication and the beautiful symmetry of the Caucasian skull— capturing the attributes of nature's original design for our species—that distinguished humans from all other creatures.

Until the nineteenth century the Christian biblical narrative was not simply a religious way of looking at the history of the world; it *was* the history of the world—at least within broad brushstrokes.[72] As the historian of science Martin J. S. Rudwick has shown, biblical history *as* world history meant "other secular events, above all the life of society and its constituent persons, received meaning by being seen in their appropriate place within the [biblical] narrative structure."[73] Knowledge derived from nonbiblical sources was cast into the general conceptual framework established by scripture. Although the advent of eighteenth-century biblical criticism in Germany and the establishment of the antiquity of the earth with the birth of modern geology during the early nineteenth century fundamentally reversed the relationship between the Bible and secular knowledge—and effectively decoupled human history from history of the earth—natural historians until the time of Darwin continued to fit secular knowledge about human descent and variation into a biblically delimited time frame.[74] The human species was thought to be only about five thousand years old at the time of Blumenbach's racial taxonomy. Yet nowhere in the *Natural Varieties of Mankind* does Blumenbach consider the length of time needed for white Caucasians to degenerate into other human types. As the historian John C. Greene explained,

> In his time scale, too, Blumenbach remained a traditionalist. Although he recognized that the evidence afforded by mummies seemed to indicate that the Egyptian people had changed very little in physical make-up in the course of several thousand years, he seems never to have wondered how much time had been required to produce the diversity of type exhibited by the various races of the human species.[75]

We might say that eighteenth-century secular knowledge about human variation was inevitably packaged to conform to the "facts" of Christian ideas about the antiquity of humankind and the interrelatedness of species.

By drawing attention to how theological premises surrounded Blumenbach's thinking about human descent and race, it is clear that the Christian heritage of natural history played a much more significant role than is often realized in contemporary discussions of racial taxonomies during this period. Blumenbach's racial science was conceived out of mongrel epistemology, the illegitimate mixture of Christian creationism and the longing for a secular account of our human origins. It is a mistake to consider the racial typologies of the eighteenth century as merely iterations of Platonism. The case of Blumenbach, the father of modern racial science, proves that they were also profoundly Christian.

Shared Theological Inheritance, Symmetrical Racial Reasoning

Just as Blumenbach's racial science was influenced by his theological inheritance, so too were broader social and political ideas about race and citizenship within late eighteenth-century Germany. Blumenbach's ethnology and the newly emergent idea of German citizenship were committed to covert forms of racial hierarchy inspired by Christian theology. That is, the universal citizen was of the same conceptual variety as Blumenbach's scientific explanation for the emergence of all the races. Both discourses proclaimed to have a true understanding of our political and biological lives. Both were also invested in marginalizing the Jewish origins of modern Christian Europe. Understanding the political and economic setting of late eighteenth-century Germany is crucial for understanding the epistemological ground shared between modern racial science and modern political reason.

Prussia in the mid-eighteenth century was a vast and disjointed geopolitical territory transitioning into what we now recognize as Germany. The region was experiencing a surge in population and recovering from the aftereffects of the Thirty Years' War, one of the longest and most destructive conflicts in European history.[76] The conflict had stifled Prussia's economic productivity by causing sharp population declines throughout the region and virtually depleting the resources available to local princes who ruled over its many provinces.[77] This was exacerbated by the rapid increase in trade activity across the Atlantic during the mid-seventeenth century as well as by famine and epidemics that wreaked havoc across Prussia.[78] But between 1700 and 1750, the population in Prussia grew by 25 percent, reaching 6.4 million, and by the end of the century the population would balloon to 8.8 million.[79]

During this period of demographic change Prussia was remarkably weak, unstable, and lacked a uniform conception and application of laws and rights for its subjects. In fact, its inhabitants were not equal before the law. As the historian David Blackbourn has noted, "Nobles, clergy, burghers, craftsmen, peasants: all enjoyed different rights (rights that were limited and highly specific) and were subject to different jurisdictions, according to the 'estate' to which they belonged."[80] The vested nobility and princes had significant power over their local states, but there were no universal rights that extended across states and principalities.[81] Social mobility, both economically and geographically, was nonexistent. Social order was largely held together by often-conflicting privileges sanctioned by princes, intermediate authorities, guilds, religious traditions, and family ties in which Germans worked, married, and died in same place. Infant mortality was extremely high, and only 10 percent of Germans lived beyond the age of sixty.[82] Communication and movement across various states were dangerous as there was no infrastructure for safe interstate travel. The few protections subjects did enjoy were all but lost if they ventured beyond the locales they called home.

Within this disjointed society where laws were unevenly distributed, Jewish life was highly regulated while at the same time marginal to German social life. Jews were a minority with numbers near 175,000 across the various German states by the end of the eighteenth century.[83] They constituted a community set apart as a result of their ancestry, language, faith, and economic activity.[84] In most states Jews were subject to local rulers who created *Judenordung*, "Jew Statutes." These laws determined where Jews could live, the forms of economic activity they could conduct, and terms of their *Schutzgeld*, or "protective money," which was required to secure the limited privileges they did enjoy.[85] Agreeing to these terms, which revolved largely around their ability to perform specific economic services, Jews were allowed internal autonomy and could establish synagogues, schools, and cemeteries free of outside influence.[86] The status and rights of the Jews depended on their ability to reside in a given locale. This privilege, however, was entirely dependent on the whims of a local authority. Most Jews were unable to secure this right, and a great number were effectively homeless and forced into a stateless existence with fundamentally no protections, rights, or privileges.[87] Throughout the eighteenth century, Jews could not settle in major German states, which included Bavaria, Saxony, and Wurttemberg.[88] Although the largest community of European Jews was found in Germany, their numbers were restricted by legislative enactments that controlled the number of sons allowed to marry.[89] These enactments favored wealthier Jews with the means to pay *Schutzgeld*.

By the mid-eighteenth century some semblance of social and political change was on the horizon, change that would bring more cohesiveness and unity across the German states. Key to this transformation were the legal, economic, and political reforms set in motion by King Frederick II. Frederick the Great was a curator of the arts and sciences who believed modern government should be inspired by Enlightenment principles rather than traditional religious orthodoxy or the hereditary rights of the nobility.[90] Frederick II believed that the social order should emanate from a state that was efficient, enlightened, and bound by laws that encouraged and inspired the allegiance of its citizens. To this end he pushed for a new legal code, which culminated in the General Land

Laws, published eight years after his death in 1794.[91] These codes encapsulated Frederick's aspirations for modern statehood, which he carried throughout his rule over the Prussian Empire between 1740 and 1786. Frederick hoped to establish a legal system that was more enlightened than the religiously grounded communities of justice, which existed in the Old Reich. At the same time he hoped to provide a coherent set of rights that overcame the inconsistent forms of protections applied arbitrarily across the various German states. As the historian Jonathan Sheehan has noted, Frederick II "sought to create a new kind of man, a citizen—what significantly enough, Germans called a Staatsbürger—who would exist outside the particularist confines of family, caste, or community."[92]

Jonathan Hess has shown that the emergence of the German state involved reconfiguring its theological relationship and civic responsibility to Jews whose perceived ethnocentrism, backwardness, and moral degeneracy provided German intellectuals with the problem of developing a secular ideal of universal citizenship that could transcend the perceived limits of Jewish identity.[93] If the terms of German citizenship were to be broad enough to gain the allegiance of all its subjects, then the norms of this political community could not be determined by any one member. At least this was the ideal form of political membership. In practice, however, Jews were signified as an especially problematic racial and religious other, whose cultural and social particularity had to be renounced to gain access to protections of the new body politic. This was consistent with the reasoning strategies of Christian intellectual history in which Jewish life served as the essential other against which Christian thinkers could shore up and police the boundaries of its ideal political order. What emerged at the end of the eighteenth century was a vision of German citizenship that was uniquely modern yet profoundly Protestant in its claim to having created a set of universal values that transcended the cultural and social life of Jews. Thus, German political identity at this time was not merely a problem of political philosophy; it was also a racial problem intimately tied to Europe's Christian theological heritage. As Hess notes, "In considering the integration of Jews into a modern state, Germans were necessarily dealing with the legacy of Christian universalism, with Christianity's claim to normative status in the modern world."[94] The universal values and perceptions of the modern subject following the Enlightenment were continuations of Christian intellectual history, not a rupture or radical departure.

In this climate of legislative and bureaucratic modernization the German academy would play an increasingly important role in establishing a common national culture that would unify the fragmented social and political landscape and eventually challenge the authority of the vested nobility.[95] The University at Göttingen was an important site for shaping the national and racial identity of what would eventually become modern Germany.[96] It was also the institution where Blumenbach spent his entire professional career. One of the preeminent academic institutions in Europe, Göttingen constituted a uniquely modern infusion of the secular and sacred. Created at the behest of King George II in 1734, by the mid-eighteenth century Göttingen (originally called Georgia Augusta) was responsible for the scientization (*Verwissenschaftlichung*), deconfessionalization (*Entkonfessionalisierung*), and nationalization (*Verstaatlichung*) of the generation of bureaucrats, legislators, and intellectuals ascending into positions of leadership during the reign of Frederick II. Göttingen was also home to one of the most innovative departments of academic theology during the Enlightenment, due in large part to the biblical scholarship of Johann David Michaelis.[97]

Michaelis was the leading Orientalist scholar of his generation, a field devoted to studying the linguistic, cultural, and philosophical traditions of the Middle East, South Asia, and Southeast Asia. He was the son of a Lutheran theologian and Orientalist, came of age under the influence of pietism, and would later be inspired by English deism. He wrote widely on ancient law, the philosophy of language, and theology. Michaelis was responsible for establishing the academic study of Hebrew during a time when university reformers devalued the primacy of academic theology.[98] Theologians and biblical scholars at Göttingen, however, were unlike other European faculty during the Enlightenment. Rather than engage in apologetics or scorn biblical knowledge, Göttingen biblical scholars such as Michaelis attempted to reform and inspire a new appreciation of Christian orthodoxy that made theology and the Bible a relevant resource for understanding modern aesthetics, political power, and legal rationality and fostering a historical understanding of society. The legal reforms proposed by Michaelis in the wake of Frederick II were racialized and involved removing the Jewish origins of European political reason.[99]

In 1745, at the age of twenty-eight, Michaelis joined Göttingen as an assistant professor of Oriental languages. Moving up the ranks of the academy, eventually directing the Academy of Sciences at Göttingen, Michaelis remained on the faculty until his death in 1791. Blumenbach arrived there in 1776 at the age of twenty-four and near the twilight of Michaelis's career. Blumenbach held the same academic chair for six decades, and he and Michaelis were colleagues for fifteen years; this was enough time for Blumenbach to witness the transformations taking place in Christian scholarship at Göttingen under the leadership of Michaelis.[100]

One of Michaelis's significant contributions to the emerging field of historical biblical criticism came in the form of a six-volume commentary on the laws of Moses, published between 1770 and 1775. Michaelis wrote *Mosaisches Recht* with the intention of reshaping the European court system and using the conceptual tools of the Enlightenment to reform penal codes across the German states.[101] In this regard, Michaelis's work as an Orientalist reflects the larger national interest of legal reform inspired by Frederick II. When *Mosaisches Recht* was published, the laws of Moses were still regarded as divine law and were viewed as important in many states across Europe.[102] Michaelis sought to reframe the authority of Mosaic law by historicizing its origins and in the process separate its connection to and authority over present-day forms of German legal reasoning. To this end Michaelis reconstructed Moses as a cultural ambassador between the ethnic and theological traditions of the ancient Israelites and the legislative wisdom of the Egyptian world:

> When, therefore, I fully consider what in [Moses's] system is new and unknown to the ancestors of the Israelites, and more especially what displays the most remarkable proofs of a highly refined legislative wisdom, I am compelled to ascribe it in a great measure to Egyptian experience. . . . If we but knew more of the comprehensive, and far-extended legislative knowledge of [the Egyptians], very probably our own political system, so far at least as connected with agriculture, and as directed to the peaceful increase of our internal strength as a nation, might receive material improvement.[103]

The purpose of this distinction between Israelite and Egyptian legislative wisdom was to identify pre-Jewish forms of governance that could inspire modern-day economic and legal reforms in Lutheran Germany. During the second half of the eighteenth century new innovations in planting and farming led to the commercialization of crops in Germany and made agricultural production a remarkably profitable enterprise. By the end of the eighteenth century three hundred thousand tons of grain were being shipped each year out of Danzig, Elbing, and Konigsberg.[104] Michaelis was an advocate for German economic independence that would be centered on domestic crop production.[105] With the emerging profitability of agriculture across Germany Michaelis believed that the Egyptians, who apparently also thought highly of domestic crop production as a means to achieve economic autonomy, could be of value to the contemporary statesman, farmer, and landed aristocracy.

Beyond reading political and economic interests back onto the ancient world, Michaelis tried to identify forms of knowledge that predated Jewish law and in the process diminished and displaced the authority of ancient Israel for contemporary Lutheran Germany. As the historian Jonathan Hess has shown, Michaelis sought to undermine the lingering hold that the laws of the ancient Israelites had over the emergent Protestant German nation-state, ultimately "purging the contemporary judicial system of traces of its Oriental heritage." Michaelis thus can be understood as engaging in "a project of political supersessionism, a supplement to the Pauline pronouncement on Jewish law that accomplished for the realm of jurisprudence what early Christianity did for the realm of religion."[106] Hess powerfully draws our attention to how Michaelis envisioned a reformed German legal system that would supersede and supplant the laws of Moses by excavating and adopting the Egyptian forms of jurisprudence that predate the laws governing the ancient Israelites.

This displacement of Jewish thought also manifests in Michaelis's writings on biblical geography—at the time a subdiscipline of academic theology that attempted to fuse biblical criticism and the emergent field of modern geology to identify the present-day location of events that took place in the Bible.[107] In the year before Blumenbach published *On the Natural Varieties of Mankind*, Michaelis completed the second of two influential volumes written between 1769 and 1780 that attempted to map out the drama of the earth's creation as detailed in the Bible. In these works Michaelis eliminated what he held to be the distorting influences of "Jewish mysticism" over scriptural accounts of the earth's creation. In this effort Michaelis placed the Garden of Eden in the region comprising Kashmir and Tibet. He also claimed that Abraham's native country, Chaldaea, was near the Black Sea toward the Caucasus, not Mesopotamia, the implication being that Abraham was white. The historian H. F. Augstein has noted that Michaelis's attempt to Europeanize the patriarchs of the ancient

Israelites was taken seriously by German intellectuals at Göttingen and influenced Blumenbach's decision to designate the Georgian population as the immediate descendants of the first human.[108]

This attempt to Europeanize the beginning of human history took place in an openly anti-Jewish political climate. By the end of the eighteenth century German statesmen were occupied by debates over the emancipation and political integration of Jews into an emergent modern European state.[109] At the center of the controversy was a famous proposal written in 1781, *On the Civic Improvement of the Jews,* by Christian Wilhelm Dohm, a politically ambitious civil servant of the Prussian state inspired by the ideals of the Enlightenment. Dohm argued that the moral, political, and physical state of degeneracy that marked European Jews was the result of their oppression and neglect at the hands of Christian rulers who discriminated against them because of their religious and cultural differences. To redress their disenfranchisement, Dohm put forth a comprehensive political solution that demanded the state intervene on their behalf, granted Jews civil protections under the law, required that they serve in the military, and proposed means to transition them into the agricultural economy, thereby moving them out of the practice of trade and moneylending. Dohm had previously collaborated with his colleague and friend Moses Mendelssohn to intervene on behalf of Alsatian Jews living in French territory, who were facing a current of anti-Jewish sentiment. Dohm's *On the Civic Improvement of the Jews* was translated into French in 1782 and would sit at the center of several French treatises that eased some anti-Jewish restrictions and ultimately set the stage for the much larger debates on Jewish emancipation that ensued in the aftermath of the French Revolution.[110]

At stake in Dohm's proposal was the viability of a modern secular conception of citizenship and the capacity of the state to transform its citizenry. If the Jews, who were perceived as morally, culturally, and physically degenerate, could be changed into productive citizens in Germany and France, this would demonstrate the success and superiority of a modern, secular state founded on the universal values of the Enlightenment.[111]

Of course, not all of Dohm's contemporaries shared his vision about the regeneration and integration of the Jew into the modern state. In fact, Michaelis proved to be one of the more vocal critics of Dohm's proposal. In 1782 Michaelis published a forty-page refutation of Dohm's proposal in *Oriental*

and Exegetical Library, a highly regarded journal edited by Michaelis himself.[112] His critique revolved around the perceived separatist nature of Jewish
law and the inherent biological differences of Jews. Drawing on arguments
made in Mosaic law, Michaelis insisted that Jewish law made Jews' integration
into the secular state as citizens impossible, as they would remain a nation
within a nation. Drawing on the racial reasoning charted by Blumenbach in
the second edition of the *Natural Varieties*, published just the year before,
Michaelis argued that the effects of the climate of ancient Israel had rendered
modern Jews physically unfit to serve in the military or be successful in the
domestic agricultural economy. Michaelis's solution to the "Jewish Problem"
was the relocation of Jews to colonies in the Caribbean where a climate similar to that of ancient Israel would enable them to be economically productive
for the German state.[113]

Given the Jews' small numbers and marginalization across German states,
it seems surprising that they would occupy such a large space within the burgeoning German nationalist imagination. This is a question raised by Hess,
who insightfully observed, "The project of Jewish emancipation provided the
ultimate test, in practice, of the rational ideals of the Enlightenment, the perfect arena for speculating about translating the lofty premises of Enlightenment
universalism into concrete practice."[114] Jews were the ideal other to conceive of
the prospects and limits of universal citizenship.

It is imperative that we see the conceptual displacement of the Jew during
the second half of the eighteenth century (as in Michaelis's *Mosaisches Recht*)
and the call for their civic conversion (as in Dohm's proposal) as being consistent with the antecedent racializing practices of Christian intellectual history.
Again, these were practices in which the signification of ethnic, religious, and
racial others enabled Christian thinkers to shore up and police the boundaries of their seemingly inclusive community. Jews occupied a precarious place
within the budding modern German imagination: They were actively being
written out of German intellectual history while at the same time sat at the center of debates over the limits of modern secular citizenship. The simultaneous
denigration and use of Jewish life to shore up the boundary of German identity
also appear in Blumenbach's racial ethnology.

Indeed, of the many ethnic groups noted in *Natural Varieties*, Jews appear
literally in the margins of Blumenbach's ethnology. Jews are white, a point that

must be surmised from Blumenbach's mentioning in a footnote in the 1775 edition that the white variety includes "that part of Asia which lies toward us, this side of the Obi, the Caspian sea, mount Taurus and the Ganges, also northern Africa."[115] In the final 1795 edition the "white variety" would take on the name "Caucasian." Yet Blumenbach makes special note to argue in this final edition that Jews constitute a peculiar variety of Caucasian. Unlike the other white races, they appear incapable of transformation into different varieties and lack the aesthetic comeliness of their German counterparts:

> The ancient Germans gave formerly instances of the unadulterated countenance of nations unaffected by any union with any other nation, and to-day the genuine Zingari, inhabitants of Transylvania do the same; and above all the nation of the Jews, who, under every climate, remain the same as far as the fundamental configuration of face goes, remarkable for a racial character almost universal, which can be distinguished at the first glance even by those little skilled in physiognomy, although it is difficult to limit and express by words.[116]

Blumenbach elaborates on this racial character in a footnote to the 1795 edition:

> The great artist Benjamin West, President of the Royal Academy of Arts, with whom I conversed about the racial face of the Jews, thought that it above all others had something particularly goat-like about it, which he was of opinion lay not so much in the hooked nose as in the transit and conflux of the septum which separates the nostrils from the middle of the upper lip.[117]

For Blumenbach, Jews possessed fixed racial traits whose recognition was common sense to even the most unscientific observer, and their perseverance and uniformity nearly baffle the skilled ethnologist. Jews are white Caucasians, but lack the pluripotency to yield new racial forms and blend seamlessly into other human varieties. Like in the surrounding political climate the Jew was both displaced and provisionally integrated into Blumenbach's theory of human diversity.

Blumenbach's Eurocentric ethnology was crafted during a time when Germany attempted to create legal and economic stability over a vast and fragmented territory, populated by subjects ruled by various principalities and regional authorities. While Blumenbach used his theologically loaded *Bildungstrieb* to bring order and coherence to the natural world and defend the biological unity of the races, Germany's central leadership looked to create modern legislation founded on the ideal of citizenship, which in turn established order and regularity in the lives of those within Germany's border. The former legislated biological order; the latter, political stability. Both were invested in race, and both were forms of governance that reoccupied the conceptual space once held explicitly by Christian ideas. The formal symmetry shared by Blumenbach's *Bildungstrieb* and the ideal of citizenship belies the purity of racial science, revealing instead the epistemological link between Christian intellectual history and modern attempts to conceptualize our biological and political selves.

Racial Science as Christian Theology by Other Means

Blumenbach is accredited with the initial articulation of contemporary scientific divisions of the human species, whose roots are found in the eighteenth century. Like all roots, however, they are covered in the soil that nurtured them. Blumenbach's racial typologies, although based on empirical observation and accounted for by his theory of *Bildungstrieb*, were framed by a long-standing tradition of Christian opposition to the Jew, ideas of common human descent, human distinction from the animal world, and the recent creation of human life.

The retention of these ideas should force us to rethink the claim that Blumenbach—as an Enlightenment figure—separated science from theology and positioned anthropology on purely secular grounds. [118] Although Blumenbach adhered to the norms of naturalistic observation for his theory of racial formation, his ideas continued to be bookended by Christian assumptions. This is a form-content issue. Surely the content of his theory was secular in the sense of being an expression of naturalistic philosophy and reliant on empirical observation. However, the rational forms of his argument—the general parameters of his thinking about the origin and ends of human life, his aspirations to create a universal story of human becoming that transcends the chronologies of Jewish and ethnic groups, his belief that the original humans have no antecedent form—remained delimited by Christian thought. Unlike Darwin nearly a century later, Blumenbach was not of the mind that humans evolved out of the animal world or that an "ape-man" preceded the human form. There is no evidence of a complete break in Blumenbach's thinking from Christian theology.

The typological thinking epitomized in the thought of Blumenbach, particularly with its covert harboring of Christian racial reasoning, would carry over into the nineteenth century and aid naturalists in their attempt to rank and classify the various racial groups. The racial theories of the eighteenth century, which turned human differences into scientific objects of study, sowed the seeds for what would become nineteenth-century polygenist accounts of human origins that explicitly renounced the supernaturalism of the Christian creationist narrative and with it the belief in common human descent. American polygenism represents Christian universalism turned upon itself. Instead of Judaism becoming the target of displacement and negation, as we saw among German intellectuals in the eighteenth century, Christianity would become a site of contestation for American ethnologists looking to carve space for a science of human becoming that transcended the assumed limits and backwardness of religious orthodoxy.

2

SUPERSEDING CHRISTIAN TRUTH
The Quiet Revolution of Nineteenth-Century American Science of Race

AMERICAN ETHNOLOGISTS in the nineteenth century grasped one of the shortcomings of the biblical narrative that eighteenth-century naturalists took for granted: Common descent from a shared ancestor could not be accounted for under the Christian time line of recent human creation. Racial diversity appeared too extensive for the first human to have turned into the various populations alive during the nineteenth century—and to do so in less than six thousand years. This paradox was not lost on nineteenth-century American polygenists who believed in separate human creation events. Josiah Clark Nott (1804–73), an American naturalist and renowned surgeon, took as his mission to bring this problem to the attention of the American public and in the process transcend the hold of Christianity over the scientific imagination and the modern study of race.

His first chance came in the winter of 1844. Nott was asked by the Mobile Franklin Society to participate in a lecture series for the educated and well-to-do citizens of his hometown in Alabama. Nott agreed to the invitation and later published his *Two Lectures on the Natural History of the Caucasian and Negro Races*. These lectures would later give Nott the reputation of America's most vocal critic of the theory of common human ancestry. Just a decade earlier, the English-born American paleontologist George Robbins Gliddon (1809–57) discovered Egyptian paintings depicting each of the major races with the same traits and characteristics seen in the mid-nineteenth century.[1] With Gliddon's discovery in mind, Nott argued in his lectures that these Egyptian depictions either meant that each of the various races acquired its unique traits in the few centuries between the Deluge and the life of Moses or that these paintings were proof that each race had been created, from the very beginning, with permanent and distinct traits and therefore did not share an ancestor.[2]

Nott argued that under the biblical time line monogenists were forced to claim that either the environment was capable of rendering different human forms in a considerably short period of time or the various racial groups were created instantaneously through a "direct act of providence." Nott found neither explanation satisfactory, as both contradicted common sense and lacked empirical evidence.[3] Nott was on to something. There were no compelling arguments during the early nineteenth century explaining if and how long it took environmental factors to create a new racial group. Neither was there any consensus among naturalists on how such changes were passed down to the succeeding generations.[4] Moreover, the idea that the creator could transgress natural law was unpalatable to nineteenth-century anatomists and physicians such as Nott who held a refined appreciation for scientific methodology.

Rather than concede the rapid emergence of racial groups through environmental factors or assume the work of direct supernatural intervention, Nott turned to an alternative hypothesis charted initially by his colleague Samuel Morton (1799–1851), the esteemed anatomist based in Philadelphia, who by 1839 began to question the plausibility that races could degenerate into other types.[5] Following Morton, Nott declared, "There is a Genus, Man, comprising two or more species," and each racial group possessed a unique ancestor. With this polygenist understanding of human origins Nott wanted to put to rest, once and for all, the theory of common human ancestry by showing the limits of the biblical time line of human descent and the incapacity of humans to turn into other racial forms, let alone within a matter of a few centuries. Nott emphatically claimed that under no conditions should we assume that the physical effects of the environment on the human form could "change a White man into a Negro."[6]

American polygenism was a provocative scientific movement whose controversial ideas about the separate origins of the human races fomented controversy among naturalists and the lay public beginning in the 1830s. Charles Caldwell, Samuel George Morton, Samuel A. Cartwright, George Gliddon,

Josiah C. Nott, and Louis Agassiz were its leading theorists. This group of scientific men took up a rigorous study of the various human populations across the globe and worked collaboratively to develop the idea that racial variation stemmed from immutable physical differences passed down from one generation to the next, and therefore the races could not have shared an ancestor. With their doubts concerning the biblical account of creation, skepticism toward shared human ancestry, and insistence that racial traits were the fixed design of nature, American polygenists called into question the persistent Christian theological commitments that shaped scientific ideas about human racial ancestry.[7] Polygenism was not a temporary moment within the history of science but grew out of an unresolved conflict dating back to the seventeenth century—a conflict between a sacred account of human history and secular knowledge from non-European cultures that called into question the truth and primacy of the Christian creation narrative.[8] American polygenists were similarly faced with the challenge of reconciling Christian ideas about recent human creation and new evidence from the skulls of the different races suggesting common ancestry was implausible. They believed this reconciliation betrayed sound logic and reason, ultimately forcing science to endorse common human ancestry on religious grounds.

Josiah Nott was particularly vocal and passionate about the need for the study of race to overcome the trappings of its Christian theological heritage and affirm a consistently secular account of our origins or, as Nott put it, "to cut loose the natural history of mankind from the Bible, and to place each upon its own foundation, where it may remain without collision or molestation."[9] With this mission in mind Nott was committed to popularizing the theory of separate human creations among scientists, proslavery politicians, legislators, and the vested elite. By 1851 he became a leading voice of American polygenism, synthesizing and defending its main premises against critics who upheld traditional Christian ideas regarding shared human origins.[10] Nott was one of the first American naturalists to publicly declare that modern science and the Bible were at odds concerning the study of race.[11]

It would seem that Nott and his fellow polygenists would be at pains to distance themselves from Christian thinking. But we find that much as it was for Johann Blumenbach, the religious intellectual history they inherited could not be so easily cast aside; indeed, it made the dilemma of race intelligible in the first place. Common human ancestry could be a problem for polygenists only as long as they implicitly believed that creation of humans was recent and that our species was ontologically distinct from the animal world. The farther in the past one placed human beginnings, as Darwin would do a few decades later, the more time there was for different racial traits to emerge from an original ancestor. Nott and his colleagues, much like Blumenbach, did not endorse the ancient antiquity of the human race nor did they believe the human form was derived from animals. Moreover, the racial theories of the American polygenists were fundamentally premised on a divinized understanding of organic life that *reoccupied* (to invoke Blumenberg) the power and labor of the God in the Genesis narrative. Nott's ethnology—and the American brand of polygenism he represented—remained squarely within the tradition of Christian ideas about the natural world from which he intended to emancipate race thinking

The case of American polygenism illustrates the degree to which modern racial science is indebted to a religious intellectual history it has tried to deny and supersede. In the work of Nott and his colleagues we begin to see how a secular understanding of race shifts from being achieved by a denial of the Jewish origins of modern thought—as we saw with Blumenbach and Johann Michaelis in the previous century—to a denial of Christianity itself. American polygenists helped seed what would be carried to full term in the next century following the spread of Darwinian evolution and the professionalization of modern science: a scientific understanding of race whose objectivity and claim to truth were secured through an outright disavowal and replacement of the religious intellectual history that came before it. The racial thinking of American polygenism is a manifestation of Christian supersessionism turned upon itself—an attack on its own theological foundations that would further remove explicit reference to religion and lay the groundwork for the present-day misunderstanding about the secularity of biological theories of race.

The Bible and the "Science" of Human Origins

The first polygenists were not Americans. In the seventeenth century Isaac de La Peyrère, a Calvinist of Portuguese Jewish decent from Bordeaux, was the first to offer a systematic defense of the theory of separate human origins.[12] In 1655 La Peyrère published his heretical treatise *Prae-Adamitae* (Men before Adam). Using biblical criticism and cartography, he concluded that races of men were created before the birth of Adam. The grounds for La Peyrère's poly-genist theory rested on his ability to reconcile two ambiguous biblical passages: Paul's Epistle to the Romans, where it is suggested that human sin existed in the world before Adam (Romans 5:12–14); and the implication in the book of Genesis 4:17 that Cain took a wife from a population not derived from Adam's stock.[13] La Peyrère reasoned that ceremonial Judaism existed before the birth of Adam through various laws and ordinances given to pre-Adamite people. The fall of humankind, however, occurred only after Adam's unique transgression against God's law in the Garden of Eden.

La Peyrère's polygenist theory was innovative not simply because he posited the existence of humans before Adam. He was also bucking the trend common among European biblical scholars and historians who dismissed the "pagan" chronicles of the Egyptians, Greeks, Babylonians, Chinese, and Americans be-cause they placed humans on earth thousands of years before the Christian chronology.[14] To deal with the challenges these ancient chronicles posed, Eu-ropean historians such as Georg Horn (1620–70) and Giovanni Battista Vico (1668–1744) made a distinction between "fabulous history" and "sacred his-tory."[15] Fabulous history referred to all accounts of human history that fell be-yond the time line narrated in the Judeo-Christian scriptures. Sacred history was considered factually true and believed to be the length of time actually lived by humankind according to the biblical narrative. In 1650, just five years before the publication of La Peyrère's *Prae-Adamitae*, the distinguished church historian Archbishop James Ussher of Ireland announced that he had calculated the origin of creation to be October 22, 4004, BCE.[16] Ussher did not use a literal reading of the Bible to arrive at this estimate. Taken literally, the Bible does not offer a coherent account of the number of years that transpired between the life of Adam and the present; the various Greek, Latin, and Hebrew sources for the Bible offer varying accounts for the length of human history.[17] Ussher arrived at his estimate of six thousand years for the life of humankind on earth through exegetical gymnastics that synthesized Hebrew genealogy, ancient Middle East-ern manuscripts, Greek marble inscriptions, and a clever use of astronomical chronicles to fill in dates not accounted for in scripture.[18] European histori-ans trying to defend the sacred history described in the Bible turned to the Ussherian chronology to help draw the line between history that was "factually" true and history that had been fantasized by "primitive" nations.[19]

Breaking with scholarly custom, La Peyrère challenged the Christian chronology traditionally understood. He also parted from the practice of dismissing the historical reality of non-European accounts of human experience. He took "pagan" histories at face value, arguing that they detailed the actual historical time experienced by pre-Adamite populations. With the claim that humans predated Adam, La Peyrère clearly inverted the biblical narrative. Yet he was careful to insist that Adam was a distinct human being, not a descendant of the populations created by God before him. With this subtle move La Peyrère reasoned that the Bible was true insofar as it was understood to be an account of only the descendants of Adam's European descendants.[20] In this scheme globally significant events such as the great Deluge were to be understood as a local incident, not a universal experience shared by all humankind.

Prae-Adamitae was swiftly denounced nearly moments after the ink set on its heretical pages. On Christmas Day in 1655 the Belgian bishop of Namur publicly denounced the book. A month earlier the president and council of Holland and Zeeland had done the same.[21] Within a year of its publication *Prae-Adamitae* had received numerous refutations from acclaimed historians such as Isaac Voss (1618–89), Edward Stillingfleet (1635–99), and George Horn. Then in 1657 La Peyrère was summoned to Rome by Pope Alexander VII and forced to renounce his theory.[22] In the wake of La Peyrère's pre-Adamite scandal, orthodox visions of common human descent and recent human creation would continue to be reaffirmed as the true account of the origin of racial differences and the proper framework from which to view human history.

The idea that humans had been on earth for less than six thousand years would prevail in the minds of the intellectual elite until the late nineteenth century. Ussher's chronology would not fall out of favor among the Christian lay public until the mid-twentieth century.[23] Here we arrive at a common point of confusion regarding the status of biblical ideas about human origins during the rise of nineteenth-century American polygenism. It is often assumed that the belief in recent human creation was abandoned after geologists at the turn of the nineteenth century began to discover vast periods of time that extended beyond the Ussherian framework. This, however, is not true. As Martin Rudwick argues, defenders of sacred history were able to separate the time line of the earth's creation from the time line of human creation.[24] When estimates for the earth's age extended beyond the Ussherian chronology, human and earth history were severed. In effect, the idea of recent human creation and nineteenth-century geological claims about the ancient age of the earth co-existed in the minds of many scholars: deep geological time was simply understood as belonging to pre-Adamite history.[25] Even the discovery of seemingly ancient human artifacts and fossils in Suffolk, England, in 1797 and in Engis, Belgium, during the early 1830s could be dismissed by naturalists who believed in the Judeo-Christian time line of recent creation.[26] Before Darwinian evolution carried the day, naturalists often believed that seemingly ancient human fossils either belonged to extinct animal species or were simply recent human remains wrongly identified.[27] By the early nineteenth century professional geologists avoided altogether the question of human origins to stay above the partisan conflict between traditional chronologists and the secularizing concerns of eternalistic theories of the earth.[28] As a result, nineteenth-century geo-

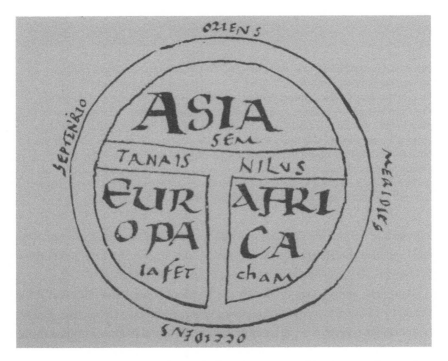

IMAGE 4. A tenth-century rendition of a "T-O" map inspired by the *Etymologiae* of Isidore of Seville. The continents of Asia, Europe, and Africa are shown as the domains of the sons of Noah: Sem (Shem), Jafet (Japheth), and Cham (Ham). Source: Harvard University map collection at Widener Library.

IMAGE 5. A twelfth-century rendition of a "T-O" map from the *Liber Guidonis compositus de variis historiis*, a compilation of historical and geographic texts from Pisa. In this version the continents of Asia, Europe, and Africa are shown without explicit reference to the three sons of Noah. This rendition, however, features more prominently the cross of Christ, which makes up the waterways dividing these three geographic territories. Also noteworthy is that the continental division of world into three separate spaces marks the ancestral beginnings of Noah's three sons without having to explicitly name them. Thus, this map represents the formal continuity of ancestral reasoning and unstated habitual modes of apprehending the world. Source: Harvard University map collection at Widener Library.

logical claims about the deep antiquity of the earth had very little effect on how most nineteenth-century scholars viewed human history until the publication of Darwin's *Origin of Species* (1859) and *Descent of Man* (1871).

American polygenists rekindled the flame of controversy that had been stoked by La Peyrère nearly two hundred years earlier. Like La Peyrère, American polygenists created an alternative and controversial theory of human racial origins that challenged the traditional Christian vision of humanity's shared ancestry and the temporal parameters of human existence. They also used the chronologies of non-European nations to question the universal validity of biblical anthropology. But unlike La Peyrère, American polygenists relied on more than simply the historical records of non-European nations. They also analyzed the bodily history of the other races. By the 1830s American polygenists were armed with new scientific data about primeval and persistent cranial traits passed along in the skulls of the different races. They also noted other physical and behavioral differences such as skin color, hair texture, intellect, and moral dispositions believed to be passed down consistently from the original ancestors of the present-day races. These secular *biochronologies* were used to cast doubt on the scientific validity of the traditional view of human descent from a common ancestor and the Christian time line of recent creation.

"The inspired writings must be abandoned"

Although Josiah Nott was the most outspoken and passionate of the American polygenists, the American School of Ethnology to which he belonged was largely indebted to the work of Samuel Morton. Morton's *Crania Americana* (1839) and *Crania Aegyptiaca* (1844) were seminal texts for early nineteenth-century American ethnologists and contributed to the debate among naturalists on both sides of the Atlantic over the long-standing belief in shared human ancestry.[29] In both works, Morton measured the skulls of each of the five major races (Caucasian, Mongolian, Malaysian, American, and Ethiopian) following in the footsteps of Blumenbach.[30] He created a facial goniometer, a device that could determine the angle of the forehead of any given skull. The device was a three-sided frame with adjustable ear rods and a vertical bar. A skull could be placed inside the goniometer such that the jaw sat parallel with the ear rods and the forehead was more or less parallel with the vertical bar. A facial angle could be captured mathematically based on the distance between the forehead and the vertical bar. After noting that the crania of each group contained consistent facial angles and unique skull capacities, Morton inferred that the intellectual and moral abilities of each race were also different.[31] The specific skull features of each race and their constant heredity suggested to Morton that climate and environment had little effect on the human form.[32] From this Morton concluded not only that racial traits were fixed but also that it was highly unlikely each group descended from a common ancestor.[33]

Morton, however, never openly denounced the theory of common human origins. He turned out to be a reluctant polygenist who acknowledged that "it was a wiser plan to present the facts of unbiased theory and let the reader draw his own conclusions."[34] Morton was also a devout Christian, having been raised a Quaker and later becoming an Episcopalian as an adult. His religious beliefs left him unwilling to draw out the full implications of his ethnology concerning the separate origins of the races.[35] This responsibility fell on the shoulders of the younger members of the American School who were willing to push Morton's discoveries to their logical conclusion—even if it meant an outright attack on scripture.

No one was more successful at this than Josiah Nott, who became the most vocal of the American polygenists following Morton's death in 1851. Born in South Carolina, Nott received his medical degree from the University of Pennsylvania in 1827. After postgraduate training in France, he began surgical practice in Mobile, Alabama, in 1836.[36] Nott quickly established a reputation as one of the most skillful surgeons in the South, where he also specialized in gynecology. While in Mobile, Nott set up a private infirmary for African Americans, which began operations in 1848 and continued to treat patients until after the Civil War.[37] Nott is also given credit in a paper that appeared in the January 1848 issue of the *Charleston Medical Journal and Review* for discovering that yellow fever was transmitted through mosquitoes.[38]

Nott's place within the pantheon of modern racial theorists is rightfully shrouded in controversy because of his proslavery political commitments. These political beliefs and their implications for the reception of his scientific thinking are discussed later. What concerns us now is that Nott and the American School of Ethnology represent a halfway point between the racial classification systems of the Enlightenment and the biological and anthropological theories of race of the early twentieth century. Much like Blumenbach and other ethnologists of the eighteenth century, Nott was part of a tradition of physicians–turned–amateur biologists who relied on evidence-based knowledge to make claims about human variation. Nott used Morton's skull measurements of present-day populations to infer the biological purity and phenotypes of past ancestors. Statistical analysis played a prominent role in the thinking of the American polygenists—a trend that continued with the study of race types by the American anthropologist Franz Boas at the turn of the twentieth century.[39] The challenge American polygenists brought to the theory of common ancestry was driven by statistical averages of the cranial capacity of each race along with the measurement of facial angles. This new evidence base helped them imagine what the ancestors of each race looked like and in the process forced them to create a new narrative about the heterogeneity of human origins and the fixity of racial traits.[40] Finally, and perhaps most significantly, Nott's explicit aspirations for a secular understanding of human origins—although controversial for its time—had become the status quo by the twentieth century.

Unlike Morton, Nott held no commitments to any Christian denomination. Nott renounced his Presbyterian faith during his adult years, distinguishing him from the other polygenists who maintained their Christian beliefs despite their scientific work. He was a freethinker on religious matters and a materialist in regard to medicine and science. He lost his faith while earning his bachelor's degree at South Carolina College, which in the 1820s was a haven for religious unorthodoxy and radical freethinkers.[41] Later as a medical student at the University of Pennsylvania Nott became an adherent to the theories of François Broussais and the French School of Physiological Medicine during a time when the French exerted a strong influence on the best-trained American physicians. The physiological theory of medicine developed by Broussais rejected previous metaphysical speculations about the workings of the human body, stressing instead the importance of observation and analysis.[42] Because of his freethinking temperament and materialist medical training Nott had no reservations about using science to contest Christian beliefs.

Nott's unorthodox religious views were apparent even to his contemporaries. In his obituary a Mobile newspaper wrote that "[Nott's] ideas on religion were confused and he was never disposed to argue about it."[43] Nott did in fact hold a peculiar view of religion, one that swayed from a quasi interest in the "modernization" of religious truth to an outright disdain for the way Christianity compromised the pursuit of science. We find in his writing that Nott believed the Bible was actually ambiguous regarding the single origins of humankind. Nott claimed, "The unity of the races can only be deduced from forced constructions of the Old and New Testaments, and a persistence in this error is calculated to subvert and not to uphold our religion."[44] Nott even asked,

Has God anywhere said that he never intended to create another man, or that other races were not created in distant parts of the globe? I would ask, after all these admitted truths, is there any thing so revolting in the idea that a Negro, Indian, or Malay, may have been created since the flood of Noah, or (if the flood was not universal) before this epoch?[45]

On the surface these statements suggest Nott was interested in bringing greater harmony between biblical truths and the facts of modern science. But given his corpus of writings on race and human origins, it is clear that Nott had little concern for what his theory of polygenesis might mean for American Christians whose belief in the redemptive significance of Jesus Christ rested on the idea that all humans were inheritors of universal sin by sharing a common ancestor in Adam. Obviously, polygenism undermined this crucial axiom of Christian faith. Although Nott gave lip service to the idea that "the plurality of species in the human race does no more violence to the Bible, than do the admitted facts of Astronomy and Geology," he relished that his lectures on race were known to "stir up hell among the Christians."[46]

Nott's antireligious views garnered heated opposition from conservative Christians who believed his denial of the inerrancy of scripture and his rejection of Adam as the patriarch of all humankind was nothing short of blasphemy.[47] But in the face of this opposition Nott remained "indifferent to the censure of those who hold up Christ as their model, while they are pouring out phials of wrath."[48] Nott wanted nothing less than the separation of the Bible from the pursuit of scientific truth, which he hoped would precipitate "the day when the natural history of man will burst the trammels which have so long held it captive." Nott believed that "the inspired writings must be abandoned, unless they can be reconciled with the clearly ascertained facts of science."[49]

Races Designed by Nature

Concerning Nott's scientific thoughts about human ancestry, his *Two Lectures* prefigures the ideas developed later in his more popular text, *Types of Mankind*, and therefore offers a glimpse into his thought while in its early formation.[50] Moreover, Nott's reputation as an ethnologist was born from the controversy created by these lectures, making them as important for the legacy of American polygenism as Morton's *Crania Americana* and *Crania Aegyptiaca*.

In these lectures Nott took the opportunity to share his thoughts on how recent discoveries in ethnology were incompatible with the biblical account of common human descent. Nott's argument revolved around two key issues: first, the length of time needed for humans to develop into different races; and second, the problem of what appeared to be the fixed nature of racial traits. Together these two issues became the grounds for Nott's refutation of the theory of common human descent.

In the tenth chapter of the Genesis narrative, Noah's three sons (Shem, Ham, and Japheth) repopulated the earth after the Deluge, yielding the various races that apparently existed during the nineteenth century. According to the biblical chronologist Joseph Justus Scaliger (1540–1609), the flood was thought to take place in the year 2348 BCE.[51] Later the Irish Protestant bishop James Ussher would concur with this dating of the flood, believing it took place roughly fifteen hundred years after the creation of Adam. These dates were printed in the margins of the Authorized Version of the Bible (known as the King James translation) and carried the weight of authority among English-speaking Christian naturalists in Europe and America well into the twentieth century.[52]

Nott would decipher from this chronology what had otherwise been overlooked for centuries by ethnologists and natural historians: the length of human history provided by Ussher gave virtually no time between the flood of 2348 BCE and the birth of Moses, which, during Nott's time, was believed to have occurred sometime after the reign of the Egyptian king Menes in 2272 BCE.[53] Roughly one hundred years separated the sons of Noah and Moses—the assumed author of Genesis. This length of time for racial differentiation struck Nott as implausible largely because he observed that racial traits appeared stubbornly resistant to change. He, for example, was aware of George Robbins Gliddon's discovery of Egyptian paintings that depicted Africans, Asians, and Europeans with the very same traits they possessed in the nineteenth century. Nott reasoned that if the biblical account of common human descent were true, humans must have developed their racial differences during the very limited period when Shem, Ham, and Japheth repopulated the earth between 2348 and 2272 BCE.[54] The problem for Nott was how to account for the development of different racial types within the parameters of this remarkably short time line while not appealing to supernatural explanations.

Before we see how Nott resolved this dilemma, it is important that we understand the metaphysical assumptions that informed his thinking about race. It appeared to Nott that each of the races was formed within climates and environments where it was properly suited to thrive. In this theory Nott would divinize nature, believing it was capable of giving order and purpose to the organic world, spawning fixed and enduring traits that continued to permanently distinguish the various races. He arrived at these conclusions after assessing Samuel Morton's ethnological work on human crania.

Beginning in the early 1830s, Morton established a relationship with Gliddon, who was conducting archeological studies of the Egyptian monuments while serving as the US consul for the city of Cairo.[55] Morton convinced Gliddon to send him the skulls of the Egyptians and the cranial remains of other populations he discovered along the Nile, eventually amassing one of the largest collections of ancient human skulls by any naturalist working in the nineteenth century.[56] Morton classified the various skulls of Egyptians and other nations with which they had come in contact according their racial traits. He identified skulls belonging to "the Celts"; "the Scythians," also known as the ancient Iranians, populations located in Greece and Italy; "the Semitic nations"; "the Hindoos"; "the Arabs"; and "the Negroes."[57] To determine which nations belonged to the ancient Egyptian lineage, Morton organized the skulls according to the similarities of their size and volume—the latter of which Morton determined by filling the skulls with lead and grain seeds to calculate their skull capacity. Morton was able to distill these ethnicities down to the following four classifications: "the Artco-Egyptians," which entailed the "purer Caucasian nations" as seen in Semitic and Pelasgic nations; "the Austro-Egyptians," where it appeared that "the cranium blends the characters of the Hindoo and Southern Arab"; "the Negroloid crania," which were admixed populations with the crania of present-day "Negroes" but shrouded with "harsh and sometimes wiry" long hair; and the "Negro," with the least-developed crania and the smallest brain volume of all the skulls compared.[58]

With his cranial typology, Morton plotted the location of "pure Caucasian heads" near and around Egypt, "at Memphis, near the mouth of the Nile," noting that "as you ascend the river into the interior of Africa and approach Nubia, the Caucasian character is gradually lost—they become mingled with Negro and other tribes."[59] Morton concluded that Egypt was originally peopled by the Caucasian race, claiming that the presence of true Caucasian skulls began to dissipate farther up the Nile into the heart of Africa. Ussher's time line of recent creation suggested to Morton that if the Egyptians possessed Caucasian skulls, they had to be direct descendants of the first human, for there simply was not enough time for them to become African. On this point Morton, as well as Nott, would follow Blumenbach's theory that the first human was the white Caucasian.

As a man of faith Morton assumed the story of Noah's flood provided insight into the race of the first humans. He, however, was opposed to the theory that humans were derived from a common stock that then developed physical differences after adapting to various climates. In *Crania Americana* Morton raised the question, "Is it not more consistent with the known government of the universe to suppose, that the same Omnipotence that created man, would adapt him at once to the physical, as well as to the moral circumstances in which he was to dwell upon the earth?" For Morton it was "difficult to imagine that an all-wise Providence, after having by the Deluge destroyed all mankind excepting the family of Noah, should leave these to combat, and with seemingly uncertain and inadequate means, the various external causes that tended to oppose the great object of their dispersion."[60] Morton believed that races were designed for specific places.

Nott also held this view but, unlike Morton, did not designate God as a causal factor in the formation of the races. Instead, he collapsed God and nature, as Blumenbach had done in the previous century, believing that the organic world possessed the capacity to govern the physical constitution of living things. In Nott's divinized understanding of life no plants could "be propagated out of the climate to which they are adapted by nature—and man forms no exception to the general law."[61] Nott explained:

> [Humans] are not spread over the earth by chance, or without local relations, but the different regions of the world, may be said to have given origin to peculiar kinds, adapted respectively by their organization, to subsist under the local circumstances, among which they appear first to have been called into existence.[62]

Given the natural order of things, Nott believed the races were in fact separate species "marked by peculiarities of structure, which have always been constant and undeviating."[63]

Nott would record his own anatomic differences between the races. Focusing almost exclusively on black and white variations, he began with an assessment of the cranial traits of both groups, explaining that "when the Caucasian and Negro are compared, one of the most striking and important points of difference is seen in the conformation of the head. . . . The head of the Negro is smaller by a full tenth—the forehead is narrower and more receding, in consequence of which the anterior or intellectual portion of the brain is defective."[64]

Nott also claimed that "the arm of the African is much longer than that in the Caucasian" and that "the chest of the Negro is more compressed laterally." He added that among Africans "the bones of the pelvis in the male are more slender and narrow; the muscles on the sides of the pelvis are less full, but more full posteriorly." Differences in the bend of the knee; the shape of the calves, feet, and heels; and, most important, skin complexion are also cited. According to Nott, all of these anatomical differences beg the question,

> Can all these deep, radical and enduring differences be produced by climate and other causes assigned? It is incumbent on those who contend for such an opinion, to show that such changes either have taken place, or that similar changes in *the human race are now in progress.*[65]

Nott reasoned that it had been "about two centuries since the Africans were introduced into this country, the 8th or 9th generation is now amongst us, and the race is unchanged. The Negroes have been improved by comforts and good feeding which they have been unaccustomed to; but they are Negroes still."[66] The unchanged physical constitution of so-called American Negroes proved, according to Nott, that races were fixed, not malleable or readily subject to the influence of the environment.

The source of these racial differences, Nott argued, was to be found in the inherent logic and design of nature, not outside environmental factors working themselves on the human form: "Two races are considered specifically different, if they are distinguished from each other by some peculiarities which one cannot be supposed to have acquired, or the other lost, through any known operation of physical causes." These peculiarities, created by nature, made each race suitable for only a limited range of environmental conditions. Like fauna and flora, "the white man cannot live in tropical Africa, or the African in the frigid zone."[67]

Nott was also caught within the Christian worldview. Although he avoided making God directly responsible for the "peculiarities" of the races, as Morton had done, Nott's idea that nature was capable of producing fixed characteristics carried with it the attributes of the creator God found in the book of Genesis. In this regard Nott's thinking followed not only Blumenbach's but also that of the late seventeenth-century natural theologian John Ray (1628–1705).

In his seminal work, *The Wisdom of God Manifested in the Works of Creation* (1691), considered a classic among the generation of naturalists who came of age with Charles Darwin, Ray professed the widely held belief in the stability of the basic structures of life. There was a theological basis for this view of nature as both static and purposive. Ray argued that God had created all that has existed and that has been "conserved to this Day in the same State and Condition in which they were first made."[68] The created world was static because at its inception God endowed plants and animals with traits and attributes that best prepared them to thrive in the environments where they were originally distributed. This distribution also occurred according to a divine plan. In effect, God's wisdom was mirrored in the features each organism manifested as well in the locale of his creations.[69] This understanding of nature fleshed out the implications of the claim in Genesis that God gave shape to a world that was void and formless. This same view of nature lay behind Nott's continental understanding of race: human differences were governed by an order where nature served as God's surrogate.

Nott believed that there were consequences to breaking natural law. Death and extinction could ensue if racial groups were taken out of their habitat or if they mixed with one another.[70] Regarding the latter he wrote, "No one can calculate the results which may result from crossing races."[71] Foreshadowing the fears of race mixing that marked Jim Crow America during the next century, Nott claimed that the offspring of black-white unions "are shorter lived, and . . . that they are more liable to be diseased and are less capable of endurance than either whites or blacks of the same rank and condition." In light of the mulatto's perceived poor health, physical constitution, and low reproductive rate, Nott asked, "Is it not reasonable to believe that the human hybrid may also have its peculiar laws," and perhaps might one of "these laws be (which is a reasonable inference from foregoing data) that the mulatto is a degenerate, unnatural offspring, doomed by nature to work out its own destruction[?]"[72] Like the God of the Old Testament, not only was nature purposeful; it was also vengeful, capable of retribution if a transgression was made against its laws. For Nott the wisdom of God was mirrored in the order and traits of the races. With nature and the divine collapsed within his thinking, theological ideas had a profound influence on his metaphysical assumptions about the organic world and the existence of species traits.

No Universal Adam

Now that we are clear about Nott's understanding of nature, we can return to the issue of how he accounted for the development of different racial types. Nott believed that Morton's ethnological research showing Egyptians with Caucasian skulls and his own anatomical observations of the American "Negro" presented a formidable challenge to either the idea of recent human creation or the common ancestry of the races. If the science of our origins were to stand on its own, one of these traditional assumptions had to go. If the Deluge was universal, then non-Caucasians had been spawned separately after the flood; these groups would not have existed prior to the flood, as there would not have been enough time for them develop within the fifteen hundred years between the creation of Adam and the time of Noah's flood. If the flood was a local event, then only Caucasians were affected and the other races did not belong to Adam's descendants.

Nott's solution to this problem was to reject the idea of a universal Adam, affirming instead that Noah's sons accounted only for the origins of Caucasians. Nott believed that the Egyptians, as descendants of Noah, could not have been black: "In the allotment of territories to the offspring of Noah, Egypt was given as an inheritance to Mizraim, the son of Ham. . . . Mizraim, being a descendant of Noah, was of course a Caucasian." If Ham's descendants, who were white, had repopulated Egypt, it was unreasonable to assume that the black population found in sub-Saharan Africa could have also been the offspring of Ham, coming into being in the one hundred years that followed Noah's flood. Nott pleaded that "if there is any miracle in the Bible more wonderful than this, I should like to know what it is."[73] In light of this inconsistency, Nott maintained that the story of Noah and his three sons accounted only for the descent and migration of Caucasians across the globe, and other populations could have developed separately from Adam's bloodline.[74]

Nott's thinking was consistent with the racial reasoning found in Martin Luther's 1534 Bible. In Luther's artistic rendition of the story of the great Deluge, Noah's three sons are all drawn with European features. Nott's argument that Noah's descendants were Caucasian was not an entirely new proposition.

Had Nott rejected the idea of recent human creation, he could have used the story of Noah's sons to explain the origin of all races. By 1840, most naturalists were aware of Charles Lyell's argument in *Principles of Geology* (1830–33) for an extended age of prehuman history, which effectively freed the study of the earth from the biblical tradition.[75] Extending the time line of human history backward would seem to dovetail with Nott's commitment to advance modern science beyond the conceptual constraints of the Bible. Nott, how-

IMAGE 6. Noah and his three sons, Shem, Ham, and Japheth. The scene on the left is after the Deluge. At the right is the setting for the curse of Ham, which occurs under Noah's tent. Notice in this depiction from Luther's 1534 Bible that Noah and his sons are all represented as European; one of Noah's sons is blond, another is brunette, and a third appears to have red hair. God is also depicted as a brunette with European traits as he sits above in heaven following the cessation of the flood. Source: Luther Bible, 1534 edition, Herzogin Anna Amalia Bibliothek, shelf mark vol. 1:CI:58b. Courtesy of Klassik Stiftung Weimar, Herzogin Anna Amalia Bibliothek.

ever, was unable to abandon the biblical chronology of recent human creation without also giving up his argument for immutable racial traits. An older human chronology better served the argument for monogenesis because it theoretically allowed more time for humans to develop their so-called racial differences after descending from a common ancestor. An extended human chronology also weakened the argument for fixed racial traits by suggesting that humankind, like animals and plants, was subject to the same laws of physical change when pressured by the environment over extended periods. But most mid-nineteenth-century ethnologists were unwilling to wage a defense of monogenesis at the expense of the belief in recent human creation.[76] Although for different reasons, Nott also had a stake in maintaining the idea of the recent creation of humankind: he simply could not take down the theory of common origins without also affirming a condensed time line for human history.

Reassessing the Politics of American Polygenism

American polygenism came into maturity during the period of social, political, and economic unrest that led to the American Civil War.[77] In 1820, a hard-fought battle between proslavery and antislavery factions in Congress resulted in the Missouri Compromise, which balanced power in the Senate between both sides of the slavery debate. The compromise aroused fears in the South that a strong federal government posed a threat to the institution of slavery and provided the motivation for the secessionist agenda of the Confederacy.

Ten years later, the presidency of Andrew Jackson (1829–37) introduced changes to America's race relations that would endure well into the following century. On May 26, 1830, Jackson signed into law the Indian Removal Act, which divested an estimated one hundred thousand Native Americans of their property throughout the South, particularly in the state of Georgia. Also under Jackson's watch, Congress implemented a Gag Rule between 1836 and 1844, which banned petitions opposing slavery from being introduced before the US House of Representatives. This was a considerable blow to the efforts of abolitionists to persuade Congress to do away with America's "peculiar institution." Finally, Jackson was responsible for appointing Roger B. Taney as chief justice of the US Supreme Court. In 1857, Taney authored the majority opinion of the famous *Dred Scott v. Sandford* case, claiming that "Negroes" were "beings of an inferior order, and altogether unfit to associate with the white race . . . and so far inferior that they had no rights which the white man was bound to respect."[78] In the wake of this decision, African Americans were denied full citizenship across the nation.

In this setting, American polygenists presented proslavery politicians new scientific theories about the inferiority of black Americans. Here again Nott was particularly vocal. He argued that Egyptian depictions of Africans in slavery at the beginning of human history suggested that they were naturally predisposed for servitude.[79] Melissa Nobles has also noted that in 1849 Nott attempted to influence a contentious congressional debate, through the help of his friend and Kentucky representative Joseph Underwood, over increasing the amount of demographic data collected about slaves in the upcoming 1850 census.[80] Just two years earlier Nott had published an article in *Commercial Review* that championed the importance of statistical data on the health and longevity of black slaves for the insurance industry.[81] Through Underwood, Nott was hoping to gather census data to track the health, disease, and mortality rates of slaves with recent white ancestry and empirical data to support his theory that racial miscegenation produced hybrids that were less healthy, more prone to disease, and ultimately inferior to their parental stock. Nott's bid proved successful; the category "mulatto" appeared for the first time on the 1850 census and continued to be used on US census forms until 1920.[82]

Nott's political commitments were unquestionably vile. It is an entirely different matter, however, to argue that his racial theories were driven solely by politics. There is ample evidence suggesting that his ideas, although surely shaped by the politics of slavery, were the consequence of genuine scientific observation and a latent Christian intellectual history he had inherited. In other words Nott's ideas about race stemmed from both scientific and Christian ideas. More often than not, polygenism is understood to be merely a scientific version of proslavery politics that belongs to the legacy of pseudoscience.[83]

For example, George Fredrickson argued that political temperament and racial bias compromised the scientific ideas of Nott and the other polygenists:[84]

> The most fervent of the scientific apologists for the American system of racial
> subordination was Dr. Josiah C. Nott, who became the leading exponent of the

new ethnology after the death of Morton. Preconceived racial attitudes probably drew him to ethnology in the first place and influenced his inquiries.[85]

Frederickson believed that Nott's politics overdetermined his views of race, and therefore the conceptual roots of his scientific account of racial variation were irrelevant. In Frederickson's view, Nott's writings "would seem to belong at least as much to the history of proslavery and racist propaganda as to the history of science." To put Frederickson's reading simply: Nott's science appears to be little more than window dressing for his racist politics.[86]

It is undeniable that American polygenism emerged from within a sociopolitical setting that was eager and willing to naturalize racial inequalities. However, the taint of nineteenth-century southern proslavery politics should not prevent us from looking deeper into the conceptual origins of this controversial theory. To dismiss polygenism as unscientific on the basis of underlying political views or discredit Nott as lacking the credentials to speak about human origins is to fundamentally misunderstand the ethos of antebellum science. In an age before the professionalization of formal scientific disciplines, the relationship between science, politics, and religion in the "Old South" was remarkably porous.[87]

Nott's reception among his contemporaries, however, sheds light on whether or not his scientific ideas were merely extensions of his political commitments. In the April 1845 issue of the *Southern Quarterly Review*, the American botanist and Episcopal minister Moses Ashley Curtis published a scathing review of Nott's *Two Lectures*. In his defense of monogenism Curtis argued, "The common origin of the several languages of the earth, involves of necessity a demonstration of the unity of the human race, and will so far afford collateral proof of the truth of the sacred narrative." Curtis also claimed that Nott placed too strict an interpretation on the laws of nature and had overgeneralized the geographic distribution of animal and plant life. Curtis believed that "many of the most useful species, both of animal and vegetable kingdoms, are capable of easy transfer and acclimation in regions far remote from their original habitations."[88] The malleability of the human form, in Curtis's view, was therefore not an exception to the natural law, so human descent from a common ancestor still seemed plausible to Curtis, even though he conceded that

[Nott] was certainly correct in saying, that the assertion of a "direct act of Providence" in affecting [change to the human form] "is an assumption which cannot

be proven" because there is no record of such any act. It might still be true however. When the true cause of any fact is unknown, we have a right to assume any
adequate possible cause as the probable true one, until it be disproved.[89]

Thus, in response to the question of whether "a White man may have been
changed into a Negro 'by direct act of Providence,'" Curtis claimed to "see no
absurdity in attributing the change to such a cause." For Curtis, Christian-
minded scientists "should certainly adopt this theory rather than that of a
plurality of species in the human race."[90] Concerning Nott's claim that racial
hybrids transgressed the laws of nature, Curtis argued that racially mixed people were prolific, as evidenced by the thriving numbers of mixed people in the
English colonies located within the Pacific and Caribbean.[91]

The Lutheran minister and proslavery botanist John Bachman (1790–1874)
of South Carolina also attacked Nott's polygenist theory. Bachman's criticisms
allow us to see the limits of viewing American polygenism as simply racist propaganda. He argued that there was ample linguistic and anthropological evidence to support the belief in shared human ancestry and the human genealogy
described in the Genesis narrative was compatible with science.[92] Bachman believed, like many of his southern contemporaries, that there were explicit biblical warrants consistent with the facts of science to support the belief in white
superiority and the biological inferiority of blacks and other races:

> The fact that nature has stamped on the African race the permanent marks of
> inferiority—that we are taught by their whole past history the lesson of their
> incapacity for self-government, and that the Scriptures point out the duties of
> masters and servants, should be sufficient to dispel every improper motive in an
> unbiased search after truth alone.[93]

With Bachman's affirmation that both nature and the Bible declared that the
African was an inferior race and incapable of "self-government," one would
assume that he, Morton, and Nott would be intellectual allies, particularly if
we buy stock in Frederickson's thesis and believe that "Nott was somewhat less
attached to polygenesis as a scientific hypothesis than to the 'practical fact' of
inherent Negro inferiority, however it might be explained."[94] But Nott, Morton,
and Bachman turned out to be bitter combatants.[95] Bachman disagreed with
the polygenist definition of species as inherently fixed, believed polygenists

overstated the sterility of racial hybrids, and ultimately claimed that the concept of race itself should be abandoned given the shared ancestry of the human species.[96] Morton and Nott were unmoved by Bachman's criticisms and were largely exasperated by his seemingly amateur defense of common human ancestry.[97] Nott in particular was unwilling to acknowledge the scientific grounds for Bachman's defense of monogenism, claiming that Bachman's commitment to Lutheranism was an intellectual handicap that predisposed him to defend the idea of a universal Adam.[98] After reading Bachman's review of his work, Nott wrote that he and his polygenist colleagues

> have never, in the whole course of our lives, risen from the perusal of any work with such bitter feelings of mortification and disappointment—mortification, from its utter want of Christian charity and courtesy, and disappointment, from its loose statements of facts, its endless assumptions, and entire want of rigid, scientific reasoning.[99]

Nott simply did not believe Bachman possessed the impartiality of a proper scientist, forcing Bachman to routinely defend his credentials as a botanist and justify his qualifications to weigh in on the question of human beginnings.[100]

If Nott's intentions were to garner broad support for restricting the freedom of blacks via a scientific theory endorsing their biological inferiority, his rejection of the truth of the Bible was certainly counterproductive. Most Christians were unwilling to abandon the truth of scripture in support of polygenism. Bachman's monogenist theory, for example, was a more favorable scientific position for many Christians, particularly in the South, because it offered a defense of black inferiority while also upholding the veracity of scripture and the idea of common human origins. After all, Nott's rejection of common human ancestry also called into question the universal significance of Jesus Christ, who Christians believed redressed the universal sin all humans inherited from Adam. If Nott were drawn to polygenism for political reasons alone, he could have conceded Bachman's monogenist position, which would have allowed Nott to defend his theory of black inferiority. But Nott was explicit that modern science did not support the biblically based idea of common human descent. He was willing to aid the march of science on this point even if it meant having "piles of wrath reaped upon [his] head" and professing an utter disregard for the inspired writings.[101]

Under the Frederickson hypothesis we would have to explain this as a poor political strategy, which then raises serious doubts about the extent to which politics actually drove Nott's scientific analysis. Nott came from a political family and understood the nuances of social governance; his father was elected to Congress in 1798 from the state of South Carolina and later became mayor of Columbia in 1807. Moreover, Nott himself garnered considerable social capital while earning a reputation as one of the most skilled medical men in the South.[102] If Nott were driven by politics, there was nothing to gain by wasting social capital on a scientific theory that did not sit well with the majority of either religious southerners or southern senators unwilling to collect statistical data to aid his research.

A more reasonable explanation is to take Nott's science at face value and admit that although polygenism was used to support a proslavery agenda, Nott was driven to his position by what he understood to be scientific interests. Having the fortune of historical distance, we can see that these scientific interests were constructed with ideas that had their root in Christian intellectual history; Nott's view of race was born out a mongrel epistemology that made use of religious concepts that had long since become a formal part of the discipline of natural history. Christianity helped facilitate Nott's own "progressive" views about race—even though he seemed largely unaware of this.

Toward a Secular Account of Race

What made Nott's theory of polygenesis so troubling for nineteenth-century naturalists was that it was grounded in many of the presuppositions shared by monogenists. They believed in a natural order sustained by God. They also assumed human creation was recent. Yet to make these beliefs cohere with new ethnological "data" about racial difference, Nott arrived at a different set of conclusions regarding human unity. Polygenesis was a plausible explanation because it could account for the differences between the races while maintaining the traditional chronology and the widely held belief in the natural order of things. Moreover, polygenists provided a scientific explanation for commonsense ideas about the fixity of racial difference. Indeed, the appeal and threat of polygenism rested on the fact that Morton and Nott simply asked the American public to consider that racial differences had always been what they were now rather than assume complex processes of descent from a common ancestor over an ambiguous period of time.

Nott's polygenist theory, however, was not a radical break from the Christian tradition but one that worked with it by marshaling long-standing religious precepts. His insistence that racial traits were permanent clearly carried over the influence of Christian natural theology.[103] This was a heritage whose theological origins predisposed thinkers to view the world as an ordered, stable, coherent system, not a universe in flux and riddled by chance and contingency as Darwin had grasped in his account of evolution by random natural selection.[104] Ideas of clearly defined, discrete, and fixed racial types were concepts indigenous to a *Weltangschauung* that assumed the organic world was sustained by a divine order—as Blumenbach had assumed in the previous century.[105] This explains the divinized conception of nature Nott used to bolster his claims about the races being designed exclusively for specific geographic locations. Darwin saw that nature was an open system that could not support the existence of permanent natural kinds; he argued that change, not fixity, was a constant feature of organic life. Natural species and associated ideas about discrete and fixed racial types belonged to an earlier tradition of reason, which informed at least half of Nott's thinking. Following Darwin's publication of the *Descent of Man* in 1871, Nott shared with his close friend James Henry Hammond, a proslavery politician in South Carolina, that he simply did not agree with the

> School of Naturalists among who are numbered the great names Lamarck, . . . Darwin, and others, which advocates the development theory, and contend not only that one type may be transformed into another, but that man himself is nothing more than a developed worm.[106]

Until his death in 1873 Nott was a critic of evolution, affirming instead his belief in the fixity of species and the inherent order of the natural world.

In their unsuccessful attempt to sever the ties between Christian thought and racial science, American polygenists furnished a series of techniques and methods to study human variation and re-create our ancestral populations. Morton's facial goniometer, for example, translated physical traits into data points used to make explicit assumptions about the purity of our ancestors. They were also front-runners in deploying these statistical data—which quantified race types—to argue that biological inheritance, not the environment, culture, or society, was the determining factor shaping the destiny of racial groups.

American polygenists gave credence to the idea of racial biological determinism well before Francis Galton and Charles Davenport, who defended similar ideas at the end of the nineteenth century.

American polygenists are hardly given credit for the fact that the techniques and reasoning strategies they used for measuring race would remain a lasting feature of the tradition of modern racial science. This becomes apparent in the following chapters as we explore how a divinized conception of nature transformed into racial biological determinism and how the assumption that humans descended from three or four pure ancestors became translated into genetic representations of our beginnings.

It is important to see, however, that these ideas and the questions they engendered did not merely expand modern scientific ideas about race; they also facilitated the turn of Christian supersessionism upon itself. Polygenists were using secular knowledge to contest the Christian intellectual history that came before them—a history that was perceived as a roadblock to a purer, more modern, and less partisan truth. On this point Nott wrote:

> Scientific truth, exemplified in the annals of Astronomy, Geology, Chronology, Geographical distribution of animals, &c., has literally fought its way inch by inch through false theology. The last grand battle between science and dogmatism, on the primitive origin of races, has now commenced. It requires no prophetic eye to foresee that science must again, and finally, triumph.[107]

The triumphalism here is not merely about the march of science. Also at stake was the replacement of a religious conception of human history. American polygenists wanted a scientific account of humankind that superseded Christian knowledge—much like the early church fathers saw Christianity as the replacement and perfection of the law given to the Israelites, or the historians of the seventeenth century who believed sacred history of the church was more perfect than the chronologies of non-Europeans.

American polygenists helped make a supersessionist vision of truth a more pronounced feature of racial science. Thus, Nott posed the question, "How could the author of Genesis know anything of the true history of the creation, or of the races of men, when his knowledge of the physical world was so extremely limited?"[108] What had been implicit among eighteenth-century ethnologists American polygenists made explicit: the science of our beginnings was true if it corrected and supplanted the limits of religious truth.[109] This supersessionist approach to the science of our beginning would be reoccupied by twentieth-century biologists and anthropologists, who organized professionally under the spirit of both secularism and scientific positivism.[110] American polygenists are a link between early modern forms of Christian supersessionism aimed at denying non-Christian accounts of human history and contemporary scientific theories of race that no longer recognize its Christian prehistory. Ironically, Nott and Morton would become victims of the supersessionism they championed. This explains the tendency to see American polygenism as merely pseudoscience or a footnote en route to Darwinian evolution. We see in the next chapter how this replacement model creates obstacles for recognizing the persistence of Christian intellectual history within modern science throughout the twentieth century.

3

THE GHOST OF
CHRISTIAN CREATIONISM
Racial Dispositions and Progressive Era
Public Health Research

DURING THE PROGRESSIVE ERA many American social scientists and physicians were convinced that the ancestry of a racial group determined its members' health, behavior, and life chances. In 1896 the German statistician Frederick Hoffman published his widely influential *Race Traits and Tendencies of the American Negro*.[1] Drawing on state and military medical records, Hoffman claimed that African ancestry explained black Americans' disposition for high infant mortality, tuberculosis, communicable illnesses, and heart disease. *Race Traits* gained attention at the same time that Charles Davenport and his fellow social Darwinists were inspired by the Malthusian population theory and a rudimentary understanding of Mendelian heredity to create the eugenics movement. Eugenicists believed that biological inheritance shaped the destiny of racial groups, and consequently sterilization and segregation were the most effective means to improve the racial purity of the nation.

Not only were turn-of-the-century public health researchers debating if the environment was a relevant factor shaping health outcomes; they were doing so while considering if distinct racial ancestry was a more viable explanation for the disparities in health recorded in the statistical studies of figures like Frederick Hoffman and government institutions like the Freedman's Bureau and the US Public Health Service. The idea that "blacks," "Mexicans," or the "yellow races" were more predisposed to diseases than white people living in the same environment carried with it latent ideas about the irrelevance of shared human ancestry or even a shared biological experience. For some public health researchers polygenism was an explicit problem to be considered; for others it was an unspoken but powerful organizing principle that helped structure medical-scientific conclusions about the predispositions and biosusceptibilities of racial groups.

At the heart of the matter was a set of unresolved conceptual problems about the links between racial ancestry, biological inheritance, and the role of the environment in shaping disease outcomes, problems that continue to trouble present-day disputes over the source of health disparities between racial groups.[2] In the absence of a clear understanding of why the races had varying dispositions to certain diseases, a polygenist understanding of human ancestry provided twentieth-century health researchers a useful tool for making sense of America's public health landscape.

Within this setting African American thinkers attempting to reform and enhance the health, behavior, and life chances of black Americans found themselves in a difficult situation. On the one hand, they were critical of the racism and pro-segregationist arguments resting behind scientific claims that black biology was inherently different from white biology. On the other hand, black reformers saw value in regulating the reproduction of the unfit and encouraging the proliferation of the "Talented Tenth." This was a term coined by the black sociologist W. E. B. Du Bois that referred to the 10 percent of black Americans who were exemplary and possessed the potential to lead the race to its full potential. As the historian Michele Mitchell noted, black reformers "realized that the continued existence of black Americans literally relied upon biological reproduction." Thus, black physicians and social reformers invested in racial uplift drew on the ideology of eugenics to transform the sexual habits and hygienic practices of black Americans.[3] Black doctors teaching medicine at black institutions were particularly supportive of eugenic reforms as they worked to modernize their academic curriculum while embracing Progressive Era ideals of professionalization and practical empiricism, which were shaping mainstream medical training across the nation.[4]

Charles V. Roman (1864–1934) was one of many black physicians swept up in the rising tide of Progressive Era racial science and the seemingly positive benefits of eugenics and social hygiene reform.[5] He was one of the South's leading black physicians and social hygienists working out of Meharry Medical College in Nashville, Tennessee. Roman was concerned that the attention white public health experts and social Darwinists placed on black ancestry as the cause of their susceptibility to disease—and ultimately their being unfit for democracy—threatened to undermine the notion that humans share a common biological heritage. Roman argued that ethnologists paid lip service to the notion that "there is but one human family," yet their studies demonstrate that "nature has favorite children, that she has written the decree of favoritism in the tissues of their bodies."[6] Roman worked to challenge the idea of so-called race-specific diseases, arguing that humans possessed a shared ancestral heritage and therefore their traits and dispositions were also common across the color line. He also affirmed that there were moral, social, economic, and political factors that had direct consequences for the health, biology, and various "traits" of a population. This was certainly true for black Americans, as Roman reasoned that the injustices of slavery and Jim Crow were inscribed on their bodies and were the cause of present-day differences between black and white Americans. He believed the health and behavioral differences between the races could be amended through proper education and socioeconomic reform.

Roman would eventually work for the US Public Health Service (PHS). As a health officer Roman, like many black reformers of the period, delivered eugenically loaded lessons about the importance of sexual hygiene, continence, and the reproduction of the "fit" as key for the survival of the race. Roman and other black reformers could not ignore that high infant mortality levels, low birthrates, and many diseases were ravaging black communities across the country. For Roman, part of the solution was to encourage black communities to adopt the sexual practices of middle-class white America, thereby discouraging the reproduction of the unfit and locating sexual reproduction more firmly within the realm of marriage and the heterosexual family.[7]

Historians have argued that the eugenics movement and the pro-segregationist politics of the American South largely drove the racial science of the early twentieth century.[8] This conventional reading, although accurate in many respects, has largely believed that turn-of-the-century thinkers widely assumed the races shared a common ancestor. This chapter, however, interrogates the racial logic of Progressive Era scientists and argues that a polygenist view of human ancestry informed the ideas of public health specialists studying venereal disease and other communicable illnesses in black communities. This in turn helped produce a deterministic view of inherited disease expression. What many of these Progressive Era medical thinkers and scientists left unresolved, however, was how these dispositions were inscribed onto black bodies to begin with. Polygenism would help relieve these thinkers of this responsibility. It was not merely racial prejudice that stood behind medical assumptions about black dispositions to disease at this time. Also at work was a divinized conception of the organic world, or what I call "secular creationism." The notion that nature creates human groups with specific dispositions and vulnerabilities that can be traced back to their original ancestors freed Progressive Era thinkers of having to reconcile claims about black dispositions to disease with an explanation for the ontology of their race-specific illnesses. By invoking the logic of biodeterminism, public health researchers could attribute black susceptibility to a given disease to their ancestral past—ignoring in the process the role of history, the environment, and any notion of shared human ancestry—without ever having to explain who or what force in nature originally endowed these populations with these enduring racial traits.

We will also see how black thinkers such as Charles V. Roman were acutely aware of the polygenist implications of Progressive Era studies of communicable diseases. For this reason Roman stressed shared human susceptibilities across the color line, as well as the social and environmental factors determining health outcomes. If the American polygenists of the nineteenth century turned the racial logic of Christian supersessionism upon itself to achieve an objective science that discredited equality among the races, black medical thinkers like Roman during the Progressive Era attempted to reverse this trend by offering an account of health outcomes that was explicitly partial to Christian reasoning and attempted to defend the notion of shared disease susceptibility.

Specter of Polygenism
in Progressive Era Racial Science

Near the end of the nineteenth century, naturalists on both sides of the Atlantic debated if and how scientists were to reconcile the idea of shared human ancestry with contemporary human differences. When Charles Darwin weighed in on this dispute, he acknowledged that "the existing races of man differ in

many respects, as in colour, hair, shape of the skull, proportions of the body";
however, when "their whole structure [is] taken into consideration they are
found to resemble each other closely in a multitude of points."[9] By stressing
the "whole structure" of the human form, Darwin was drawing attention to
the overwhelming physical and behavioral traits shared between European and
non-European populations. This rather obvious convergence, he argued, suggested shared ancestry:

> When naturalists observe a close agreement in numerous small details of habits,
> tastes, and dispositions between two or more domestic races, or between nearly-
> allied natural forms, they use this fact as an argument that they are descended
> from a common progenitor who was thus endowed; and consequently that all
> should be classed under the same species. The same argument may be applied
> with much force to the races of man.[10]

Darwin would go further, adding that many of the differences attributed to
each racial group

> are so unimportant or of so singular a nature, that it is extremely improbable that
> they should have been independently acquired by aboriginally distinct species
> or races. The same remark applies with equal or greater force with respect to the
> numerous points of mental similarity between the most distinct races of man.[11]

It would appear then that Darwin shut the door on the theory of separate
human origins with the argument that the "habits, tastes, and dispositions"
shared across the races was evidence of their sharing a common ancestor.

The path to polygenism, however, would remain open. The idea of race
continued to have analytic value for Darwin's evolutionary account of human
development, which in turn allowed facets of polygenism to remain plausible—
even if these elements crept through the back door of scientific ruminations
about human difference. Although Darwin expressed doubt "whether any
character can be named which is distinctive of a race and is constant," he
never explicitly tackled the question of whether races were merely a figment
of the naturalist's imagination or if racial categories did in fact capture something constant, fixed, and ancestral.[12] This unresolved conceptual problem kept
open the possibility for naturalists and future scientists to lose sight of the very
philosophical intervention Darwin hoped to make on the debate over human

origins: Attention to the whole structure of the human form was key for appreciating the common ancestry of the species and therefore also the habits, behaviors, and dispositions shared across populations. If the composite parts that make up this whole structure were merely singled out (i.e., mental ability, physical attributes, or disposition to disease) and colored as population specific, not only could biologists reaffirm the validity of the race concept; they could also give new life to polygenic assumptions about distinct ancestry as the true cause of human differences in behavior and disease outcomes.

Between the end of the nineteenth and the start of the twentieth century anthropologists in the United States and across Europe were increasingly invested in studying differences between the races, even at the peril of losing sight of common human ancestry. This point, all but forgotten in recent scholarship on the history of science, was made by George Stocking, who argued, "The European physical anthropology that developed in the last forty years of the nineteenth century may appropriately be regarded as a continuation of the naturalistic current of pre-Darwinian polygenism."[13] Stocking noted that the racial theories developed by Paul Broca, Karl Vogt, and Paul Topinard provided turn-of-the-century scientists on both sides of the Atlantic a new language for recovering polygenist styles of reasoning about human difference.[14] Stocking explained that "freed from the specific context of the earlier debate, many polygenist positions became part of a free-floating body of racial assumption that was often incorporated into the argument of those who were Darwinian and in that sense monogenist on the issue of ultimate human unity."[15] According to Stocking, scientists were able to refashion pre-Darwinian polygenism into three widely pervasive assumptions held by many American, British, and German scientists by the end of the nineteenth century: modern racial groups descended from biologically distinct types, racial traits were inherited, and the environment had little to no effect on the traits and dispositions of the human body.[16]

Polygenist assumptions were not limited to the field of physical anthropology. They also influenced early twentieth-century medical-scientific reasoning about disease expression in black communities, especially venereal diseases. The presence of polygenism within public health research presents a challenge to Stocking's claims about it being a free-floating discourse. It was true that Progressive Era thinkers were not explicitly concerned with reconciling the science of human variation with Christian orthodoxy or scripture. In this sense scientists who supported a polygenist view of race were freed from having to engage in theological justifications of their work. However, the presence of polygenist reasoning within early twentieth-century public health science shows that this conception of meaningful ancestral differences was not actually free; it traveled with a series of unstated assumptions about the laws of the organic world that grew out of Christian intellectual history. The uptake of these laws about human biology had two powerful effects when coupled with polygenist thinking. First, they transformed our inherited biology into a divinized force that governed racial difference. Second, assuming that human racial differences were governed by laws within the organic world settled the question of whether race was a figment of the naturalist's imagination or if racial categories did in fact capture something constant and with deep ancestral roots.

The Racial Ideology
of Progressive Era Public Health

The United States first devoted federal resources to the task of fighting the spread of venereal disease in 1918, when President Woodrow Wilson made the PHS a part of the military just three days before America entered World War I.[17] In 1912 Congress voted to transform the Marine Hospital Service—which was previously responsible for caring for sick and disabled servicemen, conducting medical inspections of immigrants, and helping state and local governments enforce quarantine regulations—into the PHS. The PHS was given the power to disseminate public health information, conduct research into the causes and spread of disease, and regulate the pollution of the nation's lakes and waterways.[18] Physicians associated with the PHS also conducted medical inspections of Asian, Jewish, and southern and eastern European immigrants into the country to determine who was healthy and who might harbor visible or hidden disease.[19] The growth of its purview eventually included the PHS's transformation into the National Institutes of Health in 1930.[20] Physicians and public health experts from across the country were summoned to join the PHS in its effort to prevent the spread of infectious diseases.

President Wilson was concerned that poor sanitation conditions within military camps and major industrial centers supporting military production could contribute to the spread of disease and compromise the health of US forces.[21] Working with the military, the PHS became responsible for supervising local sewage and water supplies, as well as vaccinating the public against typhoid and smallpox, particularly in areas surrounding military camps. Of its many tasks, the PHS spent considerable effort in educating military men about the hazards of sexually transmitted diseases.[22] Between 1917 and 1919 military officials reported substantial economic losses due to the number of servicemen taken off active duty after contracting venereal diseases.[23] Thus, controlling sexually transmitted diseases was as much about the health of servicemen as it was the economic ramifications of the illness, along with the health and defense of the nation more generally. Getting to the source of the problem was crucial. The PHS understood prostitution as a social vice largely responsible for the contraction and spread of venereal disease and therefore lobbied state legislatures to prohibit the sex trade. As a result of this pressure forty states eventually passed ninety-six laws attempting to limit prostitution. Then in 1918, Congress provided even more authority to the PHS with the Chamberlain-Kahn Act, which established an Interdepartmental Social Hygiene Board to research the cause and spread of venereal disease. Under the act all instances of venereal disease, both within and outside the PHS, had to be reported to the local health authorities with criminal consequences for physicians who failed to do so. Moreover, the Chamberlain-Kahn Act gave state boards of health the power to control the travel and mobility of victims of venereal infections to prevent the spread of the disease. The act also provided the PHS resources to establish clinics to diagnose and treat those who were infected and gave the PHS the authority to administer grants-in-aid to the states to help subsidize their efforts at controlling the spread of venereal diseases. This was the first use of federal aid to the states for health purposes.[24]

By the start of World War I social-scientific surveys were giving credibility to the idea that African Americans were biologically predisposed to sexually transmitted diseases and suffered from illnesses such as syphilis at rates significantly higher than those expressed by white Americans. In its campaign against venereal disease the PHS took a particular interest in African American military men because they appeared to suffer from the disease at higher rates

than white soldiers. In this effort the PHS partnered with the American Social Hygiene Association (ASHA) as the United States entered the war. African
American soldiers formed one-tenth of the military forces, and with the start of
the war there were growing concerns by military officials that the contributions
of black soldiers would be diminished by their high rates of venereal disease.[25]

Eugenic ideology no doubt played a role in how public health officials involved with the PHS thought of race and illness during the war. According to
historians Paul Lombardo and Gregory Dorr, there was very little distinction
between public health and eugenics during the first half of the twentieth century.[26] They argue that eugenic ideology shaped the way physicians, particularly
in the South, theorized black susceptibility to syphilis and other communicable
diseases. Lombardo and Dorr also note that members of the intellectual leadership of the PHS were trained at the University of Virginia Medical School,
where exposure to eugenics updated the racial medicine of the nineteenth century, "establishing it on firmly modern, scientific grounds."[27]

However, in their attempt to show that public health and eugenics were
united during the Progressive Era, Lombardo and Dorr overstate the significance of eugenics as a theoretical source for conceptualizing racial ancestry:

> According to eugenic theory, people of different races inherited not only dif-
> ferences in appearance, moral character, and sexual behavior, but also differ-
> ential susceptibility to disease. Doctors schooled in eugenic theory included
> these "racial" distinctions as part of their diagnostic expectation, understanding
> disease susceptibility and medical outcomes differently for black and white pa-
> tients. Between approximately 1900 and 1950, this perspective was built into the
> curriculum at Virginia; to perceive medical therapeutics in eugenic terms would
> not have seemed strange to doctors trained there.[28]

Lombardo and Dorr create the impression that the theory of differential susceptibility to disease and the inheritance of racial traits originated within the
eugenics movement. Such an impression, however, wrongly attributes eugenicists as the authors of racial theories. Eugenics was the pragmatic application of
preexisting racial ideas, not an actual account of ancestry or race per se.

Francis Galton himself defined eugenics not as a theory of ancestry or
even race but "the science which deals with all influences that improve the
inborn qualities of a race; also with those that develop them to the utmost

advantage."[29] Likewise, Madison Grant understood eugenics to be an applied science in which "under existing conditions the most practical and hopeful method of race improvement is through the elimination of the least desirable elements in the nation by depriving them of the power to contribute to future generations."[30]

Where we do find eugenicists theorizing about race, their ideas are largely derivative of other intellectual sources. Nancy Stepan has made this point, arguing that Galton's ideas about race were poorly defined and built largely on anecdotal evidence "because he took the reality of racial types and the inferiority of certain races to be self-evident, or else well established in anthropology."[31] The eugenicist Charles Davenport's views of race were equally derivative. Following in the footsteps of contemporary biologists, he wrote,

> [The] modern geneticists' definition differs from that of the systematists or old fashion breeder. A race is a more or less pure bred "group" of individuals that differs from other groups by at least one character, or, strictly, a genetically connected group whose germ plasm is characterized by a difference, in one of more genes, from other groups.[32]

Davenport argued that mixing the distinct traits of two racial groups—as defined previously—would result in "racial hybrids" that were maladapted for their immediate environment.

We have seen that American polygenist Josiah Nott defined "race" in nearly the same terms as Davenport. Nott argued that "two races are considered specifically different if they are distinguished from each other by some peculiarities which one cannot be supposed to have acquired, or the other lost, through any known operation of physical causes."[33] According to this polygenist view the traits that distinguished the races were the result of biological differences, not environmental influences. Nott then used this definition of race to argue that racial crossing between blacks and whites had disastrous consequences, as these individuals were "the shortest lived of any class of the human race" and were "more liable to be diseased and are less capable of endurance than either whites or blacks of the same rank and condition."[34] Foreshadowing Davenport's stance against dysgenic mixing of the races and his rejection of environmentalist accounts of human difference, Nott used his polygenist view of human ancestry to argue against providing aid and education to newly emancipated blacks by the Freedman's Bureau. Nott, much like eugenicists in the next century, believed charity and other resources would not change the innate "physical" limitations of the black race.[35]

How are we to explain this continuity between polygenist and eugenic reasoning on the question of innate racial ancestry and its social consequences? According to Stepan, "apart from the new emphasis given by eugenics to heredity and intelligence, eugenicists' views of race were clearly variations on existing racial themes, not new compositions. Their views gave support to, but did not fundamentally alter, the racial paradigm in science."[36] American eugenicists did not offer physicians in the PHS a theory of race or ancestry but instead provided a theory of social planning that would instantiate preexisting racial theories into law and social practice. Lombardo and Dorr are correct in their claim that eugenics modernized racial science. This modernization, however, was achieved by applying established racial ideas to address social concerns. Eugenicists inherited, rather than invented ex nihilo, ideas about race-specific disease susceptibility and other inherited traits.

Polygenism was surely part of the intellectual inheritance of American eugenicists who believed biology trumped environmental influences. This should not come as surprise.[37] Eugenicists in the United States were generally opposed to the idea that racial differences were the result of environmental factors and therefore rejected the idea that the condition of each race could be improved with adjustments to social and political structures.[38] A polygenist view of racial ancestry complied well with this understanding of race. Eugenically minded scientists and physicians could simply reference the ancestral traits of blacks and other groups as the true cause of the differences between the races.

Of course, this would imply that races were stable units, an assumption that was philosophically at odds with Darwin's deconstruction of racial fixity articulated in *The Descent of Man*.[39] According to Peter Bowler the turn of the twentieth century was a period when fundamentally nonevolutionary ideas about species traits and heredity eclipsed Darwinism. Darwin's theory that the selection of favorable traits within a species or organism occurred through an open-ended and random process was met with great suspicion by biologists who endorsed evolution but believed there was a natural order to change.[40]

Darwin suggested that the structures within an organism functioned autonomously—that is, without the guiding influence of God or some other teleological force in nature—in relation to the selection pressures of the environment. Bowler writes that non-Darwinian alternatives

> [were] clearly supported, in part, because they seemed to preserve an element of teleology that would counteract the apparent materialism of neo-Darwinism. Naturalists who were reluctant to concede that evolution is a haphazard, trial-and-error process argued that living development is constrained to advance in a purposeful or orderly manner by forces affecting the production of new variations. They suggested that variation is guided by the intelligent activity of individual organisms, or by forces inherent to the process of individual growth.[41]

With random natural selection in doubt biologists turned to other theories to explain how organisms attained their traits and developed over time.

The rejection of random natural selection also influenced medical-scientific reasoning about human traits under Jim Crow. Physicians at the turn of the twentieth century made use of a polygenist framework to explain how racial groups inherited their dispositions. These non-Darwinian theories allowed medical-scientific thinkers to assume that there was a natural order that explained why some racial groups had greater dispositions to disease and were destined to perish. Ideas about innate ancestral traits would cast a shadow over the common human ancestry of the so-called races, rendering monogenesis virtually meaningless in medical-scientific discourse about changing rates of disease between racial groups.

The Transformation of Venereal Disease into a Racial Disposition

As Darwinism started to be eclipsed by nonevolutionary theories about race and heredity, Hoffman published *Race Traits*, which was nothing short of a social-scientific treatise demonstrating that subsequent to emancipation blacks throughout the nation were degenerating as a race. They were thought to experience high rates of infant mortality, suffer from greater illnesses than other races, and have the shortest life expectancy in the country. Hoffman made his case by researching and quantifying state and military medical records on the health of African Americans since the time of the Civil War. Of the many afflictions African Americans faced, Hoffman seemed particularly interested in what appeared to be the extraordinary number of black men and women, as well as "mulatto" children, suffering from the effects of venereal diseases. Hoffman reported that of a total 22,053 white patients in treatment at the hospitals of the Freedman's Bureau, venereal diseases affected only 379, but 10,887 "colored" patients were treated for venereal conditions out of a total of 430,466.[42] Hoffman also reported that the number of deaths from scrofula and venereal diseases in Alabama between 1890 and 1894 was 66 for whites and 249 for blacks.[43] According to Hoffman, the disparity between the number of whites and blacks who contracted venereal disease also held true in the North. In Baltimore and Washington, D.C., Hoffman found that, between 1885 and 1890, 6 white people and 24 black people died from venereal diseases for every 100,000 persons. Hoffman concluded that comparable disparity in black-white deaths from venereal disease in Baltimore, Washington D.C., and Charleston made "plain the fact that the prevalence of these two diseases and the consequent mortality have greatly increased since the war."[44] Despite the low number of deaths from venereal disease Hoffman insisted on the statistical significance of these figures. He postulated that since

> the disease is closely related to other diseases, principally consumption, and an excessive infant mortality, that the rapid increase of scrofula and venereal disease among the freed people becomes a matter of the greatest social and economical importance.[45]

In other words, venereal diseases were often associated with other common illnesses and collectively had devastating implications for entire generations of African Americans. This, according to Hoffman, warranted national consideration. He believed that the increasingly poor health of African Americans would shift race relations in favor of whites, who, on the whole, appeared to be more robust and resistant to communicable diseases as African Americans were "dying out."

Hoffman's "scientific" explanation for the excessive incidence of death from venereal disease among blacks reflects a tripartite conflation of biological determinism, disease, and morality. Hoffman reasoned that

> the root of the evil [of black decline] lies in the fact of an immense amount of immorality, which is a race trait, and of which scrofula, syphilis, and even

consumption are the inevitable consequences. . . . It is not in the *conditions of life*, but in the *race traits and tendencies* that we find the causes of the excessive mortality. So long as these tendencies are persisted in, so long as immorality and vice are a habit of life of the vast majority of the colored population, the effect will be to increase the mortality by hereditary transmission of weak constitutions, and to lower still further the rate of natural increase, until the births fall below the deaths, and gradual extinction results.[46]

Hoffman rejected the idea that the environment could account for the differences in the death rates between black and white Americans from venereal disease. Rather, innate black dispositions and heredity were seen as the cause for the differences between individuals with African and European ancestry. This line of reasoning was caught in a reinforcing tautology that made any notion of common human ancestry irrelevant for understanding the source of this health disparity. In this post-Darwinian polygenist framework the biological constitution of American blacks was dependent on their innate moral dispositions, which in turn were an expression of the racial traits thought to be unique to their African ancestry. These traits were inherited, and the diseases they manifested were believed to have occurred independently of the environment. Thus, the conclusion was obvious: blacks were destined to perish under the weight of their own unique ancestral tendencies and inferior biological constitutions as free citizens in North America.

Hoffman claimed that his study had the backing of statistical science, and his German-born status also helped guarantee that his perceptions of the "Negro problem" were objective and free from the racial prejudice that compromised the work of other American researchers on this question.[47] This claim to objectivity was typical of turn-of-the-century social scientists, who increasingly relied on statistical analysis as a resource for gaining insight into the causes of the nation's most pressing social problems. Almost overnight *Race Traits* made Hoffman one of the country's premier experts on the health and life expectancy of the American Negro. His studies were widely cited by physicians, social scientists, politicians, and proslavery apologists. *Race Traits* also received the prestigious backing of the American Economic Association.[48] Perhaps most important, his ideas were understandable to the general public and were on the minds of laymen well into the twentieth century.[49]

The impact of Hoffman's *Race Traits* on medical scientists, physicians, and social scientists in the United States was tantamount to the cultural and political impact of *Uncle Tom's Cabin* before the Civil War.[50] Hoffman's conflation of biology, disease, and morality had the effect of dividing American physicians on whether or not the poor health of the Negro was tied to the unique biological ancestry of blacks or was a consequence of deprived social and environmental conditions that could be changed through sanitary and moral education. Some public health researchers understood the deteriorating conditions of black health to be an expression of their poor biological constitutions and African origins. In fact, by the early twentieth century it was not uncommon for white medical societies to openly claim that the African ancestry of black Americans was the direct cause of their poor health, low intelligence, and immoral behavior. All three of these racial traits were thought to pose a threat to white Americans: the plight of blacks during the start of the twentieth century had been famously coined the "Negro Problem."

Addressing the problem of blacks' seemingly high susceptibility to communicable diseases was a concern of many medical societies across the country during the start of the new century, especially in the South. For example, on February 20, 1900, in Charleston, South Carolina, Paul Barringer, president of the Medical Faulty of the University of Virginia, delivered an address before the Tri-State Medical Association of Virginia and the Carolinas, "The American Negro, His Past and Future."[51] Barringer was a physician and highly influential leader at the University of Virginia. He was also a vocal advocate of using eugenic measures to eliminate racially inferior populations. Barringer's influence on southern medicine was enormous. As president he restored the University of Virginia to prominence as the elite medical institution of the South. Influenced by the progressive ideals of scientific professionalism and practical empiricism, Barringer helped establish clinical training of medical students at Virginia and reformed the medical school curriculum to include courses on eugenics.[52] Barringer's ideas influenced generations of Virginians, and after his reforms, the University of Virginia established a pipeline of eugenically trained talent for the PHS.[53]

Barringer had been asked by the secretary of the Tri-State Medical Society to offer reflections on the raison d'être for this new southern medical society. Barringer's response was that the Tri-State Medical Society, which was a con-

sortium of physicians, dentists, and other medical practitioners, should hold a
series of meetings on the Negro Problem facing the South, as this would prove
to be the most important issue for the nation heading into the twentieth century.[54] His suggestion was well received, and Barringer's address spearheaded a
debate on the influence of heredity as the cause of the Negro Problem among
medical practitioners within the society. Although several papers were delivered throughout the course of the February 20 meeting, Barringer's address was
only one of two essays that gained the unanimous vote of the association for it
to be printed and sent to all medical societies in the South.[55]

Much of Barringer's essay reflected the rhetoric of proslavery apologists
and southern paternalism typical of writers who championed the "Negro Degeneracy" myth.[56] Like Hoffman and other social Darwinists, Barringer insisted that the underlying causes behind the degenerate health and behavior
of southern blacks were the racial traits unique to their African origins. Barringer drew from the adage coined by the social Darwinist Ernst Haeckel that
"sociological problems are in most cases biological problems" and the Negro
Problem is best summarized by the "short, crisp biological axiom, which reads
'the ontogeny is the repetition of the phylogeny.'"[57] According to this axiom,
living organisms advanced through the same stages of development as all
other previous members of the same species. In Barringer's terms this could
mean that "freely interpreted the life history of any individual, of any type, unless modified by forces of an exceptional character, will tend to conform to the
lines of ancestral traits."[58] According to this line of reasoning, the descendants
of Africans, who inherited the racial traits of their ancestors, were inevitably
doomed to relive and act out the dispositions, behaviors, and health problems
that were a permanent part of the phylogenic history of the race, unless they
happened to be spared by the gift of "exceptional character." This meant that
the prospect of improving the Negro's situation was truly a matter of chance,
as social forces could not easily, if at all, alter the biological forces responsible
for the poor health of blacks. As Barringer addressed his audience, he made
it clear that

> the question for us to-day then, and the question of questions for the South,
> is, "What is the cause of the change and what can be done to remedy the evil?"
> The first thing is to seek out the truth, however unpalatable it may be, and in

my opinion it is very simple. The young negro of the South, except where descended from parents of exceptional character and worth, is reverting through hereditary forces to savagery. Fifty centuries of savagery in the blood can not be held down by two centuries of forced good behavior if the controlling influences which held down his savagery are withdrawn as they have been in this case. The language and forms of civilization may be maintained, but the savage nature remains.[59]

And what were the racial traits that marked "the Negro's" regression? Barringer cited increased tendencies toward crime, preference for squalid social conditions, "no self-control," "absence of sustained will-power," complete inability to "resist his impulses," "cruelty," and proclivity for the raping of white women unheard of during the time of slavery.[60] Concerning the question of rape, Barringer believed that the "degenerating Negro" possessed "a sexual development, both anatomical and physiological, unapproached except among the lower animals."[61] Like Hoffman, Barringer singled out the sexuality of black males as a unique threat to the overall health and safety of the nation.

However, not all white medical men were of the opinion that the health and sanitary conditions of blacks were hopelessly lost causes. In 1915 the *American Journal of Public Health* dedicated a special issue to the health of the Negro.[62] The physicians who authored opinions argued that inferior sanitary conditions, overcrowding, and a general ignorance about social hygiene caused the poor health of blacks.[63] These were social, not simply biological, conditions that could be changed if whites marshaled the appropriate political will. Unlike the hard hereditarianism championed by eugenicists, these physicians believed that an environmentalist account of race better explained the differences in disease susceptibility between whites and blacks.

In the face of the disagreement over the cause of communicable diseases among white medical men, ideas about venereal diseases being a natural racial trait of the American "Negro" nonetheless gained more power among American medical scientists and laypeople when the US surgeon general's report for 1918 claimed that black soldiers suffered from venereal disease at a rate that was 2.8 times higher than that of white soldiers.[64] Given the highly subjective nature of diagnosing venereal diseases at the time of the First World War, it is unclear whether these statistics were accurate. What is clear, however, is that unlike white men, black men with venereal disease were accepted into military service because military doctors assumed that all blacks had a biological predisposition for sexually transmitted diseases.[65] This assumption and corresponding recruitment practice likely increased the proportion of black soldiers with venereal illnesses in relation to whites. In other words, assumptions about black biology directly contributed to the overreporting of black men with venereal disease.

Thus, we can identify three major factors that contributed to the transformation of venereal disease into a racial trait that reinforced whites' concerns that blacks were a conduit of disease and posed a threat to the nation: social-scientific studies that harbored polygenist assumptions and claimed that heredity rather than the environment was the source of black disposition to venereal disease; faulty assumptions about the role venereal disease played in other common illnesses blacks suffered from more frequently than whites; and racist views about the moral fortitude of blacks and their inability to resist dangerous sexual activity.

Charles V. Roman, the Physician

Although some white physicians challenged the racist connections between black ancestry and disease, black doctors were acutely aware of how this negative association threatened to eclipse the idea of shared human ancestry and with it the notion of shared human traits and equal claims to participating in democratic life. Charles Roman was one of several prominent Progressive Era black thinkers whose critique of race-specific dispositions to disease centered on the idea of shared human ancestry and therefore both identified and challenged the polygenist carryovers shaping public health science.[66]

Charles Victor Roman was a remarkably influential but less well-known African American medical practitioner, public health reformer, and ethicist during the early twentieth century. Roman was born on July 4, 1864, in Williamsport, Pennsylvania. At the age of ten Roman and his family moved to Ontario, Canada, where he was educated at the all-white Hamilton Collegiate Institution.[67] Roman was the first African American to graduate from Hamilton and excelled in his studies, completing a four-year study course a year early.[68] When Roman first returned to the United States in February 1889, he worked as an office assistant to Robert F. Boyd, a physician and professor at Meharry Medical College in Nashville, Tennessee, and founder of Mercy Hospital, Nashville.[69] At this time Mercy was the largest hospital in the South to be owned and managed by African Americans.[70] In 1887 Roman enrolled in a three-year medical program at Meharry.[71] After completing his degree in 1890, he pursued additional studies at the Post-Graduate Medical School and Hospital of Chicago. To complete his medical education, he then attended the Royal Ophthalmic Hospital and Central London Ear, Nose and Throat Hospital in England. After his postdoctorate studies, Roman opened his first medical practice in Dallas, Texas.[72] In October 1904 he relocated to Nashville, where he helped found and chair the Department of Ophthalmology and Otolaryngology at Meharry Medical College. Roman would serve as professor of medical history and ethics from 1904 to 1931.[73]

At the beginning of his term as chair of the department, Roman was appointed president of the National Medical Association (NMA) in 1903.[74] Originally called the National Association of Colored Physicians, Dentists, and Pharmacists, the NMA was founded in 1895 by a consortium of the country's leading African American physicians and medical students after they were denied entry into the American Medical Association, which had been established in 1847. The NMA was established to promote the professional development and national collaboration of African American physicians and other medical practitioners while also addressing the larger health issues facing African Americans more broadly. The NMA made it a mandate to tackle illnesses such as hookworm, tuberculosis, and pellagra.[75] It was also the leading African American professional association lobbying for universal health care beginning at the turn of the twentieth century.[76] Roman, who was a member of the NMA while studying at Meharry as a medical student, was given the task of writing its mission statement:

> Conceived in no spirit of racial exclusiveness, fostering no ethnic antagonism, but born of the exigencies of the American environment, the National Medical Association has for its object the banding together for mutual cooperation and helpfulness, the men and women of African descent who are legally and honorably engaged in the practice of the cognate professions of medicine, surgery, pharmacy and dentistry.[77]

Indeed, Roman took seriously the important social obligations that African American physicians bore. In a 1908 address on medical ethics to the Rock City Academy of Medicine and Surgery, he declared,

> The real mission of medicine is to benefit mankind by healing the sick and preventing disease, not the enrichment of its votaries. The true physician gathers his emoluments because he deserves them, not because he seeks them. His rewards follow as a consequence of duty done. His right thereto is based upon the highest ideal of civilization—the triple extract of ethics, religion and common-sense.[78]

Roman and the members of the NMA were strong advocates of viewing the delivery of health care as the moral application of scientific knowledge and the fullest expression of one's duty as a democratic citizen. Following his tenure as president of the NMA, in 1908 Roman became the first editor of the *Journal of the National Medical Association* (*JNMA*)—a post he held for a decade.

Roman's Environmental Account of Race and Disease

In the year after he stepped down as editor of the *JNMA*, Roman was recruited by the PHS to discuss social hygiene in African American communities.[79] As a medical student at Meharry Medical College he had written his graduating thesis on preventive medicine.[80] As editor of the *JNMA*, Roman also wrote regularly about the benefits of proper social hygiene in the fight against communicable disease. He honed his skills as an orator, Christian ethicist, and critic of racial prejudice while leading a layman's Bible class at St. Paul A.M.E. Church in Nashville beginning in 1904.[81] Roman's "layman discourses" were widely popular among Nashville residents and were regularly attended by the faculty and student body of Meharry. Roman's sermons discussed the moral and political challenges facing African Americans and the importance of fostering cultural and social awareness among blacks—referred to at the time as "race psychology"—in the struggle for equity. In fact, his discourses were so well received that they occasionally replaced the Sunday sermon at St. Paul's.[82] As early as 1917 Roman was lecturing to students at historically black colleges about how improved public sanitation and advancements in medical science were tools for young physicians and medical practitioners in the fight to advance the health of African Americans.[83]

Throughout his large body of writings and public lectures on race and social hygiene Roman articulated a vision of medical science and its relationship to race and social reform that would likely appear unorthodox to many present-day readers, given the secular approach of contemporary medical practitioners. Even though the early twentieth century was a period when contemporary medical science underwent a process of secularization—developing professional, institutional, and conceptual autonomy from other areas of society—medical practitioners and social hygienists such as Roman and others involved in the ASHA continued to disseminate knowledge about disease, sexuality, and race to lay audiences explicitly framed by moral and religious concepts.[84] For Roman, the Christian belief in shared human ancestry (monogenism) was crucial to his theory of health outcomes.

Indeed, key to Roman's understanding of race and disease was his insistence that social and historical factors shaped public health. All races were vulnerable to these forces as a result of their shared ancestry. Therefore, talk of innate biological dispositions overshadowed not only humans' shared vulnerability to illness but also the social and historical conditions that structure disease outcomes.

Roman's clearest articulation of why the Christian idea of common human descent mattered for medical science appeared in his major work, *American Civilization and the Negro: The Afro-American in Relation to National Progress*.[85] It provided a systematic critique of scientific racism and the politics of racial discrimination in the United States, both of which he saw as clear obstacles to improving the life chances of African Americans and their contribution to American democracy. Published in 1921 and more than four hundred pages long, this work offers a view of the breadth and complexity of Roman's thinking on medical and scientific racism, the living legacy of slavery within the United States, the importance of morality for the progress of civilization, and the promise of American democracy. Roman wrote *American Civilization* while working with the PHS; thus, this work offers a deeper understanding of the philosophical assumptions he held when confronting disease in black communities.

Roman demonstrated in *American Civilization* an impressive command of the history of natural philosophy and ethnology, drawing from the work of Carl Linnaeus, Johann Blumenbach, George Cuvier, Ernst Haeckel, Thomas Huxley, Jean Louis Armand de Quatrefages, and Franz Boas.[86] For Roman this literature made it clear that "a careful scrutiny of the data of anthropology . . . will show that nature has not separated her human children by impenetrable walls. Racial differences are not innate and permanent; but are superficial, environmental, and transitory."[87] Racial differences in Roman's mind were fleeting, and human varieties were not distinct but blended into one another:

> Humanity passes with facility from one variety to another, as it does from one class to another. From whatever angle we approach, scientific investigation forces us to the conclusion that the only just way to measure men, either physically, mentally or morally, is to measure them individually. Society is measured by the individual; the development of the individual man is the model of social progress.[88]

In the spirit of Progressive Era individualism Roman saw that the way out of America's fixation with race was to measure the character and biology of each citizen individually. Moreover, he acknowledged that his critique of distinct human groups stood within the long tradition of monogenist conceptions of race as modeled, for example, in the work of Johann Friedrich Blumenbach:

> Blumenbach, true founder of scientific anthropology, has summed up the whole question from the physical standpoint in words that have lost nothing of their force since they were penned a hundred years ago. He asks whether everywhere in time or place mankind has constituted one and the same, or clearly distinct species; and he concludes: although between distant people the difference may seem so great that one may easily take the inhabitants of the Cape of Good Hope, the Greenlanders, and Circassians for peoples of so many different distinct species, nevertheless we shall find, on due reflection, that all, as it were, so merge into the other, the human varieties passing gradually from one another, that we shall scarcely if at all be able to determine any limits between them.[89]

From this Roman concluded that "there is black blood in the whites as assuredly as there is white blood in the blacks." It was also equally clear that "there is but one species of man. These propositions are so established that no one with any just pretense to a scientific education would attempt to dispute them."[90]

Of course, Roman was well aware that there were early twentieth-century men of science who, in denying the common origins of humankind and the effect that the environment had on the human form, "sought assiduously for scientific justification of the tenets of racial inequality." Roman explained that "we have reached a stage of scientific knowledge when evolution is accepted as an elementary truth at the foundation of a rational conception of the universe. Yet wild theories of emotional ethnology still persist among us."[91] Roman thought that those who continued to champion pre-Darwinian theories of racial distinction "lack[ed] neither ingenuity nor industry" but that these persistent theories of "emotional ethnology" continued to thrive because of practitioners' cultural beliefs in racial hierarchy:

> They now admit all . . . propositions [of common descent], claiming however, that while there is but one human family, nature has favorite children, that she has written the decree of favoritism in the tissues of their bodies. In other words, they concede the Negro's theoretical rights as a man, but deny his capabilities as a citizen. They claim the artifice of man is built upon the necessity of nature.[92]

Roman here was spelling out the logic of post-Darwinian polygenism: There are behavioral and health consequences to inferior racial heredity that overshadow any notion of common human ancestry. Insofar as politics ought to mirror the intentions of nature, not all populations should to be treated equally under the law. What is remarkable here is that not only was Roman describing how science participates in social inequality during his own time, but he also was capturing the role of science during the intolerance against Jews during the time of Blumenbach and certainly also the discrimination against blacks by the American polygenists.

For Roman it was precisely because of our shared human ancestry that the "permanent characteristics of mankind are common to all varieties; and the differences that characterize the varieties are transitory."[93] If the traits that distinguish the races were shared across the color line and proven to be ephemeral, then there were no grounds to treat racial differences as fixed or claim these differences had behavioral and health implications. There was also no biological evidence to deny the citizenship of certain populations on the basis of their ancestry. His belief in common descent and that all humans share the same range of physical and behavioral traits had direct health implications for the entire nation; all races are equally disposed to the same diseases and illness:

> The most insidious and destructive diseases of civilized life show no racial predilection. Gonorrhea, and syphilis, opium, alcohol and cocaine, respect no

racial lines. The high and increasing mortality of middle life from Bright's disease, apoplexy and heart disease is a national not a race problem.[94]

There were no race-specific dispositions, just equally vulnerable biology shared
across the color line.

With this as a guiding premise, Roman accounted for the apparent differences in the races by using an environmentalist argument, claiming that species
change was driven by the effect of external forces on the human form rather
than an innate essence that was impervious to the environment. He expressed
this environmental account of race in a lecture delivered at Howard University
on March 2, 1917:

> Health problems begin with the souls and not with the bodies of men. San-
> itation is but a reflex of cerebration, and hygiene is a matter of appetite and
> instinct, impulse and conduct. Health is to be measured in terms of psychol-
> ogy rather than in terms of physiology. What a man thinks is more fateful than
> what he eats. . . . A man has a body, but is a soul. Physical condition is made
> or marred by psychical and social conditions. The key to the mortality table is
> to be found in the educational, economical and political situation. Progress in
> sanitation and health is a reciprocal factor of progress in liberty, virtue and intel-
> ligence. No modern discovery has abrogated [this] moral law.[95]

Roman's intentions were to give an account of the improvements and continued obstacles to positive African American health conditions while also refuting long-standing myths about the inferiority of black biology represented in
the statistical studies of Frederick Hoffman at the turn of the twentieth century.
Roman believed that "an impartial examination of vital statistics does not war-
rant, in fact, flatly contradicts, many of the deductions and prophecies of Hoffman, whose 'Race Traits and Tendencies of the American Negro' has been such
a solace to Negrophobiana."[96] Roman argued that Hoffman's work fomented
the politics of racial prejudice and distorted perceptions of black health within
American medicine:

> Race prejudice has cast its baneful shadow athwart the pathway of medical sci-
> ence and chromotopsia has characterized the vision of medical men. The re-
> sponsiveness of medicine to outside influences has materially enhanced the
> Negro death-rate. Vital statistics are interpreted in terms of ethnography and

mortality returns are taken as a measure of racial fitness; pathology has become
the handmaid of prejudice and the laboratory a weapon of civic oppression.[97]

According to Roman, racial prejudice in medicine made it difficult to see that
health and hygiene were determined not by innate biological or physical dispositions but by the souls, psychological well-being, and moral fortitude of
human beings. These factors, he argued, shape the habits, instincts, and impulses that lead to good health and, when poorly managed, are also responsible for high mortality. Improvements in public health involved changes to
the inner life of the human being, his or her moral dispositions, and socioeconomic conditions. Roman explained how the inner life of a population is
tied to sound health:

> Health problems, I repeat, begin with the souls and not with the bodies of men.
> . . . Freedom and health are intimately and inseparably related. Segregation is the
> partner of disease and the enemy of sanitation. Honor and long life are compan-
> ions. The key to infant mortality is to be found in adult morality.[98]

Roman believed that the immoral economic and political conditions of Jim
Crow, not their innate biological constitutions, were directly responsible for the
denigrated well-being of African Americans. Roman went further:

> American mortuary returns reveal no lethal diseases peculiar to the colored
> people. Tuberculosis of the lungs, the various forms of pneumonia, organic
> heart disease and infant mortality constitute the major part of our excessive
> death-rate. These are all diseases of crowd and stress. Intemperance and late
> hours, insufficient food and rest, bad housing and immorality are powerful fac-
> tors in their production and deadliness. Many of these factors are measurably
> within our control.[99]

There was no such thing as race-specific afflictions derived from inferior biology, only social problems that could be changed through improvements within
public hygiene and the socioeconomic setting of a population. With this logic
Roman reasoned that at the root of venereal disease were social problems, not
ancestral traits. The elimination of venereal disease, therefore, required changes
in the socioeconomic situation of black Americans, as well as a transformation
in their sexual practices.

This is precisely what Roman argued when the PHS assigned him to deliver a series of lectures in 1918 to African American military men stationed in Camp Grant, located in Rockford, Illinois, and Camp Stewart near Savannah Georgia.[100] In these lectures Roman tried to persuade black soldiers that continence, moral integrity, and proper medical diagnosis and treatment were the three most effective means of preventing the spread of venereal disease. In fact, Roman likened the contraction of venereal disease to Nature's punishment for immoral sexual acts:

> Nature gives us the privilege of choosing our course but reserves the right to pay or punish according to our conduct. Nature has set her stand of disapproval on sexual promiscuity by fixing venereal diseases as a penalty for prostitution. A thing is good or bad according to the way it is used. The sexual impulse is one of the greatest influences that ever came into a man's life. Rule it and it will bless you, let it rule you and it will curse you, and the generations to follow you. The sexual act has but two purposes or places in an honorable life. It is a generative act and an expression of love. Sexual congress is the creator's high seal of approval upon the marriage vow. Sexual congress between people who do not love each other is brutal passion degrading human reason. Nature has made no provision for prostitution. Gonorrhea and syphilis are but expressions of her disgust.[101]

Weaving together an image of Nature as a retributive force and appealing to the inherent value of Christian marriage, Roman presented the etiology of venereal disease not simply in medical-scientific terms but also within an explicitly moral framework. The message was clear: black men are to harmonize their sexual practices with the moral laws embedded in nature, or there will be consequences for both the individual transgressor and his offspring:

> A man that would willfully put out the eye of an innocent baby is the meanest of criminals. Yet that is what a man does who takes clap to the marriage bed. If there is any Hell, I think the hottest place in it ought to be reserved for the man who willfully spreads venereal disease. A man with no respect for a pure woman is not fit to live. I believe I am right when I think you want to be good soldiers and good men, that you want to defend your country and protect your mothers, wives, sweethearts and children.[102]

Roman's emphasis on having "respect for a pure woman" and the duty of black soldiers to be "good men" who protect their "country," "mothers, wives," and "children" is an example of the overlapping message eugenicists and social hygienists conveyed to black and white audiences on how prudent and well-informed sexual choices improve the "fitness" of a population and potentially that of the nation.[103] In this framework the love of one's country meant more than a willingness to take up arms in its defense; it also meant the defense of good sexual hygiene. At stake in the sexual practices of these black soldiers in particular, and black men in general, was the fitness of the race as a whole and ultimately the contributions of blacks to American civilization.

Roman's understanding of the social determinants of health and the fallacy of race-specific illnesses, particularly venereal disease, reflected a historical and environmentalist account of human difference shared by many other advocates of social hygiene during this period. Indeed, an environmentalist account of race reverberated among leading social hygienists in the 1920s, such as Roscoe C. Brown, who was also recruited by the PHS; Franklin O. Nichols, director of the Southern Regional Office of the National Urban League and hired by the ASHA; and Arthur B. Spingarn, the Jewish director of the National Association for the Advancement of Colored People (NAACP) hired by the US Army to work with African Americans. As the historian Christina Simmons has noted, all three of these social hygienists claimed that high rates of venereal disease and other illnesses among African Americans could be explained as the effects of history, the environment, and class.[104] They argued that the legacy of slavery wreaked havoc on the communal support structures of black family life, leaving African Americans more exposed to sexual and communicable diseases. This vulnerability was exacerbated by the politics of racial prejudice. Poor funding and lack of resources for public schools effectively robbed blacks of the institutional support structures capable of facilitating moral values and other important social skills. Roman, along with Brown, Nichols, and Spingarn, argued that the contraction and spread of venereal disease could not be understood without giving attention to these marked effects of slavery and racism.[105]

According to Roman these social and moral determinants of health could easily be eclipsed by medical men, anthropologists, and politicians who bought stock in theories of biological determinism that attributed high rates of infant mortality and disease among blacks to their African ancestry:

> The greatest difficulties confronting us from a sanitary and hygienic standpoint arise not from the physiological weakness of the colored man but from the psychological strength of the white man. The white man's immunity to fact is a more destructive force than the colored man's susceptibility to disease.[106]

Roman understood that the links made between racial ancestry and illness were a major factor in the misrepresentation of blacks as a biologically unfit population in which social conditions were not taken into consideration concerning blacks' vulnerability to disease and hopes for health. In other words, a high rate of disease in black Americans was a conceptual and political problem, not a genetic one.

Race toward the Twenty-First Century

At the beginning of the twentieth century American social scientists and medical practitioners believed that each race possessed different susceptibilities to venereal disease. This assumption became part of a medical-scientific discourse that associated unique racial ancestry with higher rates of illness. American public health researchers effectively brought back to life the logic of nineteenth-century polygenism, drawing connections between distinct biological pedigree and inherited racial dispositions. The shared heredity of the races was virtually irrelevant for early twentieth-century public health researchers—such as Frederick Hoffman and Paul Barringer—who were convinced that blacks possessed an innate disposition to contract venereal disease. In effect, a common illness was transformed into a racialized disorder.

But from the perspective of physicians more attentive to the significance of shared human ancestry and the environmental factors shaping health outcomes, the links between ancestry and venereal disease were rife with contradictions. For the social hygienist Charles V. Roman, monogenism provided a conceptual anchor for his critique of scientific racism, allowing him to decouple false correlations between black ancestry and communicable disease. By taking seriously the common descent of all racial groups, he turned to the environment to explain the disparities in health that existed across the color line. Social hygienists committed to this progressive view of race understood that human health and behavior changed in relation to the cultural, political, and economic history of a population. With this logic, the living legacy of slavery and the immediate effects of Jim Crow directly shaped the health of African Americans. In other words, sociopolitical institutions were the cause of high rates of disease among blacks, not innate biological dispositions stemming from unique racial ancestry. With common descent in full view an ever-broadening understanding of the environment became the key to explaining perceived differences between so-called racial groups. Diseases like syphilis could be framed as a race-specific trait only when medical thinkers lost sight of the shared biological experience that links all racial groups.

Roman's vision of the social determinants of health provides a window onto the ethical implications that were carried along by the idea of common human descent. Monogenism was an ethical concept by virtue of its ties to Christian thought, which, according to Roman, kept alive the physicians' sense of responsibility for the care of all racial groups. Yet for Roman, the notion of common human ancestry was also a scientific idea that compelled thinkers to develop more sophisticated accounts of why humans varied while sharing a set of biological experiences—either from the ancient past or the more recent present. Roman's marriage of Christian values with public health reform was a precursor to civil rights era activists who saw that medicine and morality were necessary counterparts in the struggle for equal life chances for all racial groups in the United States.

With the gradual advance of twentieth-century genetics and medical research, we will continue to see intellectual investment in studying the origins and source of human variation. The problem to which we now turn is that the proliferation of new tools and techniques to measure race, along with the unbridled optimism this brings, divided scientists on whether race is a valid scientific concept. Part of the opposition stemmed from the gradual awareness, on the part of biologists and social scientists, of illegitimate metaphysical assumptions about human ancestry and racial traits that remain a feature of even the most cutting-edge genetic research on human populations.

4

NOAH'S MONGREL CHILDREN
Ancient DNA and the Persistence of Christian Forms
in Modern Biology

ON JUNE 2, 1857, Johann Carl Fuhlrott, a gymnasium teacher in Elberfeld, Germany, and Hermann Schaaffhausen, a professor of anatomy at the University of Bonn, presented to the Natural History Society of Prussian Rhineland and Westphalia what appeared to be the remains of an ancient human race.[1] The fossils, which included about half of the bone structure of a complete body, were found by accident the year before by workers at the Kleine Feldhofer Grotte in the Neander Valley near Düsseldorf, Germany. On the day of their fortuitous discovery, September 4, 1856, canyon workers had presented the remains to Fuhlrott, assuming they belonged to an ancient cave bear—an increasingly common find by quarry workers in Germany and other parts of Europe during the mid-nineteenth century. Fuhlrott, an amateur but well-known fossil collector, saw that the prominent brow ridges and narrow skullcap were too humanlike to belong to an ancient animal. This was true even though the thickness and weight of this creature's massive femur bones were unlike any he had seen in modern humans. With a humanlike bone structure whose antiquity appeared obvious given the extent of mineralization that had collected on the fossils and the depth at which the remains were found, Fuhlrott concluded that the quarry workers had actually discovered the remains of an ancient human type. Word of Fuhlrott's discovery spread quickly to Hermann Schaaffhausen. Eventually the two met, and Schaaffhausen corroborated Fuhlrott's claim that an ancestral human had been discovered in the Neander Valley. Their collaborative presentation of the world's first "Neanderthal" in June 1857 prompted a furious debate across Europe and America about the origins of modern humans and the biological links that humans might have with ancestral hominids buried deep below the earth's surface.

In May 2010, almost a century and a half later, the Neanderthal Genome Project (NGP) announced a discovery that shed new light on human ties to our hominid ancestors, the Neanderthals. Hidden within the six billion base pairs that make up the modern human genome, the NGP identified potential regions within "the human genome reference sequence" (a collection of all known human genes covering 99 percent of the human genome) where Neanderthals and humans are thought to have mixed through interbreeding.[2] To corroborate their theory, modern scientists have compared Neanderthal DNA with human DNA from six individuals who in most people's minds represent continental racial types: two individuals from China, one from France, one from Papua New Guinea, one from South Africa, and one from West Africa. Their conclusions were rendered in broad, sweeping terms; the project discovered that Asians and Europeans were more genetically similar to the Neanderthal than Africans were, with an estimated 1–4 percent of their genome containing Neanderthal DNA.[3] Thus, some 150 years after Fuhlrott and Schaaffhausen's discovery, scientists now claim to have verified the actual biological links between humans and Neanderthals. Although all contemporary humans did not equally share the genetic legacy of the Neanderthal, the line between our closest extinct relatives and us proved more porous than had been expected.

The discovery of gene flow between humans and Neanderthals was aided by novel scientific methods that allow biologists to access and conceptualize the genetic traits that separate populations. Using this innovation, geneticists were able to discover Neanderthal genes in humans by looking for Neanderthal traits in the descendants of what are believed to be the three most cohesive and ancestral populations that make up our species: African, Asian, and European. Given the history that has been covered in previous chapters, this division of humans into three ancestral groups should not strike us as an arbitrary move. Geneticists did not invent this practice of reducing human diversity to three original populations. They inherited it from a Christian intellectual history. Indeed, this ontological division between African, Asian, and European represents a form of secular creationism, yet one in which geneticists can imagine the formation of

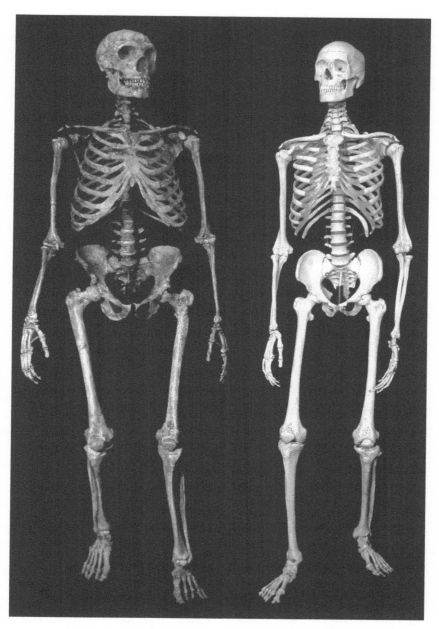

IMAGE 7. Reconstruction of a Neanderthal skeleton found in the Neander Valley during the mid-nineteenth century (left) and a skeleton of a modern human (right). Source: Reconstruction by Gary Sawyer and Blaine Maley, Anthropology Division of the American Museum of Natural History; photo by Ken Mowbray.

a stable, coherent, and "pure" population without having to provide an account of a creator. This represents what Blumenberg referred to as "the reoccupation of answer positions that had become vacant" and the pursuit of questions that cannot be resolved under the epistemological constraints modernity has set for itself. Hence the paradox of contemporary genetic studies of race: God the creator remains an organizing principle for conceptualizing human ancestry while at the same time it is believed that God's power has been eliminated from the inner workings of modern life. The effects of the creator God of the Genesis narrative are apparent even though God is believed dead. We will see in this chapter how creationist assumptions have been built into the algorithms used to simulate the human genetic diversity of the past. The discovery of the Neanderthal genome offers a brilliant display of how inherited assumptions from Christian intellectual history literally frame contemporary scientific thinking about race.

This was also true of the scientific encounter with the Neanderthal during the nineteenth century. Just over 150 years ago early ethnologists used "racial traits" derived from human crania to first differentiate the human races according to a relatively stable set of four original racial types. The racial traits found in the skull of each population were then used to discern the evolutionary link between Neanderthals and human beings. Yet also left unexplained was how nature—which according to evolutionary thinking was not supposed to be driven toward specific biological ends—was capable of forming ancestral populations with clearly defined traits that so easily divided the human species. Present-day geneticists who have unlocked the secrets of the Neanderthal genome have made a very similar move. Instead of cranial traits, genetic traits (SNPs) have been used to divide humans into three ancestral populations to shore up our genetic links to the Neanderthal. Thus, in both centuries we see how the scientific encounter with the Neanderthal exposes the latent secular creationism, derived from Christina intellectual history, that has informed how scientists have imagined and explained the origins of the races.

The Problem: Recurring Visions of Race

Until recently scientific theories of race have been explained according to the following narrative.[4] Race emerged as a coherent scientific concept during the nineteenth century, when scientists assumed all humans could be reduced into three or more basic racial groups or typologies. This way of approach-

ing race was indebted to the classification systems of post-Enlightenment figures, such as Carl Linnaeus and Johann Friedrich Blumenbach during the late
eighteenth century. Biological conceptions of race eventually fell into disfavor
during the first two decades of the twentieth century due in large part to the
pioneering work of the Jewish-German anthropologist Franz Boas and the
African American sociologist W. E. B. Du Bois. Boas in his two most noteworthy works, *The Mind of Primitive Man* (1911) and *Changes in Bodily Forms of
Descendants of Immigrants* (1912), severed the link between race, language, and
culture, which was a fundamental premise of racializing evolutionary theories
and social Darwinism.[5] By separating biology from culture, he called into question the scientific validity of race, arguing that Westerners lack the ability to
objectively evaluate the cultural life, and by extension the evolutionary development, of other social groups. The value of each culture had to be taken on its
own terms, as there were no grounds for sorting humans into a "natural" hierarchy. Boas also disputed the widely accepted notion of fixed and heritable racial traits by collecting ethnographic data demonstrating that the bodily forms
of immigrant groups—specifically their skull measurements—varied as a result
of the environment and other social factors.

Although working in the field of sociology, Du Bois made a similar attempt
to decouple the link between race, culture, and biology. In his work *The Philadelphia Negro* (1896) and *An Essay toward an Anthropology of a Race Concept*
(1943) Du Bois confronted the scientific racism that motivated the views of social Darwinists in the United States and abroad. Du Bois argued that economic
and social factors, not innate biological deficiencies, were responsible for the
poor health and dire social conditions of African Americans. Moreover, much
like Boas, he argued that it was illegitimate to use the cultural forms of a social group as a proxy for determining their biological worth or evolutionary
progress.[6] According to the decline of the scientific racism narrative, Boas and
Du Bois helped precipitate a paradigm shift in the way scientists visualized the
perception of race and ultimately opened the door for more robust critiques of
racial determinism and the use of race as a tool of scientific analysis during the
remainder of the twentieth century.

Eventually the development of population genetics through the work of
Ronal A. Fisher, John B. S. Haldane, Sewall Wright, and Theodosius Dobzhansky in the 1920s and 1930s helped further complicate the notion of fixed racial

types.[7] These early pioneers of population genetics synthesized the Mendelian theory of genetic inheritance with the Darwinian view of evolution through natural selection.[8] They came to see human groups as dynamic biological units or "populations" in which the genetic composition of a group was believed to change as a result of the operation of various factors such as natural selection, genetic drift, mutation, geographic isolation, and migration.[9] With this vision of the human species as a porous and potentially unstable biological entity, population geneticists realized that the idea that race was something consistently passed down from one generation to the next was oversimplified and inaccurate.[10] Instead, they maintained that the differences between so-called racial groups could be better understood in terms of the frequency and concentration of certain alleles (or genes) across a given population and geographic region.[11]

According to the story of the decline of scientific racism, the end of World War II is believed to mark another important paradigm shift in the way Western scientists conceptualized human variation. In 1945 the United Nations Educational, Scientific, and Cultural Organization (UNESCO) was formed to promote international collaboration on issues dealing within peace, security, justice, and human rights through education and scientific and cultural research. Given the blatant role that scientific racism played in the Holocaust, UNESCO was asked in 1949 by the UN Economic and Social Council to develop a program for disseminating scientific facts designed to remove racial prejudice. UNESCO convened a Committee on Experts on Race Problems, comprising primarily social scientists working in the field of cultural anthropology and sociology. This committee drafted a statement on race refuting the misconceptions that race determines mental aptitude, temperament, or social habits. After several revisions and reviews by a designated group of scientists in biology, genetics, social psychology, sociology, and economics, the first UNESCO "Statement on Race" was issued on July 18, 1950.[12]

Following the 1950 "Statement on Race," objections were raised concerning the analytic value of racial concepts. Scientists also argued that the original statement lacked authority of those groups most competent to discuss the biological aspects of human variation because its authors did not include input from geneticists and physical anthropologists. Thus, the debate over the status of race after the modern evolutionary synthesis went unresolved.[13] On June 4–8, 1951, UNESCO invited a panel of physical anthropologists and geneticists to draft a supplementary statement representing the views of the biological sciences. This supplementary statement, "Statement on the Nature of Race and Race Difference by Physical Anthropologists and Geneticists," was published in 1952 and made two important revisions to the 1950 statement.[14] First, scientists involved in the second statement challenged the claim that intellectual and emotional differences between the races did not exist. The framers of the second statement continued to affirm that innate differences between human groups could in time be demonstrated and that the pursuit of this question should not be removed from the agenda of scientists solely for political correctness.[15] Second, they took issue with the claim that the equal treatment of human beings through the law and economic relations should depend on the assumption that all humans are biologically similar. The framers of the second statement believed that racial categories could still be helpful analytic tools for understanding human variation as long as they were freed of ideological influences and divorced from larger social needs. This opened the door for further revisions to the race concept during the 1960s as population geneticists, following the lead of Dobzhansky, attempted to define race as a dynamic subgroup within the human species.[16] In this view races were not discrete biological units but fluid natural populations that emerged in response to the pressures of natural selection.

Given the pushback of physical anthropologists and population geneticists, Reardon argues that it is important not to be misled into believing that the seemingly "nonpolitical" conception of human difference articulated by the framers of the second statement marked an end to the concept of race within modern science.[17] Instead, the second statement reveals deep disagreement among scientists over the use value of racial classifications and the proper relationship between science, ideology, and society. Framers of the second statement agreed that the political uses of race by scientists should be avoided, but scientists themselves should not abandon racial categories in their own work.

The defenders of the first statement, however, believed that a populationist conception of race did not avoid the conceptual problems of nineteenth-century racial typological theories.[18] Thus, rather than view the UNESCO statements as precipitating a paradigm shift in racial thinking, we must see a continuity between pregenetic history of racial thinking and the emergence of population genetics.[19] This continuity has resulted in scientists remaining divided about whether there is a genetic basis to race.

Indeed, at the turn of this millennium the notion that races were not clearly defined populations or that there were no genes for race was confirmed with the complete sequencing of the human genome. Geneticists found that the surface differences expressed between any two "races" constitutes less than half a percent of our total genome.[20] This vision of human *similarity* became the recognized view of many scientists when in June 2000 the geneticist Craig Venter, head of the private sequencing company Celera Genomics, announced publicly that humans are 99.9 percent the same genetically.[21] Now able to view the structure of human DNA, some population geneticists believed that once again the use value of racial categories had been called into question. Many geneticists saw that the phenotypic variations between so-called racial groups were truly inconsequential in light of the overwhelming amount of genetic information shared between populations who on the surface appeared different from one another. With this new vision of human similarity advocates of genomic science believed that it would be possible to provide personalized genomic medicine that would move beyond the restrictions of race and make good on the liberal democratic value of promoting the well-being of all citizens.[22]

After the discovery that humans are 99.9 percent the same genetically, it would seem increasingly difficult, if not impossible, for scientists to continue using race as a metric for understanding what it means to be human at a biological level. Yet in the last decade social scientists have drawn attention to the return of racial typological thinking within the life sciences.[23] By looking at the most divergent qualities of the most geographically separated individuals, contemporary geneticists have been able to increase the likelihood of detecting differences between populations, thereby amplifying the significance of the less than half a percent of genetic material that distinguishes human groups.[24] Specifically, scientists have sought out SNPs, which are variations in the DNA nucleotide base pair pattern of A-T-G-C.[25] Population geneticists interested in human difference claim to have found SNPs unique to the four major continental populations (Africa, Asia, Europe, North America) from which contemporary humans have descended.[26] With regard to human origins, these SNPs have been given the technical term "ancestry-informative marker" (AIM) and indicate to researchers the ancestral heritage of present-day populations. In this most recent form of typological thinking, geneticists are able to hypothesize the various ancestries (genetic admixture) any given individual might possess.[27] In recent years the public has increasingly grown familiar with this technology due to the popularity of various television documentaries on human genetic ancestry as well as the increased availability and affordability of direct-to-consumer DNA testing.[28]

As in the 1950s and 1960s there has been some resistance to this resurgence of racial thinking within science. Both social scientists and geneticists have pointed out that geneticists continue to cast human variation in terms of racial typologies even though the association between any given individual with an assumed ancestral past is probabilistic and far from certain. Many argue that there are other ways to define an individual's genetic makeup or geographic origin. Medical anthropologist Duana Fullwiley writes that "although the language of scientists who invented this panel of AIMs is now that of 'biogeographical ancestry,' the conceptual configuration of human racial typology remains intact even though [they have] the ability to employ a larger interpretive frame when pressed."[29] Moreover, there appears to be no consensus among geneticists whether or not the SNPs thought to differentiate populations have actually played a relevant role in human evolutionary history.[30] These inconsistencies and gaps in knowledge have led both social scientists and geneticists to question the epistemology that guides the use of SNPs to discern ancestry. Some have argued that the notion that there once existed three or four homogeneous parental populations from which present-day groups have descended is fundamentally non-Darwinian.[31] The implication is that through admixture technology geneticists have engaged in new forms of secular creationism that divide individuals into the same racial typologies deployed by nineteenth-century naturalists and twentieth-century racial theorists who relied on Christian intellectual history.[32] The starting point for the modern genetic study of human variation is not marked by an intellectual defect or a void in the understanding of scientists concerning where we come from. On the contrary, contemporary biologists have a rich intellectual heritage that prefigures the scientific perception of race. The effects of this heritage have been particularly apparent across the history of scientific study of the Neanderthal.

Racialized Crania during the Nineteenth Century

Following Darwin's *Origin of Species* evolutionists faced two major problems in the attempt to defend their account of human development.[33] Evolutionists first had to provide a culturally palatable and scientifically consistent explanation of how natural selection was responsible for the higher faculties thought to be exclusive to the human mind. They also had to establish a scientific case for the link between humankind and the animal world. Naturalists such as Charles Lyell and Alfred Russell Wallace tried to resolve the former issue by rearticulating the Christian view of humankind's biological uniqueness. Both were led to the conclusion that the attributes of humanity were the result of a supernatural interference within the natural laws of evolution. This solution was unsatisfactory in the eyes of Darwin and Thomas Huxley, who insisted that humans did not constitute an exception to the laws of continuous evolution from lower life-forms.[34]

In fact, Huxley made one of the first attempts to offer a consistently naturalist explanation of how humans acquired their novel traits in his work *Man's Place in Nature*, originally published in 1863. Huxley argued that based on the shared physical characteristics between humans and the great apes—particularly the hands, feet, and skull—the human species should be properly classified in the same order as the other primates.[35] Even though there were clear morphological similarities between humans and the apes, this alone did not prove that they shared an ancestor. Huxley and other evolutionists had to show within the fossil record that there existed a hominid antecedent to the present humans with characteristics closer to those of the apes than of modern humans. Naturalists believed that the modern human form was a recent evolutionary creation, but the ancestor shared between humans and primates was assumed to have the primitive features still expressed by the great apes. To search for the missing link between the great apes and humans, evolutionists turned their attention to the humanlike fossil remains found in the Neander Valley by Fuhlrott and Schaaffhausen, as well as the fossils discovered in Engis, Belgium, in the early 1830s. It was thought that the Neanderthal would shore up an evolutionary understanding of human development from the animal world.

The Neanderthal, however, appeared much closer to modern humans than not. Indeed, the anatomical studies of the Neanderthal by Franz Josef Carl Mayer in 1856 and George Busk in 1861 led many naturalists to conclude that the Neanderthal crania more closely resembled those of the so-called savage races such as the Mongolians and Australian aboriginals than the crania of the great apes.[36] Following his own comparative analysis of human and Neanderthal skulls from Engis and the Neander Valley, Huxley wrote,

> Although in the lower races of men now upon earth, and in the skeleton found in
> the cavern in the Neanderthal, the human characters vary a little in some particu-

lars in a pithecoid direction, the extent of this variation is very slight indeed when compared with the whole difference which separates them; and it may be safely affirmed that there is at present no evidence of any transitional form or intermediate link between man and the next succeeding form in the vertebrate scale.[37]

In fact, so similar was the skull of the Neanderthal to that of present-day humans that Mayer claimed that the remains found in the Neander Valley belonged to a horse-riding Cossack who had fought against Napoleon during the wars of liberation in 1813–14.[38]

The similarity between Neanderthals and humans made it difficult to divide both populations into separate species. For those in favor of evolution, the Neanderthal skull was too similar to existing racial types to be posited as the "missing link" between humankind and the animal world (i.e., apes). For those opposed to evolution, the similarity of the Neanderthal to modern human types, specifically Mongolians and Australian aboriginals, confirmed that this humanoid belonged to one of the existing races with its unique traits interpreted as pathological deformities.[39]

Ultimately, the Neanderthal did not turn out to be the bridge between humans and the great apes that evolutionists had hoped for. The subsequent Neanderthal remains unearthed in the Belgian La Nualette Cave in 1866 and near Spy in Belgium in 1886 shared features with the remains found in the Neander Valley and thus consistently approached the human form. Even the discoveries of the Cro-Magnons in the Dordogne region of France in 1868, as well as the "Java Man," discovered by Eugène Dubois in 1890 and 1892, proved to be strikingly human. In effect the "missing link" was absent from the fossil record.

Even though there were no concrete human remains approaching the ape form, the fossil record did show a steady improvement in the technology used by humans, evolving from primitive stone tools to the use of bronze and iron. As the historian Peter Bowler has explained, in the absence of "fossil evidence for the *biological* improvement of man, evolutionists seized on the evidence for *cultural* progress as at least indirect support for their claims." In effect, "the great development of prehistoric archaeology that took place in the late nineteenth-century allowed the construction of a sequence of cultural periods that were supposed to have succeeded one another as the human race progressed. Little thought was given to the possibility that different cultures might exist side by side in the same epoch."[40] The result was that turn-of-the-century anthropologists and prehistoric archeologists constructed a linear model of human cultural development. This model assumed that cultural progress and technological innovations were an expression of underlying biological changes within human populations as they evolved through a predetermined hierarchy of stages, with Europeans at the top of the evolutionary chain. This progressive arrangement of human development was an extension of the Christian view that life progresses toward higher forms to truth. When this religious conception of history was set within an evolutionary framework, each race was thought to develop according to its own pace, with the so-called savage races depicting how the "white race's ancestors lived in prehistoric times."[41] Modern "primitives" became, in effect, stand-ins for the missing link between animals and humans sought by evolutionists.

Thus, in its earliest articulation Darwinian evolution was shaped by two contradictory influences that left Huxley and others struggling to maintain a consistently evolutionary view of human origins and development. As Bowler explains, "On the one hand, contemporary developments in cultural evolutionism seemed to imply that development should be treated as a linear progress along a predetermined scale. On the other, [Darwin's] own theory treated biological evolution as an open-ended process in which each branch's history is shaped by unique factors."[42] Evolution by natural selection did not imply that human development advanced toward any particular form or set stages of cultural development. Evolutionists, however, were in a bind, as they needed to explain why humans appeared to possess unique attributes—such as the ability to make music and the capacity for reason—without succumbing to supernaturalism. Evolutionists believed that the attributes that made humans special had to be acquired gradually over time, not through direct divine intervention. Given the limits of the fossil record, the idea that cultural achievements reflected internal biological developments within our species allowed nineteenth-century evolutionists to argue that human culture and biology became more refined as we evolved from lower animal forms. Of course, this view implied that this refinement was still taking place and therefore the so-called primitive races, who appeared to lack complex forms of government and technological sophistication, represented early stages of human evolution from the animal world that present-day Europeans had once occupied. Bowler points out, however, that such a view of development had the unintended consequence of casting human formation "as the predestined end product of a morally purposeful system."[43] In attempting to explain the formation of the races, evolutionists created a theory that "re-occupied" answer positions that had been carved out by an explicitly Christian worldview, thus leaving their ideas framed by the very religious epistemology they sought to overcome in their critique of supernaturalism. Although a cultural evolutionary model was more acceptable than the supernaturalism affirmed by Lyell and Wallace, it was inconsistent with the view of indefinite evolutionary pathways Darwin sketched out in the *Origin of Species*. This linear view of human advancement across fixed developmental stages left evolutionists with a contradictory understanding of race, which became apparent in their comparative study of human and Neanderthal crania.

Evolutionists who affirmed the unity of the races were opposed to the polygenist idea that the various races possessed traits that warranted classifying humans into separate species. Darwin and Huxley explicitly denounced the view that the different traits of humankind were so extreme that speciation had occurred between the races. In the *Descent of Man*, Darwin claimed that those trying to rank "the races of man as distinct species" would be "much disturbed as soon as he perceived that the distinctive characters of every race of man were highly variable." Darwin "doubted whether any character can be named which is distinctive of a race and is constant." For Darwin saw that "the most weight of all the arguments against treating the races of man as distinct species is that they graduate into each other, independently in many cases, as far as we can judge, of their having intercrossed." Thus, it was "hardly possible to discover clear distinctive characters between [the races]."[44] Following Darwin, Huxley in his 1863 essay "On Some Fossil Remains of Man" wrote that "the student of anatomy is perfectly well aware that there is not a single organ of the human body the structure of which does not vary, to a greater or less extent, in different individuals."[45] Regarding the idea of race-specific characters within the human skull, Huxley claimed,

> The characters of the brain vary immensely, nothing being less constant than the form and size of the cerebral hemispheres, and the richness of the convolutions upon their surface, while the most changeable structures of all in the human brain are exactly those on which the unwise attempt has been made to base the distinctive characters of humanity, viz. the posterior cornu of the lateral ventricle, the hippocampus minor, and the degree of projection of the posterior lobe beyond the cerebellum.[46]

For Huxley, the variation that humans expressed also occurred within so-called racial groups in which "the majority of the structural varieties to which allusion is here made, are individual."[47] Clearly Darwin and Huxley were opposed to the notion that there were racial characteristics wholly unique to one population that warranted classifying humankind into various species.

Yet when comparing human characteristics with the traits of the Neanderthal, evolutionists were less consistent in their views of race. Evolutionists' critique of speciation did not necessarily translate into a complete refutation of the idea of distinct and heritable racial traits. In fact, knowledge of the cranial differences expressed between the races was key for the ability of naturalists to plot the Neanderthal form as belonging to one of the many stages of human development. It also helped evolutionists argue that the Neanderthal was an ancient specimen and not a modern human with gross or pathological deformities. Schaaffhausen, for instance, understood the large frontal sinuses and super-orbital ridges of the Neanderthal as "a typical race-character" and not simply the features of an aberrant "individual or pathological deformity."[48] This view was derived from comparing data gathered by ethnologists, such as the polygenist Samuel Morton, on the cranial traits of other races. Schaaffhausen claimed that it was

> remarkable, and important in the explanation of the [Neanderthal form] that a prominence, though in much less degree, of the supra-orbital ridges has been observed chiefly in the crania of savage races, as well as in those of great antiquity. . . . In Morton's works an unusual development of the [supra-orbital ridges] may be seen in the Peruvian, the Mexican, the Seminole, and in the skulls of other races, some of which were taken from ancient burial places.[49]

Like Schaaffhausen, Huxley thought that there were clear points of structural similarity between the Neanderthals and the racial traits of the so-called aboriginal races. In his first analysis of the Neanderthal published in his essay "On Some Fossil Remains of Man," Huxley was convinced that the cranial capacity of the Neanderthal fell within the range of contemporary races:

> Under whatever aspect we view this cranium whether we regard its vertical depression the enormous thickness of its supraciliary ridges its sloping occipital or its long and straight squamosal suture we meet with ape-like characters

stamping it as the most pithecoid of human crania yet discovered. But Professor Schaaffhausen states that the cranium in its present condition holds 1033.24 cubic centimetres of water or about 63 cubic inches, and as the entire skull could hardly have held less than an additional 12 cubic inches, its capacity may be estimated at about 75 cubic inches, which is the average capacity given by Morton for Polynesian and Hottentot skulls.[50]

Several years after this initial examination Huxley reaffirmed his beliefs on the similarity between the Neanderthal and certain races:

> It has come to be generally admitted that [the Neanderthal's] remarkable cranium is no more than a strongly marked example of a type which occurs not only among other prehistoric men, but is met with, sporadically, among the moderns; and that, after all, I was not so wrong as I ought to have been, when I indicated such points of similarity among the skulls found in our river beds and among native races of Australia.[51]

Huxley, however, wavered in his understanding of racial traits within the skull. Clearly he thought that there were no consistent differences in the brain shape and size of population groups to suggest there were different human species. But Huxley was tentatively optimistic that the current methods of analysis could yield reliable data about race-specific features. In his view, more data from human skulls coupled with novel innovations in the measurement of their various facial angles were needed to provide a "safe basis for that ethnological craniology which aspires to give the anatomical characters of the crania of the different Races of Mankind."[52]

The writings of Schaaffhausen and Huxley reveal that evolutionists came to terms with the "humanity" of the Neanderthal by observing this ancient fossil through the lens of race and nonevolutionary assumptions about population-specific characteristics. If there were no consistent features that divided humankind into clearly set groups, as Darwin claimed, then logically speaking, evolutionists should have avoided the use of ethnological data suggesting the possibility of "racialized skulls." In other words, there were no grounds to assume that an analysis of an aboriginal skull would be more informative about the link between humans and Neanderthals than an analysis of a European skull. Yet identifiable cranial traits *were* taken to be the defining characteristics

of the various stages of human development that helped evolutionists place the
Neanderthal on the lower end of what was assumed to be a gradual progression
toward the cultural achievement and biological constitution of the European.
In fact, Huxley wrote,

> Though truly the most pithecoid of known human skulls the Neanderthal cra-
> nium is by no means so isolated as it appears to be at first but forms in reality the
> extreme form of a series leading gradually from it to the highest and best devel-
> oped of human crania. On the one hand, it is closely approached by the flattened
> Australian skulls . . . from which other Australian forms lead us gradually up to
> skulls having very much the type of the Engis cranium.[53]

Racial differences that should have been inconsequential—by virtue of Darwin's and Huxley's refutation of speciation—actually proved essential when the
lifespan of human beings was placed in a linear view of evolution from the Neanderthal and the most primitive of the existing races to the European.

If humans evolved through various stages, as the evolutionists assumed,
and the primitive races functioned as stand-ins for the missing link between
humans and the animal world, then it was also assumed that these various
stages were marked with discernible characteristics. In this nonevolutionary
framework, naturalists made the mistake of viewing the various traits of the
human skull as a marker of both race and the hierarchal stages of human advancement. This understanding of human diversity carried with it the theological view of nature as a creative force capable of forming species with specific
traits, and the belief that human history was marching toward predetermined
ends. This conception of race and human development occupied the same
Christian worldview articulated by natural theologians and ethnologists during the seventeenth and eighteenth centuries. Again this was one in which a
creator God was present within nature and in which living things existed in a
world that progressed toward a meaningful end. Yet this was an understanding
of human diversity that stood in contrast to the open-ended view of evolution and renunciation of human racial speciation implied by Darwin in the
Origin of Species and the *Descent of Man*. When thinking about the relationship between humans and the Neanderthal, nineteenth-century evolutionists
paradoxically affirmed the existence of race-specific traits, which carried with

it the epistemological assumptions of Christian intellectual history, while also maintaining that the organic world did not create natural kinds with distinct and constant features. A novel form of this paradox has reiterated itself in the twenty-first-century encounter with the Neanderthal genome.

Discovering the Bit of Neanderthal in All of Us

When the NGP was initiated in 2006 at the Max Planck Institute for Evolutionary Anthropology in Leipzig, Germany, the consortium of researchers involved did not set out to discover how Neanderthal genetics would bear on scientific conceptions of race. After obtaining the first viable and complete genomic sequence of the Neanderthal, researchers were initially interested in locating potential regions where humans diverged from Neanderthals genetically since sharing an ancestor around five hundred thousand years ago.[54] Humans are not the direct descents of Neanderthals, contrary to many of the nineteenth-century speculations. Rather, Neanderthals are more of a "sister group to modern humans," sharing a common ancestor in Africa nearly half a million years ago.[55] According to the current fossil record it is estimated that the Neanderthals died out thirty thousand years ago. However, paleoanthropologists have long speculated that following "the out of Africa event"—when some of the first wave of humans left the mother continent and spread into Asia and Europe—Neanderthals and humans came into contact in the Middle East at least eighty thousand years ago and then later again in Eurasia around forty thousand years ago.

Because humans and Neanderthals took separate evolutionary paths a half million years ago, the NGP believed a Neanderthal genome sequence would provide "a catalogue of changes that have become fixed or have risen to high frequency in modern humans during the last few hundred thousand years" and would be "informative for identifying genes affected by positive selection since humans diverged from Neanderthals."[56] According to this genealogical reasoning, humans will possess traits that do not appear in Neanderthals since the two groups pursued separate genetic paths. At the same time, humans and Neanderthals share traits because they descend from a common ancestor.

Paleoanthropologists have been divided over whether or not the morphological similarities between present-day humans and Neanderthals are evidence of interbreeding or simply a remainder of the common ancestry shared between both groups.[57] Comparative studies of the mitochondrial DNA (mtDNA)—a separate and limited cache of genetic material sitting on the outside, rather than inside the nucleus of a cell, where DNA is stored—of both groups have found no links between present-day humans and Neanderthals. The reason is that typically mtDNA is species specific, which means that humans possess a range of mtDNA found exclusively in our species.

To have a more robust understanding of the pervasiveness of Neanderthal admixture within modern humans, NGP researchers compared the variants of present-day humans with those of the Neanderthal. The NGP sequenced the genomes of individuals from China, France, Papua New Guinea, South Africa, and West Africa. If gene flow from Neanderthals to humans occurred in Africa before humans diverged into these four major groups in the study, then the SNPs from each of the present-day humans would match Neanderthal variants equally. To their surprise, researchers in the NGP found that the individuals from China, France, and Papua New Guinea shared more genetic variants with Neanderthals than did the Africans used in the sample. Descendants of Eurasians appeared to match Neanderthals in ten of the twelve regions where they were also most different from Africans. NGP researchers estimated that non-African populations possess between 1 and 4 percent Neanderthal DNA.[58] By discovering that on average Eurasians shared more genetic traits with Neanderthals than with Africans, the NGP also posited that gene flow from Neanderthals to modern humans likely occurred in the Middle East one hundred thousand years ago before migration to Europe and Asia between forty thousand and fifty thousand years ago.

Neanderthals and the Three Sons of Noah

The fact that humans and Neanderthals mated successfully means that there was enough genetic similarity between both groups to produce viable offspring. But does successful procreation imply that Neanderthals were also human? There appears to be no clear or simple answer to this question largely because this distinction rests on how one defines what it means to belong to our species. Here we are stepping into philosophical territory where statistical representations of Neanderthal admixture in humans clarify as much as complicate the issue. At a genetic level, the discovery of Neanderthal admixture poses a unique problem for sorting Neanderthals and humans into separate groups because Neanderthal variation, according to the NGP, appears to fall within the range of *acknowledged* human genetic variation. In other words, the Neanderthal genome is not consistently different from the human genome, given what we know about human variation. This is true not simply because we shared an ancestor five hundred thousand years ago but also because of the gene flow that occurred between some humans and Neanderthals. As a result of relatively recent procreation, in certain parts of their genome, Asian and European populations share more genetic variation with the Neanderthal than they do with African populations.[59] In these sites, we might say non-Africans are more Neanderthal than they are African. But this certainly does not make Asians and Europeans any less human due to the total of genetic information shared with Africans. Interestingly, the same can be said about Neanderthals. In certain locations of their genome, Neanderthals are identical to Asian and Europeans and thus equally distant from Africans. Couple this with their shared ancestry with humans a half million years ago and one could make a strong case on genetic grounds that Neanderthals are also human, as if the Neanderthal is one of Noah's lost sons.

IMAGE 8. Young girl encounters Neanderthal. Source: Neanderthal Museum, Mettmann, Germany.

However, some geneticists would argue that all of this speculation about the
genetic similarity and distance of Neanderthals to certain human populations
is precisely that. Since the inception of admixture technology as a method of
analysis, many geneticists have been critical of it and the attempt to infer the
genetic ancestry of a population based on the collection of population-specific
SNPs. The grounds for this criticism are based on what some geneticists have
described as the failure of scientists interested in human difference to distinguish their study of population ancestry from nineteenth-century discourses
of race.[60]

Population geneticists Kenneth M. Weiss and Jeffrey C. Long, as well as
computational biologist Brian W. Lambert, have been some of the most recent
voices of opposition toward admixture technology and the use of computer
software programs to calculate human ancestry. They have argued that contemporary geneticists inadvertently fall back onto racial typologies when they
divide humans according to continental regions where specific genetic variations are assumed to have come into being. This has the effect of collapsing the
difference between gene flow as a result of humans mating with one another
with genetic changes that occur due to environmental factors that cause alleles
to rise in frequency. They affirm a view shared by other scientists that the lived
history of a population is far more messy and complicated than algorithmic
models of human ancestry.[61] The latter identifies a hypothesized continental
origin based on a carefully selected catalogue of population-specific traits,
whereas the former entails the lived experience of migration, mating, cultural,
and environmental pressures that might cause a variant to rise in frequency
within a given population.

According to Weiss and others, an additional problem with admixture
estimates is that the parental populations from which present-day individuals
are thought to have descended are not alive to be sampled.[62] In effect present-
day humans are tied to ancient populations that scientists have no direct way
to access. Here again we have the problem of the creation of race without
evidence of a creator. Geneticists attempt to resolve this problem by sam-
pling from contemporary populations, using their DNA to imagine and re-
create the assumed groups from which a given individual is thought to have
descended. Weiss and Lambert claim that this hypothetical representation
of the origins of human diversity would be fine as a heuristic if it were not

for the obvious fact that when these imagined parental groups are analyzed among themselves, their intragroup differences are as great as and in some instances greater than the differences that appear when being compared to members of another parent group.[63] Weiss, Long, and other geneticists stress that the existence of intragroup variation is indicative of the fact that the *lived ancestry* of a population is at the same time more gradual and more precarious than the end result of laboratory studies that model human genetic ancestry. But in an effort to render this otherwise complex lived biological history quantitatively, they argue that geneticists who employ admixture technology assume that the parental populations of present-day admixed individuals were homogeneous populations, thereby expressing the logic of secular creationism, which posits meaningful ontological cleavages between human groups. According to Weiss and Long,

> Whether the investigator uses external information or makes estimates from the samples at hand, the parental populations are abstractions that conform to only the simplest kind of genetic structure. This structure places heavy emphasis on the idea that the world once harbored distinct and independently evolved populations that have now undergone admixture of an unstated type (often seeming to connote admixture due to colonial era migrations). The ideal markers for this kind of analysis are private to, and in high frequency in, only one of the putative parental populations, or at least display major differences in frequency among the putative parental populations.[64]

Not every SNP or genetic variation can be used to infer the unique ancestry of a population. Thus, geneticists have to be discerning in their selection of variants to infer the genetic makeup of a parental population. Genetic variants in high frequency tend to be prime candidates. However, Weiss and Long add that exclusive SNPs that have reached a high frequency within one population are rare because genes shared widely within a group are mostly old, having been derived from a shared ancestor or been obtained through gene flow from other populations already in possession of this trait. They argue that variants widely prevalent in a population say more about the geographic conditions that forced certain alleles into high frequency than reveal a moment of unique population differentiation.[65] In their view, models for the frequency of a trait in one population compared to another actually explain the relative rates of possessing an allele shared with other groups, not necessarily the origin or exclusiveness of a genetic variant.

Nevertheless, Weiss and Long explain that allele frequencies are still understood by some geneticists as indicative of ancestry and population differentiation, even though "most structure-like analyses use markers that were discovered in modest size samples from only a few populations (mainly, Europe, West Sub-Saharan Africa, and East Asia), and registered in databases such as dbSNP (www.ncbi.nlm.nih.gov/projects/SNP/) or HapMap (www.hapmap .org) whose markers are intended primarily for gene mapping. How specific these markers are to a limited geographic region is often untested."[66] The result is a picture of human ancestry with populations divided according to continent-specific traits, distilling human genetic diversity down to three or four essential groups much as did Blumenbach in the eighteenth century and the racial science of the American polygenists of the nineteenth century, both of which were patterned after Christian intellectual history.[67]

There are virtues and limits to using new genetic tools to locate Neanderthal genes in humans. One clear upside is that this technology reveals the messiness of human ancestry. The genetic profile of present-day people is mixed with the ancestries of people from around the world. This mixture reflects the lived history of humans reproducing across geopolitical boundaries and, in the case of Neanderthals, with humans considered extinct. Again, humans are not pure biological units. We are instead mongrel creatures with the history of our mixed ancestors buried within our biology. Never has this been more clear than after the sequencing of the human, and now Neanderthal, genome.

Despite this realization, scientists can use SNPs to hypothesize moments in our evolutionary past when our ancestors were theoretically less mixed and more homogeneous than we are. This hypothetical reasoning—and the technology used to support this form of racial thought—organizes the heterogeneity of our mixed biological inheritance and re-creates the idea that present-day groups descended from idealistically pure ancestors. Moreover, this contemporary form of racial typology helps sustain the belief—derived from the Christian intellectual history that shaped Western racial thinking —that the single most important moment within the life of a so-called racial group is its inception and differentiation from other members of our species.

We Are All Mongrel

Finding bits of Neanderthal in our genome forces us to acknowledge the opacity of the human past and challenges our cultured assumptions about our ontological uniqueness and the division between the human and non-human worlds. For nearly 150 years scientists assumed that modern humans were free of Neanderthal ancestry. Yet as members of the NGP explain, not only was the discovery of Neanderthal DNA in present-day humans entirely unexpected; they also learned that there are potentially many other extinct early humans (such as a group they called Denisovans) whose DNA lives on in our genomes. Svante Paabo, one of the leading paleogeneticists on the NGP, explained,

> This was an amazing finding. We had studied two genomes from extinct human forms [Neanderthal and Denisovan]. In both cases we had found some gene flow into modern humans. Thus, low levels of mixing with earlier humans seemed to have been the rule rather than the exception when modern humans spread across the world. This meant that neither Neanderthals nor Denisovans were totally extinct. A little bit of them lived on in people today.[68]

We might say that all humans are mongrel, in the sense that it may be impossible to recover the many different early and more recent human ancestors who contributed to our genetic inheritance. In biological terms, mongrels are not merely organisms with a mixed heritage. They are beings in which only part of their ancestry is known or recoverable. To say that we are all mongrel, therefore, is to acknowledge that our ancestry will never be fully knowable.

Of course, to call ourselves human, and not merely advanced primates or even Neanderthals, implies that we know who and what make us unique as a species. Securing this knowledge, however, remains one of the most elusive tasks in modern science. The unexpected discovery of Neanderthal DNA in the human gene pool belies the idea that human identity is unique, stable, and transparent to our inquiring minds.

At the same time, finding Neanderthal DNA in present-day humans puts on display how biological heterogeneity, or "being mixed," is in fact the default human ontological position. Humans were mixing before they became "races." At no point in our history has there been a member of our species not mixed with another human and nonhuman group. At a biological level, being mixed is the norm, not the exception, of human existence.

Races exist only when thinking about human becoming within a specific moment in time while also assuming that this marks an ontologically novel event of human creation. These temporal and conceptual constraints are at play when geneticists assume that human diversity can be reduced to fundamentally three ancestral groups. In many respects the legitimacy of providing a scientific answer to why humans differ has yet to be fully reckoned with. Scientists in pursuit of human variation have yet to relieve themselves of the burden of explaining human existence under the terms laid out by Christian natural theology—in which life at its origination is believed to be the most ontologically meaningful and distinct. The study of the Neanderthal genome reveals that the racial formations created by scientists continue to venerate the concepts and reasoning strategies of their Euro-American Christian ancestors.

5

BEYOND THE RELIGIOUS
PURSUIT OF RACE

DOCTORS AND PUBLIC HEALTH RESEARCHERS have long noted that African Americans face lower chances of survival than other groups when diagnosed with common cancers.[1] Although many researchers have revealed the social and structural factors involved with this discrepancy, scientists have continuously searched for genetic causes. In March 2015, geneticists working at the Wistar Institute in Philadelphia claim to have found a single gene variant that may explain why black Americans with cancer are less likely to survive. The Wistar Institute was founded in 1892 as the first independent nonprofit biomedical research organization in the country and has held the Cancer Center designation from the National Cancer Institute since 1972. In this study, Wistar researchers examined the S47 variant of a tumor-suppressor gene (TP53), which is found in almost half of all cancers.[2] According to researchers the S47 variant of this suppressor gene occurs only in people of African descent and is thought to make cancer resistant to cell death. Although researchers noted that this S47 variant is present in about 2 percent of African Americans, they were convinced that this single genetic variant, as a result of its perceived exclusiveness to African Americans, could be a significant factor shaping health outcomes.[3] Given the limited number of African Americans with this variant, researchers created a mouse model to study its effects. Mice are prime organisms for researching human cancers because of their biological similarity to humans. Thus, geneticists can infer conclusions about human cancers by observing biological changes within mice genetically engineered to express a specific variant. In this case, researchers were excited to discover that in mice, 80 percent of those with the variant developed liver cancer, colon cancer, or lymphoma.[4] In the press release the lead author of the study claimed, "We may finally have a truly genetic explanation for why African-Americans are more prone to a variety of cancers."[5] She went further, noting that "this is a variant that has never been observed in Caucasian populations, so identifying people who have this variant may be crucial for providing improved prognosis and personalized treatment that will lead to better outcomes."

Social scientists have known for some time that social definitions of race do not correspond directly with the genes of populations.[6] In their study, Wistar researchers used the term "Caucasian" to note the identity of their white subjects. Caucasian, however, is a social category created in the eighteenth century and used by Johann Blumenbach to define whiteness in terms that largely ignored national and ethnic distinctions among Europeans. For Blumenbach it was also a concept that included populations in the Middle East. Caucasians are literally figments of the scientific imagination and not a reliable concept to describe with any nuance the genetic makeup of people with ancestry from a landmass that includes all of Europe, West Asia, and North Africa. "African American" is an equally imprecise category. With the advent of genetic-sequencing technology, scientists have shown that African Americans are a remarkably genetically diverse population. For example, a 2006 study published in the *New England Journal of Medicine* examined self-described persons of African American identity from Cleveland, Ohio.[7] When their genetic ancestries were analyzed, only 4 percent who understood themselves to be black had predominantly African ancestry.[8] In other words 96 percent of the self-described African Americans in Cleveland had predominantly European and other non-African ancestry. Theoretically, this means that a geneticist attempting to explain disease patterns observed in so-called African Americans within this Cleveland data set is likely to find alleles displayed by people of European ancestry, not African. Studies of this sort show why we cannot assume that the category "African American" denotes a group whose genetic profile is consistently and overwhelmingly derived from populations in Africa. African Americans are too diverse to assume a single genetic variant involved in cancer growth, but found in only 2 percent of those classified as African American, could have the explanatory power to account for the survival of the entire population.

The Wistar study also ignores the research on the social determinants of health that factor into complex disease outcomes. There is a growing body of research demonstrating that the rates at which black women contract and die from cancer involve a wide variety of social, economic, and environmental factors, including cultural biases held by physicians that influence the frequency with which black women are screened for cancer, access to health care, a general distrust of medicine that prevents black women from seeking out medical diagnosis, the role that stress plays in the contraction of complex diseases, and socioeconomic factors that shape the amount of exposure black women have to cancer-causing agents.[9] This literature has demonstrated that any attempt to understand the survival rate of breast cancer in populations known to be historically marginalized and discriminated against must consider social factors as well as the conditions surrounding gene-environment interactions. To pursue a single genetic explanation for varying rates of survival from cancer is to undertake an inquiry that willfully ignores other avenues of analysis. Although seemingly well intentioned, this study suffers from the latent belief that to account for human differences, scientists must give preference to nature over the human factors that shape the conditions under which human life develops.

Racial Science and the Conflict Thesis

Over the course of this book I have argued that modern scientists have inherited racial reasoning practices and habits of mind derived from Christian intellectual history. This inheritance has predisposed them to a variety of racial reasoning strategies which includes giving preference to nature when attempting to explain perceived differences across human populations. This has been true even in intellectual settings noted for the assumed liberation of science from cultural and other social forms. Thus, I have attempted to demonstrate how present-day scientific views of race have been built on antecedent religious ideas. In doing so, I have also attempted to "provincialize" the modern scientific study of race, revealing a very specific Christian intellectual inheritance that has shaped Euro-American science and the study of human origins that claims to have universal significance for all human populations.

By showing the connections between Christian thought and scientific racial thinking, I have intended in this work to go beyond the pervasive conflict thesis regarding science and religion. In the United States it seems almost second nature for us to believe that these two forms of knowing inhabit separate intellectual spaces, or constitute "domaining practices."[10] According to a 2015 Pew Research Study Poll, roughly 59 percent of Americans believe science and religion "in general" are at odds and belong in separate spaces within modern life. Yet when asked if science conflicts with their own personal beliefs, only 30 percent of Americans report a dispute.[11] This discrepancy suggests that Americans believe that the categories of science and religion as they exist in the collective imagination are in conflict even though privately most Americans are able to reconcile scientific and religious claims.

This paradox is a symptom of late nineteenth-century formulations of science and religion that remain a part of the US social imagination. The idea that science and religion have been locked in perpetual tension is part of an enduring myth developed by the American historians John Draper and Andrew Dixon White at the end of the nineteenth century.[12] In what was called the Draper-White thesis, conflict between religion and science became an established conceptual paradigm for most twentieth-century secular historians who defended the importance of free scientific inquiry against the influence of religion.[13] Historians and philosophers since the 1970s have steadily rejected the Draper and White thesis and have maintained that the history of science in the West is too complex to affirm metanarratives that posit science and religion to be constant adversaries.[14]

In this book I have attempted to bring the history of scientific thinking about race into these critical discussions that expose the limits of the conflict thesis. There are clear problems with viewing the study of race as a purely a scientific issue. First, this view distorts the history of how contemporary visions of race came into being through the steady influence of religious concepts on scientific assumptions. We saw, for example, in Chapter 1, how the contemporary literature on the racial theories of Friedrich Blumenbach have overlooked the influence that Christian ideas of common human descent, unique human creation, and recent human origins had on Blumenbach's thinking. Although he was instrumental in establishing anthropology as a separate scientific discipline of study, Blumenbach did not outright reject the habitual modes of thinking and religious assumptions that were a part of more explicitly Christian discussions of human descent. As it turns out, Blumenbach was more of a Lutheran on the question of race than many historians of science have realized.

Adopting the conflict thesis for viewing the history of modern racial science is limiting in another important respect. By investing in the notion that science and religion are inherently at odds, we fail to grasp how the relationship between those who look similar and different from ourselves is an enduring human existential dilemma, not merely a scientific problem. The anthropologist Jonathan Marks echoed this sentiment in *What It Means to Be 98% Chimpanzee* when he wrote, "Sameness/otherness is a philosophical paradox that is resolved by argument, not by data."[15] The human species is the only one that actively gives meaning to its members' life worlds. The scientific study of our origins is an example of this meaning-making process. Racial differences are not simply facts given to us by nature but become meaningful through the framing concepts, assumptions, and methodologies used by scientific actors who are situated within specific historical and cultural settings.

In his commentaries on the 1951 UNESCO statements on race the British American anthropologist Ashley Montagu captured the importance of recognizing the role that human assumptions play in the perception of racial differences:

> We perceive the consequences of different histories of biological experience in the races of today. Now, unfortunately what we see, what we per-ceive (*per* = by, through, *capere* = to take), is largely based on the kingdom that is within us. What we do with the objects of the outside world is to take them in and pass them through all that our experience, biological and social, has made us—the alembic of ourselves—and then judge them according to that experience. In short our perceptions come not from the objects we judge but from ourselves, and what we judge things to be depends not so much upon the things as upon what we ourselves are in terms of the history of our own past experience. That is why it is said that what we perceive is preconceived, for a perception is not a new sensation, a mere appearance reflecting reality, but it is a sensation which has been invested with meaning, a meaning entirely determined by our past experience.[16]

I take Montagu's point to be not a denial of objective reality but an appreciation for how the objects we perceive are already mediated by our past experience and our cultural and social milieu. The relationship between ideas and the world outside the mind is a central problem of modern Western philosophy that has implications for the study of human difference. Montagu is providing a contemporary gloss on what Immanuel Kant, in the *Critique of Pure Reason*, identified as the inability of human reason to capture the essence of the objects and individuals we encounter.[17] There is, indeed, a world outside the mind. The problem is that our understanding of this world and those who inhabit it remains limited to how these things appear to us and are mediated by our inherited habits of thought and rational practices. Following Montagu, we must realize that human differences are the result of the interaction not simply of genes and environment but also culture—particularly the cultural setting in which scientific work takes place. The meaning scientists attribute to human difference is a reflection of the social, political, and values they have internalized as historical subjects. Simply put, scientific perceptions of race are neither value-free nor detached from the inherited traditions of belief and reason that constitute the scientific subject.

Thus, thinking beyond the conflict thesis allows us to *humanize* the scientific study of race by drawing attention to the larger social, cultural, and religious concerns that have animated people's interest in human origins. Science participates in this search to bring closure to difficult existential questions about what it means it be human. Ashley Montagu put his finger on the uniquely human needs that rest behind the modern investment in racial classification:

> [A] race is not something fixed, permanent, and unchanging or unchangeable, but . . . is a dynamic, potentially unstable entity, which is seen to be stable only when one delimits the process of change at one's own time level. Seen at another time, at another period, in another century, another millennium, it may be a very different race, depending upon the kind of influences which have been operative upon it during the interval of elapsed time.[18]

Races are meaningful only if one reduces the human evolutionary timescale to the present. Belief in racial distinctions, be they sanctioned by theology or science, are at best proximate answers for historically contingent interpretations of the importance and meaning of human life. We can easily lose sight of the fact that we are a constantly evolving species when we allow scientific or religious discourse to frame human diversity in terms of fixed and stable demarcations between human groups. The need for enduring answers about what it means to be human, via notions of racial difference, can distort our self-understanding as a species. We are ultimately the product of evolutionary processes much older and enduring than our social time lines, defined either by the Bible or estimates of science.

Insofar as we believe human differences are rooted within our biology, the idea that races are "real" is also one of the last holdouts for the once explicitly Christian belief that the creator has planted in nature the secrets of our behavioral, health, and intellectual differences. It is a true paradox that the temptation to reduce human differences purely to genetic causes and therefore nature endures even though contemporary science has abandoned all references to the creator as the first cause behind natural phenomena. Moreover, notions of common human origin and the perception of distinct racial traits remain integral to contemporary scientific discourse even though early modern Christian naturalists helped forge these ideas. Although scientific naturalism (i.e., the belief that natural phenomena can be explained without reference to the supernatural) was an important methodological shift within the development of Western science, I have shown in this book that religious concepts did continue to frame scientific views of race—particularly when pitched in biological terms.

On this point I disagree with Ronald L. Numbers's claim that adherence of scientists to methodological naturalism at the end of the nineteenth century marked the end of Christianity's influence over scientific thought.[19] In my view much depends on the "science" that one has in mind, as well as how closely one associates Christian thought with appeals to the supernatural. In this book I have shown how actors within anthropology, medical science, and genetics were capable of translating into secular terms Christian ideas about universalism, the order of nature, human descent, uniqueness of our species, and racial diversification. These concepts were not anchored by any notion of the supernatural, and in their secular translations they played the same "framing" role as they did in more explicitly religious discussions. For example, Blumenbach's designation of the white Caucasian as the original human type was analogous to the idea that all human beings were descendants of the biblical Adam. Moreover, the biblical narrative of human creation and human descent remained valid for most scientists and lay thinkers well into the twentieth century even though biblical scholarship and historical criticism stripped away many of the supernatural elements of this narrative. The point here is that many of the "truths" of Christian ideas about race did not rest on appeals to the supernatural. The controversy over polygenism in the nineteenth century created by Josiah Nott is another illustration of this. In Chapter 2 we saw that the root issue for most Christians was not the method by which Nott arrived at his theory of multiple human origins. Rather, Nott's hypothesis was problematic because of his denial of the notion of common human descent. Thus, Christian ideas about race can be remarkably accommodating to scientific theories insofar as vestiges of the Christian creation narrative remain discernible to the religious public.

This raises important questions about our present context. According to the 2015 Pew Survey Darwinian evolution by random natural selection remains a difficult idea for many. Pew reported that only 35 percent of Americans believe humans evolved as a result of natural processes. The report also revealed that 24 percent believe a supreme being guided human evolution, and 31 percent of Americans believe that humans existed in their present form since the beginning of human history.[20] This study suggests that a considerable number of Americans remain committed to the religious belief that a creator is responsible for preserving the form and destiny of our species.

As I showed in my discussion of the algorithms used to model human ancestral populations in the recent Neanderthal genome sequence, beliefs about stable and naturally discrete human populations have been philosophically antithetical to Darwinian evolution. These beliefs, which have their root in early modern Christian thought, have the potential to foster the view that race is a stable biological reality. One must question the extent to which these persistent religious beliefs—which have been transmitted through scientific thinking about race—have made the public imagination more receptive to embrace, rather than question, the rising prominence of genetic conceptions of human variation. Indeed, given its opposition to Darwinian evolution, a considerable section of the lay public has much in common with eighteenth- and nineteenth-century naturalist historians—the Christian forebears of present-day scientists—who believed that races were stable and discrete biological entities.

Rather than move beyond racial thinking, contemporary biomedical discussions of human biological difference are finding common ground with a lay public skeptical of ideas based on evolution and sympathetic to notions of species fixity and an inherent natural order.

The complex connections between religion, race, and science in Euro-American thought are easily overlooked when we view this history as one of conflict and affirm that science and religion are philosophically at odds and therefore inhabit separate intellectual spaces within modern life. A more careful examination of this history reveals a profoundly religious heritage at work in the ways modern scientists in the West have studied and classified human beings.

Thus, the race concept in science forces us to recognize how Christian intellectual history sits with us despite our claims to being secular, rational, and modern. One of the consequences of this intellectual history is that we remain ambivalent about whether humans or God (understood in terms of nature or genetics) ultimately determines our destiny. The consequences of this ambivalence have been devastating for populations described by scientists and physicians as being predisposed to diseases or behaviors because of their genes rather than social and environmental factors that can be changed. The solutions afforded by a conception of race that naturalizes human differences have not allowed us to realize that we are the gods. Our habits of mind, epistemological commitments, and reasoning practices are what create the conditions that determine the life chances and health outcomes of human groups, not nature or genetics. If some populations die from higher rates of disease than others, or express behaviors that vary across groups, our institutions and inherited forms of thinking are to blame, not nature.

If we are to fully embrace our role in shaping the life chances of human groups, we must have some clarity about how habits of mind and reasoning practices inherited from Christian intellectual history have predisposed us to conceptualize human origins and development in racial terms. A supersessionist understanding of history—whereby scientific ideas about race are assumed to have displaced and supplanted religious thought—can be maintained only at the expense of obscuring the presence of inherited habits of mind that continue to animate our preference for naturalizing racial differences. Rather than deny the Christian roots of racial science, we must make plain the role this prehistory plays within our present racial formations. Deciphering the values and epistemic commitments these roots have inculcated within us might engender alternative habits of mind that move understanding beyond the religious pursuit of race within the biomedical sciences.

NOTES

Introduction

1. Spencer Wells, *The Journey of Man: A Genetic Odyssey* (Princeton, NJ: Princeton University Press, 2003).

2. Spencer Wells, *Journey of Man: The Story of the Human Species*, DVD, dir. Clive Maltby (Arlington, VA: Public Broadcasting Station, 2005).

3. My use of the term "missionary conversion" to describe Wells's conscription of the indigenous body into an evolutionary narrative is inspired by Willie Jennings's account of the theological moves that accompanied European colonial expansion. Jennings notes that the "age of discovery and conquest began a process of transformation of land and identity. And while worlds were being transformed, not every world was changed in the same way. Peoples different in geography, in life, in different worlds of European designation—Africa, the Americas, Europe—will lose the earth only to find it again in a strange new way. The deepest theological distortion taking place is that the earth, the ground, spaces, and places are being removed as living organizers of identity and as facilitators of identity" (Willie James Jennings, *The Christian Imagination: Theology and the Origins of Race* [New Haven, CT: Yale University Press, 2011], 39). He also notes that linking of European and indigenous bodies within this new enlightened capitalist arrangement "indicated a fundamental transforming of space. Europeans were willingly leaving their homes. Newly discovered natives were unwillingly being taken from their lands" (37). We see this missionary inheritance play out in the telling of Wells's biogenetic narrative. Wells, the European, willingly leaves his homeland in search of the natives that not only corroborate his new creationism but do so precisely at the moment that they accept the terms of his story and are therefore removed from their indigenous cosmologies (i.e., converted) and given new identities within an alternative biospatial network of ideas and beliefs about geography, migration, inheritance, and the formation of the races.

4. Wells, *Journey of Man* (DVD), 00:38:41.

5. Ibid., 00:39:03–00:39:34 (emphasis added).

6. Ibid., 00:39:47–00:39:57 (emphasis added).

7. Ibid., 01:42:52–01:42:59.

8. Ibid., 01:43:05–01:43:35.

9. Ibid., 01:44:37–01:45:02.

10. Ibid., 01:44:03–01:45:04 (emphasis added).

11. Kim Tallbear notes that Wells's understanding of the history of racial science and the possibility that genetics can end racism is remarkably ahistorical and trades in the belief that "there is discontinuity between present and past" (Kimberly Tallbear, *Native American DNA: Tribal Belonging and the False Promise of Genetic Science* [Minneapolis: University of Minnesota Press, 2013], 149). In my view Wells's ignorance about the intellectual history of the race concepts in science is not merely political naïveté or ahistoricism among scientist generally. Instead Wells's ignorance expresses a very specific reverence for the abrupt solemnity of ideas and human bodies, which itself is symptomatic of Christian conceptual commitments that privately animate and orient race thinking in science. There is in fact a parochial social-cultural history that enables Wells's disregard for the history of racial thinking that predates his own biogenetic story of human development and thus furthers the belief that a proper understanding of human diversity begins with an intellectual deficit and then moves toward truth.

12. Part of my methodology borrows from Dipesh Chakrabarty, *Provincializing Europe: Postcolonial Thought and Historical Difference* (Princeton, NJ: Princeton University Press, 2008), xiii.

13. In regard to ideas about race within the history of science and history more generally, see John C. Greene, *The Death of Adam: Evolution and Its Impact on Western Thought* (Ames: Iowa State University Press, 1959); George Frederickson, *The Black Image in the White Mind: The Debate on Afro-American Character and Destiny, 1817–1914* (1971; repr., Middletown, CT: Wesleyan University Press, 1987); Peter J. Bowler, *Evolution: The History of an Idea* (Berkeley: University of California Press, 1989); Jonathan Marks, *Human Biodiversity: Genes, Race, and History* (New Brunswick, NJ: Aldine Transaction, 1995); Audrey Smedley, *Race in North America: Origin and Evolution of a Worldview* (Boulder, CO: Westview Press, 1999); Dorothy Roberts, *Fatal Invention: How Science, Politics, and Big Business Re-create Race in the Twenty-First Century* (New York: New Press, 2012). For key comprehensive works on the history of race within religious thought, see Colin Kidd, *The Forging of the Races: Race and Scripture in the Protestant Atlantic World, 1600–2000* (Cambridge: Cambridge University Press, 2006); David Livingstone, *Adam's Ancestors: Race, Religion, and the Politics of Human Origins* (Baltimore: Johns Hopkins University Press, 2008); Sylvester Johnson, *The Myth of Ham in Nineteenth-Century American Christianity: Race, Heathens, and the People of God* (New York: Palgrave Macmillan, 2004).

14. Jonathan Z. Smith, "Religion, Religions, Religious," in *Critical Terms for Religious Studies*, ed. M. C. Taylor (Chicago: University of Chicago Press, 1998), 269–84.

15. See, for example, J. Cameron Carter, *Race: A Theological Account* (Oxford: Oxford University Press, 2008); Jonathan Boyarin, *The Unconverted Self: Jews, Indians, and the Identity of Christian Europe* (Chicago: University of Chicago Press, 2009); Richard A. Bailey, *Race and Redemption in Puritan New England* (Oxford: Oxford University Press, 2011); Rebecca Anne Goetz, *The Baptism of Early Virginia: How Christianity Created Race* (Baltimore: Johns Hopkins University Press, 2012).

16. Denise Kimber Buell, "Early Christian Universalism and Modern Racism," in *The Origins of Racism in the West*, ed. Miriam Eliav-Feldon, Benjamin Isaac, and Joseph Ziegler (Cambridge: Cambridge University Press, 2009), 111–12.

17. Justin Martyr, *Dialogue with Trypho*, in *The Ante-Nicene Fathers*, vol. 1, *The Apostolic Fathers with Justin Martyr and Irenaeus*, ed. Alexander Roberts, James Donaldson, and A. Cleveland Coxe (New York: Cosimo Classics, 2007), 200.

18. Carter, *Race: A Theological Account*, 4.

19. Boyarin, *The Unconverted Self*, 1.

20. Ibid., 1–2.

21. Viewing Christianity as a community that supplants ethnic distinctions yet also reinforces the importance of human variation has implications for modern science more generally. This is a connection Peter Harrison has made in *The Territories of Science and Religion* (Chicago: University of Chicago Press, 2015). Harrison documents the social and intellectual history that created present-day conceptions of science and religion. These circumstances have long been in the making, dating back to the early church. Harrison argues that during the first three centuries of the Common Era Christian communities conceived of themselves as possessing a belief system with claims to truth that transcended cultural and ethnic distinction. Early Christians provided a prototypical model for later belief systems that would aspire to achieve universal significance. Tracing the transformations of this belief system, Harrison notes that during the early modern period there emerged a neutral epistemic space in which Christianity was impartially judged to be the true religion in the face of other competing religious truth claims. By the nineteenth century, the notion of Christianity as an impartial and universally applicable truth was fully integrated into the new life sciences (191). At this moment, Western ideas about its superiority, which carried with it racial beliefs about Europeans, shifted from its religious beliefs to an ostensibly secular rationality. Harrison notes, "The epistemic imperialism of science was inherited from the supposedly neutral grounds of eighteenth-century natural theology from which it emerged" (190). Thus, we cannot properly understand the traits and features of modern Euro-American science without recovering the religious antecedents that helped shaped its form and epistemic inclinations.

22. Paolo Rossi, *The Dark Abyss of Time: The History of the Earth and the History of Nations from Hooke to Vico* (Chicago: University of Chicago Press, 1984), 158–68.

23. Ibid.

24. Matthew Hale, *The Primitive Origination of Mankind: Considered and Examined according to the Light of Nature* (London: Printed by W. Godbid, for W. Shrowsbery, 1677), 148.

25. Isaac Newton, *Opera Quae Extant Omnia* (London: Samuel Horsley, 1779–85), 5:142–93, quoted in Rossi, *The Dark Abyss of Time*, 163.

26. Michael Allen Gillespie, *The Theological Origins of Modernity* (Chicago: University of Chicago Press, 2008), 16.

27. Ibid., 274.

28. Greene, *The Death of Adam*, 309–39. Thomas Gossett reproduces Greene's post-

Enlightenment decline narrative in *Race: The History of an Idea in America* (New York: Oxford University Press, 1963).

29. Ideas about the declining significance of religion to racial science have not been limited to scholarship within the history of science. The "decline thesis" is also prevalent among scholars of race in America and appears in George H. Frederickson's widely influential *The Black Image in the White Mind*, as well as in Reginald Horsman, *Race and Manifest Destiny: Origins of American Racial Anglo Saxonism* (Cambridge, MA: Harvard University Press, 1980); and more recently in C. Loring Brace, *"Race" Is a Four Letter Word: The Genesis of the Concept* (Oxford: Oxford University Press, 2005); and Roberts, *Fatal Invention*. One also finds the narrative of decline in recent works on the history of Christian thought about race, such as Kidd, *Forging of the Races*; and Livingstone, *Adam's Ancestors*.

30. David Hull, *Science as a Process: An Evolutionary Account of the Social and Conceptual Development of Science* (Chicago: University of Chicago Press, 1993).

31. See ibid., 75–110. For additional examples of what I call "hard secularism," see Elazar Barkan, *The Retreat of Scientific Racism: Changing Concepts of Race in Britain and the United States between the World Wars* (New York: Cambridge University Press, 1992); Marks, *Human Biodiversity*, 55.

32. This understanding of secularization differs from Talal Asad's views in *Formations of the Secular: Christianity, Islam, Modernity* (Stanford, CA: Stanford University Press, 2003). The world is not secular because we live in an age of uncertainty. This understanding romanticizes the premodern world as a coherent and predictable worldview. Neither do I think of the secular as merely the result of specific practices that organize and assemble thoughts, behavior, and ideas. In this work, I am arguing that the secular acts as a mask for the religious. By "mask" I mean in the active sense of concealment as verb and action. What I have been arguing up to this point is that our beliefs about science as secular have been configured specifically to prevent our awareness of those Christian forms that continue to animate scientific thought.

33. Hans Blumenberg, *The Legitimacy of the Modern Age*, trans. Robert Wallace (Cambridge, MA: MIT Press, 1983), 65.

34. Ibid., 64.

35. Ibid., 48.

36. Despite recognizing the impure and hybrid nature of Christian thought, I am claiming that there are key features to this religious tradition found across the many varieties of Christian belief. There are three features particularly relevant for the narrative I am telling about the history of racial science. They involve the belief in a creator God, a rejection of Christianity's Jewish origins, and relatedly a disposition for making universally applicable claims about the history and ends of all human life. I recognize that of the three the latter does appear in other religious traditions. Unlike Talal Asad, however, I do not believe that a hallmark feature of Christianity is its belief in redemption (Asad, Formations of the Secular, 64–65). Redemption is surely key to this tradition, but I contend creationism, anti-Jewish dispositions, and universalism are more pervasive and enduring features, not simply more pivotal, but have proven to be integral to the modern worldview.

37. See, for example, Stephen Jay Gould, *The Mismeasure of Man* (New York: W. W. Norton, 1996), 401; Smedley, *Race in North America*, 163.

38. Jonathan Marks, "Race: Past, Present, Future," in *Revisiting Race in a Genomic Age*, ed. Barbara Koenig, Sandra Soo-Jin Lee, and Sarah G. Richardson (New Brunswick, NJ: Rutgers University Press, 2008), 22–25.

39. Duana Fullwiley, "The Biologistical Construction of Race: 'Admixture' Technology and the New Genetic Medicine," *Social Studies of Science* 38, no. 5 (2008): 695–735.

40. Henry T. Greely, "Genetic Genealogy: Genetics Meets the Marketplace," and Kimberly Tallbear, "Native-American-DNA.com: In Search of Native American Race and Tribe," both in Koenig, Lee, and Richardson, *Revisiting Race in a Genomic Age*, 215–23; 235–52.

41. Richard Green et al., "A Draft Sequence of the Neanderthal Genome," *Science* 328 (2010): 710–22.

Chapter 1

1. John Ray, *The Wisdom of God Manifested in the Works of Creation* (1691; repr., London: William Inney and Richard Manby for the Royal Society of London, 1735).

2. Bruce Baum, *Rise and Fall of the Caucasian Race: A Political History of Racial Identity* (New York: New York University Press, 2006), 73.

3. Karl Friedrich Heinrich Marx, "Memoir of J. F. Blumenbach," in *The Anthropological Treatises of Johann Friedrich Blumenbach*, trans. Thomas Bendyshe (London: Longman, Green, Roberts, and Green, 1865), 3–45.

4. Jonathan Sheehan, *The Enlightenment Bible: Translation, Scholarship, Culture* (Princeton, NJ: Princeton University Press, 2005), 87.

5. Audrey Smedley, *Race in North America: Origin and Evolution of a Worldview* (Boulder, CO: Westview Press, 1999), 163; Robert J. Richards, *The Romantic Conception of Life: Science and Philosophy in the Age of Goethe* (Chicago: University of Chicago Press, 2002), 216–37.

6. Richards, *Romantic Conception of Life*, 11, 222–37.

7. J. Kameron Carter, *Race: A Theological Account* (Oxford: Oxford University Press, 2008); Richard A. Bailey, *Race and Redemption in Puritan New England* (Oxford: Oxford University Press, 2011); Rebecca Anne Goetz, *The Baptism of Early Virginia: How Christianity Created Race* (Baltimore: Johns Hopkins University Press, 2012).

8. Denise Kimber Buell, "Early Christian Universalism and Modern Racism," in *The Origins of Racism in the West*, ed. Miriam Eliav-Feldon, Benjamin Isaac, and Joseph Ziegler (Cambridge: Cambridge University Press, 2009), 111–12.

9. Jonathan Boyarin, *The Unconverted Self: Jews, Indians, and the Identity of Christian Europe* (Chicago: University of Chicago Press, 2009).

10. Ronnie Po-chia Hsia, "Religion and Race: Protestant and Catholic Discourses on Jewish Conversion in the Sixteenth and Seventeenth Centuries," in Eliav-Feldon, Isaac, and Ziegler, *The Origins of Racism in the West*, 268.

11. Ibid., 270.

12. See Peter Sanlon, "Original Sin in Patristic Theology," and Robert Kolb, "The

Lutheran Doctrine of Original Sin," both in *Adam, the Fall, and Original Sin: Theological, Biblical, and Scientific Perspectives*, ed. Hans Madueme and Michael Reeves (Grand Rapids, MI: Baker Press, 2014), 85–108; 109–28.

13. Richards, *Romantic Conception of Life*, 211.

14. Ibid., 211–12.

15. Johann Friedrich Blumenbach, *Uber den Bildungstrieb und das Zeugungsgeschaft* (Göttingen: Johann Christian Dieterich, 1781); Johann Friedrich Blumenbach, "Uber den Bildungstrieb (Nisus formativus) und seinen Einfluss auf die Generation und Reproduction," *Gottingisches Magazin der Wissenschaften* 2 (1780).

16. Jacques Roger, "The Mechanistic Conception of Life," in *God and Nature: Historical Essays on the Encounter between Christianity and Science*, ed. David C. Lindberg and Ronald L. Numbers (Berkeley: University of California Press, 1986), 285–86.

17. Richards, *Romantic Conception of Life*, 212.

18. Ibid., 212–16.

19. Roger, "The Mechanistic Conception of Life," 287.

20. Richards, *Romantic Conception of Life*, 218.

21. Ibid., 219.

22. Johann Friedrich Blumenbach, *The Anthropological Treatises of Johann Friedrich Blumenbach*, trans. Thomas Bendyshe (1795; repr., London: Longman, Green, Longman, Roberts, and Green, 1865), 194.

23. Ibid., 195, 194–205, 196.

24. Ibid., 194.

25. Chapters 3 and 4 discuss this analogical method of using the traits of contemporary populations to reconstruct what are assumed to be homogeneous ancestral types, which endures within contemporary medical and behavioral science and has been particularly prominent within recent genetic studies of Neanderthal ancestry among living humans.

26. Blumenbach, *Anthropological Treatises*, 269.

27. Ibid., 269.

28. See, for example, Stephen Jay Gould, *The Mismeasure of Man* (New York: W. W. Norton, 1996), 410.

29. Jonathan Marks, *Human Biodiversity: Genes, Race, and History* (New Brunswick, NJ: Aldine Transaction, 2009), 55.

30. Reginald Horsman, *Race and Manifest Destiny: The Origins of American Anglo-Saxonism* (Cambridge, MA: Harvard University Press, 1981), 46.

31. Ibid., 47–48.

32. Michel Foucault, "Nietzsche, Genealogy, History," in *The Foucault Reader*, ed. Paul Rabinow (New York: Pantheon, 1984), 79.

33. Johann Blumenbach, *Contributions to Natural History*, trans. Thomas Bendyshe (1811; repr., London: Longman, Green, Longman, Roberts, and Green, 1865), 287.

34. Martin J. S. Rudwick, "The Shape and Meaning of Earth History," in Lindberg and Numbers, *God and Nature*, 308–9.

35. James R. Moore, "Geologists and Interpreters of Genesis in the Nineteenth Century," in Lindberg and Numbers, *God and Nature*, 322–25.

36. Ibid.

37. John C. Greene, *The Death of Adam: Evolution and Its Impact on Western Thought* (Ames: Iowa State University Press, 1959), 235–38.

38. Moore, "Geologists and Interpreters of Genesis," 322–25.

39. Catastrophism stood in contrast to uniformitarianism, which claims that the earth's surface was formed gradually and that the same forces governing life were also at play at the beginning of the earth's history. One could argue that Blumenbach actually straddled catastrophism and uniformitarianism because he believed his *Bildungstrieb* was a steady force governing life throughout all the various global catastrophes that shaped the earth. For more on catastrophism and uniformitarianism, see Charles Bodemer, "Regeneration and the Decline of Preformationism in 18th-Century Embryology," *Bulletin of the History of Medicine* 38 (1964): 20–31. See also Philip C. Ritterbush, *Overtures to Biology: The Speculations of Eighteenth-Century Naturalists* (New Haven, CT: Yale University Press, 1964).

40. Blumenbach, *Contributions to Natural History*, 283–85, 287.

41. Ibid.

42. Ibid., 294.

43. J. Greene, *Death of Adam*, 213–16.

44. Blumenbach, *Contributions to Natural History*, 329–40.

45. Blumenbach, *Anthropological Treatises*, 183.

46. Ibid., 269.

47. Blumenbach, *Contributions to Natural History*, 323.

48. M. C. Legaspi, *The Death of Scripture and the Rise of Biblical Studies* (Oxford: Oxford University Press, 2010), 39–43.

49. Ibid., 45–50.

50. Jonathan Sheehan, *The Enlightenment Bible*, 174–75.

51. Ibid.,175; James Sheehan, *German History* (Oxford: Oxford University Press, 1994), 145–60.

52. Jonathan Sheehan, *The Enlightenment Bible*, 176.

53. "Und Gott der HERR machte den Menschen aus einem Erdenkloß, uns blies ihm ein den lebendigen Odem in seine Nase. Und also ward der Mensch eine lebendige Seele."

54. "Und zum Weibe sprach er: Ich will dir viel Schmerzen schaffen, wenn du schwanger wirst; du sollst mit Schmerzen Kinder gebären; und dein Verlangen soll nach deinem Manne sein, und er soll dein Herr sein."

55. "Im Schweiße deines Angesichts sollst du dein Brot essen, bis daß du wieder zu Erde werdest, davon du genommen bist. Denn du bist Erde und sollst zu Erde werden."

56. "Und Adam hieß sein Weib Eva, darum daß sie eine Mutter ist aller Lebendigen."

57. "Und Adam erkannte sein Weib Eva, und sie ward schwanger und gebar den Kain und sprach: Ich habe einen Mann gewonnen mit dem HERRN."

58. Blumenbach, *Contributions to Natural History*, 294.

59. Ibid., 211, 269.

60. Ibid., 212.

61. Stephan Füssel, "The Book of Books," in *The Luther Bible of 1534: A Cultural-Historical Introduction* (Cologne: Taschen, 2002), 63.

62. Martin Luther, "Genesis 1:26," in *Luther's Works*, vol. 1, *Lectures on Genesis Ch. 1–5*, trans. George V. Schick (1535–45; repr., St. Louis: Concordia Publishing House, 1958) 65, 64.

63. Blumenbach, *Anthropological Treatises*, 205.

64. Ibid., 269.

65. J. Greene, *Death of Adam*, 221.

66. David Livingstone, *Adam's Ancestors: Race, Religion, and the Politics of Human Origins* (Baltimore: Johns Hopkins University Press, 2008), 42–43.

67. Blumenbach, *Anthropological Treatises*, 196.

68. Luther, "Genesis 1:26," 63, 65.

69. Blumenbach, *Anthropological Treatises*, 294.

70. Ibid.

71. Luther, "Genesis 1:26," 66.

72. Rudwick, "The Shape and Meaning of Earth History," 301.

73. Ibid., 300.

74. Ibid., 310.

75. J. Greene, *Death of Adam*, 228.

76. James Sheehan, *German History*, 74–75.

77. Terry Pinkard, *German Philosophy, 1760–1860: The Legacy of Idealism* (Cambridge: Cambridge University Press, 2002), 3–4.

78. James Sheehan, *German History*, 74.

79. Ibid., 74–75.

80. David Blackbourn, *History of Germany, 1780–1918: The Long Nineteenth Century* (Malden, MA: Blackwell Publishing, 2003), 3.

81. James Sheehan, *German History*, 25–26.

82. Blackbourn, *History of Germany*, 2.

83. Jacob Katz, *Out of the Ghetto: The Social Background of Jewish Emancipation, 1770–1870* (Cambridge, MA: Harvard University Press, 1973), 9.

84. Reinhard Rurup, "The Tortuous and Thorny Path to Legal Equality: 'Jew Laws' and Emancipatory Legislation in Germany from the Late Eighteenth Century," *Leo Baeck Institute Yearbook* 31 (1986): 5.

85. Werner E. Mosse, "From 'Schutzjuden' to 'Deutsche Staatsbürger Jüdischen Glaubens': The Long and Bumpy Road of Jewish Emancipation in Germany," in *Paths of Emancipation: Jews, States, and Citizenship*, ed. Pierre Birnbaum and Ira Katznelson (Princeton, NJ: Princeton University Press, 1995), 61.

86. Ibid.

87. Katz, *Out of the Ghetto*, 17.

88. Rurup, "The Tortuous and Thorny Path to Legal Equality," 5.

89. Mosse, "From 'Schutzjuden' to 'Deutsche Staatsbürger Jüdischen Glaubens,'" 61.

90. James Sheehan, *German History*, 67.

91. Ibid., 70.

92. Ibid., 71.

93. Jonathan M. Hess, *Germans, Jews and the Claims of Modernity* (New Haven, CT: Yale University Press, 2002), 5.

94. Ibid., 11.

95. Pinkard, *German Philosophy*, 4.

96. Legaspi, *Death of Scripture*, 27–51.

97. Ibid.

98. Ibid., 80–81, 79–80.

99. Ibid., 31.

100. H. F. Augstein, "From the Land of the Bible to the Caucasus and Beyond: The Shifting Ideas of the Geographical Origin of Humankind," in *Race, Science, and Medicine, 1700–1960*, ed. Waltraud Ernst and Bernard Harris (New York: Routledge, 1999), 67.

101. Hess, *Germans, Jews and the Claims of Modernity*, 60.

102. Ibid.

103. Johann D. Michaelis, *Commentaries on the Laws of Moses*, trans. Alexander Smith (London: F. C. and J. Rivington, 1814), Art. 4, 14–15.

104. James Sheehan, *German History*, 104–5, 105.

105. Hess, *Germans, Jews and the Claims of Modernity*, 64–65.

106. Ibid., 60.

107. Augstein, "From the Land of the Bible," 67.

108. Ibid.

109. Jonathan Hess, "Johann David Michaelis and the Colonial Imaginary: Orientalism and the Emergence of Racial Antisemitism in Eighteenth-Century Germany," *Jewish Social Studies* 6, no. 2 (2000): 57.

110. Hess, *Germans, Jews, and the Claims of Modernity*, 3.

111. Ibid.

112. Ibid., 52.

113. Ibid., 58, 59.

114. Ibid., 6.

115. Blumenbach, *Anthropological Treatises*, 99.

116. Ibid., 234.

117. Ibid.

118. Horsman, *Race and Manifest Destiny*, 46.

Chapter 2

1. William R. Stanton, *The Leopard's Spots: Scientific Attitudes toward Race in America 1815–1859* (Chicago: University of Chicago Press, 1960), 50.

2. Josiah Clark Nott, *Two Lectures on the Natural History of the Caucasian and Negro Races* (Mobile, AL: Dade and Thompson, 1844), 13.

3. Ibid., 1.

4. Peter J. Bowler, *The Eclipse of Darwinism: Anti-Darwinian Evolution Theories in the Decades around 1900* (Baltimore: Johns Hopkins University Press, 1983), 118–40; Peter J. Bowler, *Evolution: The History of an Idea* (Berkeley: University of California

Press, 1989), 208–14; David Hull, *The Metaphysics of Evolution* (Albany: State University of New York Press, 1989), 27–42.

5. Samuel G. Morton, *Crania Americana; or, A Comparative View of the Skulls of Various Aboriginal Nations of North and South America* (Philadelphia: J. Dobson, 1839).

6. Nott, *Caucasian and Negro Races*, 1.

7. These commitments would also be challenged with the arrival of Darwinism in the United States near the end of the nineteenth century. See Stanton, *Leopard's Spots*, 196; Jonathan Marks, "Race: Past, Present, Future," in *Revisiting Race in a Genomic Age*, ed. Barbara Koenig, Sandra Soo-Jin Lee, and Sarah S. Richardson (New Brunswick, NJ: Rutgers University Press, 2008), 4.

8. For more on this tension between sacred and secular accounts of history see: Paolo Rossi, *The Dark Abyss of Time: The History of the Earth and the History of Nations from Hooke to Vico*, trans. L. G. Cochrane (Chicago: University of Chicago Press, 1984); David Livingstone, *Adam's Ancestors: Race, Religion, and the Politics of Human Origins* (Baltimore: Johns Hopkins University Press, 2008); Colin Kidd, *The Forging of the Races: Race and Scripture in the Protestant Atlantic World, 1600–2000* (Cambridge: Cambridge University Press, 2006).

9. Josiah Clark Nott, *Two Lectures on the Connection between the Biblical and Physical History of Man* (New York: Bartlett and Welford, 1849), 7.

10. Stanton, *Leopard's Spots*, 69–70; George M. Frederickson, *The Black Image in the White Mind: The Debate on Afro-American Character and Destiny, 1817–1914* (1971; repr., Middletown, CT: Wesleyan University Press, 1987), 78.

11. Stanton, *Leopard's Spots*, 69.

12. D. Livingstone, *Adam's Ancestors*, 26.

13. Ibid., 33–34.

14. Ibid., 34.

15. Rossi, *Dark Abyss of Time*, 158.

16. D. Livingstone, *Adam's Ancestors*, 5.

17. James Barr, "Pre-scientific Chronology: The Bible and the Origin of the World," *Proceedings of the American Philosophical Society* 143, no. 3 (1999): 382.

18. Ibid.; D. Livingstone, *Adam's Ancestors*, 5.

19. Rossi, *Dark Abyss of Time*, 159.

20. D. Livingstone, *Adam's Ancestors*, 35.

21. Ibid., 38–39.

22. Ibid., 37–38.

23. Ronald L. Numbers, "'The Most Important Biblical Discovery of Our Time': William Henry Green and the Demise of Ussher's Chronology," *American Society of Church History* 69, no. 2 (2000): 262.

24. Martin J. Rudwick, "The Shape and Meaning of Earth History," in *God and Nature: Historical Essays on the Encounter between Christianity and Science*, ed. David C. Lindberg and Ronald L. Numbers (Berkeley: University of California Press, 1986), 307–8.

25. Rossi, *Dark Abyss of Time*, 152–57.

26. John C. Greene, *The Death of Adam: Evolution and Its Impact on Western Thought* (Ames: Iowa State University Press, 1959), 236.

27. Friedemann Schrenk and Stephanie Muller, *The Neanderthals* (New York: Routledge, 2009), 6–7.

28. Rudwick, "Shape and Meaning," 311.

29. James Cowles Prichard, *Researches into the Physical History of Man* (London: Printed for John and Arthur Arch, 1813); John Bachman, *The Doctrine of the Unity of the Human Race: Examined on the Principles of Science* (Charleston, SC: C. Canning, 1850); Charles Hamilton Smith, *The Natural History of the Human Species* (Boston: Gould and Lincoln, 1851).

30. Johann Friedrich Blumenbach, *Anthropological Treatises* (1795; repr., London: Longman, Green, and Roberts, 1865), 264.

31. Morton, *Crania Americana*, 295.

32. Samuel Morton, *Crania Aegyptiaca; or, Observations on Egyptian Ethnography Derived from Anatomy, History and the Monuments* (Philadelphia: John Pennington, 1844), 65–66.

33. Morton, *Crania Americana*, 2–3.

34. Ibid., 295.

35. Stanton, *Leopard's Spots*, 40.

36. Ibid., 69, 66.

37. Emmett B. Carmichael, "Josiah Clark Nott," *Bulletin of the History of Medicine* 22 (1948): 250.

38. Ibid., 251.

39. See Franz Boas, "Some Recent Criticisms of Physical Anthropology," *American Anthropologist* 1, no. 1 (1898), 98–106.

40. Chapter 4 explains that this pattern of reasoning was a precursor to the statistical analysis used by contemporary geneticists who model allele frequency differences among present-day groups and then infer from which of the four major continental populations (African, Asian, European, and Native American) they descended.

41. Reginald Horsman, *Josiah Nott of Mobile: Southerner, Physician, and Racial Theorist* (Baton Rouge: Louisiana State University Press, 1987), 18.

42. Ibid., 23, 27–28.

43. Carmichael, "Josiah Clark Nott," 255.

44. Nott, *Biblical and Physical History of Man*, 7.

45. Nott, *Caucasian and Negro Races*, 7.

46. Ibid., 5; Stanton, *Leopard's Spots*, 122.

47. Frederickson and Stanton disagree on the acceptance of polygenism in the South. Stanton is of the opinion that southern religiosity was too strong to accept what amounted to the rejection of biblical truth and one of Christianity's most foundational beliefs: human descent from Adam. Frederickson, however, makes a compelling argument that the popularization of polygenism in the South by figures such as Samuel Cartwright smoothed over potential conflicts with biblical scripture by showing how polygenism could be supported with creative interpretations of the story of Cain or the Curse of Ham. For more on their contrasting views, see Stanton, *Leopard's Spots*, 192–96; and Frederickson, *Black Image*, 82–90, 256–82.

48. Nott, *Caucasian and Negro Races*, 1.

49. Nott, *Biblical and Physical History of Man*, 7, 14.

50. William Stanton argues that most of the ideas contained in the widely popular *Types of Mankind* had been published or made public by the American School before 1854 (see Stanton, *Leopard's Spots*, 163). For this reason I have decided not to discuss Nott's *Two Lectures on the Connection between the Biblical and Physical History of Man* delivered in New Orleans before the Louisiana legislature in December 1849. The ideas contained in this lecture are largely captured in the two lectures discussed in this chapter.

51. Janet Browne, "Noah's Flood, the Ark, and the Shaping of Early Modern Natural History," in *When Science and Christianity Meet*, ed. David C. Lindberg and Ronald L. Numbers (Chicago: University of Chicago Press, 2003), 114.

52. Ibid.

53. Nott, *Caucasian and Negro Races*, 10.

54. Ibid.

55. Morton, *Crania Aegyptiaca*, 1–2.

56. Stephen Jay Gould, *The Mismeasure of Man* (New York: W. W. Norton, 1996), 82.

57. Nott, *Caucasian and Negro Races*, 14.

58. Ibid.

59. Ibid., 15.

60. Morton, *Crania Americana*, 3.

61. Ibid., 19.

62. Nott, *Caucasian and Negro Races*, 18–19.

63. Ibid., 18.

64. Ibid., 23.

65. Ibid., 25 (emphasis in original).

66. Ibid., 26.

67. Ibid., 18, 19.

68. John Ray, "Preface," in *The Wisdom of God Manifested in the Works of Creation* (1691; repr., London: William Inney and Richard Manby for the Royal Society of London, 1735).

69. J. Greene, *Death of Adam*, 5–6.

70. Ibid.

71. Ibid., 29.

72. Ibid., 34.

73. Ibid., 12, 14.

74. Historians of the early modern period have cautioned against assuming a continuity of meaning between premodern and modern ideas about Noah's sons. Prior to European colonial expansion into West Africa and the Americas, Western thinkers did not possess a global framework for understanding human variation. The differences recorded and studied by the likes of Hippocrates, Aristotle, Augustine, and Seville reflected regional encounters across fairly proximate national borders. Until the sixteenth century these premodern encounters were limited to interactions across the Mediter-

ranean, North and East Africa, and the borderlands of Europe and Asia. We can see this regional understanding of human difference reflected in the eleventh- and twelfth-century renditions of the "T-O maps" of Isadore of Seville (which were originally created in the fifth century). Premodern thinkers did not assume that races were derived from purely distinct groups that lived on isolated continents in the past. Without a comprehensive taxonomy separating humans on the basis of "inherited" physical traits and dispositions, or an awareness of the degree to which humans had migrated to far-reaching areas of the globe, scholars before the modern period did not see "the races" as separate biological units or subdivisions of the human species. The idea that race refers to a constantly distinct and biologically stable population is a modern invention that came into existence following the European colonial expansion and the post-Enlightenment obsession with classifying the species of the natural world. For more on how premodern definitions of race varied from what was believed by modern thinkers, see Benjamin Braude, "The Sons of Noah and the Construction of Ethnic and Geographical Identities in the Medieval and Early Modern Periods," *William and Mary Quarterly*, 3rd ser., 54, no. 1 (1997): 103–42. For more on how modern thinkers came to see race in biological terms, see Nicholas Hudson, "From 'Nation' to 'Race': The Origin of Racial Classification in Eighteenth-Century Thought," *Eighteenth-Century Studies* 29, no. 3 (1996): 247–64.

75. Mott T. Greene, "Genesis and Geology Revisited: The Order of Nature and the Nature of Order in Nineteenth-Century Britain," in Lindberg and Numbers, *When Science and Christianity Meet*, 154.

76. J. Greene, *Death of Adam*, 309–39.

77. Lee D. Baker, *From Savage to Negro: Anthropology and the Construction of Race, 1896–1954* (Berkeley: University of California Press 1998), 14.

78. Audrey Smedley, *Race in North America: Origins and Evolution of a Worldview*, 2nd ed. (Boulder, CO: Westview Press 1999), 242–45.

79. See Nott's discussion of the antiquity of the Negro type as a race perpetually in bondage in Josiah Clark Nott and George Robbins Gliddon, *Types of Mankind* (Philadelphia: Lippincott, Grambo, 1854), 248–53.

80. Melissa Nobles, *Shades of Citizenship: Race and the Census in Modern Politics* (Stanford, CA: Stanford University Press, 2000), 37–39.

81. Josiah Clark Nott, "Statistics of Southern Slave Population," *Commercial Review* 4, no. 3 (November 1847): 275–87.

82. Nobles, *Shades of Democracy*, 42.

83. Marks, "Race," 2–3.

84. Frederickson, *Black Image*, 71–96; see also Steven Jay Gould's treatment of the American School, which has become key for anthropologists, in *The Mismeasure of Man*, 62–104.

85. Frederickson, *Black Image*, 78.

86. Ibid., 79, 78–82.

87. Theodore Dwight Bozeman, *Protestants in an Age of Science: The Baconian Ideal and Antebellum American Religious Thought* (Chapel Hill: University of North Carolina Press, 1977); Alexandra Oleson and John Voss, *The Organization of Knowledge in*

Modern America, 1860–1920 (Baltimore: Johns Hopkins University Press, 1979); Michael O'Brien, *Intellectual Life in the American South, 1810–1860* (Chapel Hill: University of North Carolina Press, 2010).

88. Moses Ashley Curtis, "Unity of the Races," *Southern Quarterly Review* 7 (1845): 375, 415–16, 416.

89. Ibid., 393–94.

90. Ibid., 394.

91. Ibid., 446.

92. Bachman, *Unity of the Human Race*; John Bachman, *A Defense of Luther and the Reformation against the Charges of John Bellinger, M.D., and Others to Which Are Appended Various Communications of Other Protestant and Roman Catholic Writers Who Engaged in the Controversy* (Charleston, SC: William H. Paxton 1853); John Bachman, *A Notice of the "Types of Mankind," with an Examination of the Charges Contained in the Biography of Dr. Morton, Published by Nott and Gliddon* (Charleston, SC: James, Williams, and Gitsinger, Steam Power Press, 1854); John Bachman, "An Examination of Professor Agassiz's Sketch of the Natural Provinces of the Animal World, and Their Relation to the Different Types of Man, with a Tableau Accompanying the Sketch," *Charleston Medical Journal and Review* 10, no. 4 (1855): 482–534.

93. Bachman, *Unity of the Human Race*, 8.

94. Frederickson, *Black Image*, 81.

95. Stanton, *Leopard's Spots*, 124–36, 158, 173, 175; Horsman, *Josiah Nott of Mobile*, 117–18.

96. Bachman, "Professor Agassiz's Sketch."

97. Stanton, *Leopard's Spots*, 124–36.

98. Horsman, *Josiah Nott of Mobile*, 118.

99. Josiah Clark Nott, "Diversity of the Human Races," *De Bow's Review* 10 (February 1851): 116.

100. Horsman, *Josiah Nott of Mobile*, 118.

101. Nott, *Caucasian and Negro Races*, 1.

102. Horsman, *Josiah Nott of Mobile*, 10, 34–35, 72–74.

103. The British historian of science Peter Bowler argued that it would be a mistake to assume that the racial typologies developed in the eighteenth century by Carl Linnaeus, Comte de Buffon, Johann Blumenbach, and Immanuel Kant were truly evolutionary or could be considered intellectual precursors to Darwin. The reason is that these accounts of race assumed that nature unfolded according to a predetermined pattern or teleology. Bowler argued, "There was no possibility of a Darwinian, or open-ended view of evolutionary development until the naturalists of the early nineteenth century had overthrown [the] belief in a rationally structured order of things" (*Evolution*, 51). Until then, natural historians continued to define the natural world and the human species by relying on the argument from design, species fixity, and the inherent order of the natural world. These were ideas inherited from late seventeenth-century natural theology (ibid., 52) and were clearly present in the racial theories of American polygenists.

104. Ibid., 51.

105. J. Greene, *Death of Adam*, 304–7; Bowler, *Evolution*, 51.

106. Josiah Clark Nott, "The Instincts of the Races," *New Orleans Medical and Surgical Journal* 19 (1866): 4.

107. Nott and Gliddon, *Types of Mankind*, 60.

108. Nott, *Biblical and Physical History of Man*, 53.

109. One could say the need for scientific knowledge to supersede the religious knowledge of the past was fully naturalized with the rise of positivism and the professionalization of science that occurred in the twentieth century.

110. See, for example, J. Greene's seminal text *The Death of Adam*.

Chapter 3

1. Frederick L. Hoffman, *Race Traits and Tendencies of the American Negro* (New York: Macmillan, 1896).

2. For new epidemiological work explaining how "the social" is embodied in health outcomes, see Nancy Krieger, "The Science and Epidemiology of Racism and Health: Racial/Ethnic Categories, Biological Expressions of Racism, and the Embodiment of Inequality—an Ecosocial Perspective," in *What's the Use of Race? Modern Governance and the Biology of Difference*, ed. Ian Whitmarsh and David Jones (Cambridge, MA: MIT Press, 2010), 225–58. For work on the problems with using racialized genetic and/or biomolecular explanations to understand complex diseases, see Simon M. Outram and George Ellison, "Arguments against the Use of Racialized Categories as Genetic Variables in Biomedical Research: What Are They, and Why Are They Being Ignored?," in Whitmarsh and Jones, *What's The Use of Race?*, 91–124; Jay S. Kaufman, "Ethical Dilemmas in Statistical Practice: The Problem of Race in Biomedicine," in *Mapping "Race": Critical Approaches to Health Disparities Research*, ed. L. Gomez and N. Lopez (New Brunswick, NJ: Rutgers University Press, 2013), 53–66; Duana Fullwiley, "The Biologistical Construction of Race: 'Admixture' Technology and the New Genetic Medicine," *Social Studies of Science* 38, no. 5 (2008): 695–735.

3. Michele Mitchell, *Righteous Propagation: African Americans and the Politics of Racial Destiny after Reconstruction* (Chapel Hill: University of North Carolina Press, 2004), 12, 76–107.

4. See ibid., 12; Gregory Michael Dorr, *Segregation's Science: Eugenics and Society in Virginia* (Charlottesville: University of Virginia Press, 2008), 98–106.

5. For a discussion of other black physicians and social activists negotiating between racial science and eugenics at this time, see Gregory Michael Dorr on Thomas Wyatt Turner in *Segregation's Science*, 98–106. See also Mia Bay's discussion of Alain Locke and W. E. B. Du Bois in *The White Image in the Black Mind: African American Ideas about White People, 1830–1925* (New York: Oxford University Press, 2000), 187–217; Michele Mitchell also discusses the range of black responses to Progressive Era racial science in *Righteous Propagation*, 76–105.

6. Charles V. Roman, *American Civilization and the Negro: The Afro-American in Relation to National Progress* (Philadelphia: F. A. Davis, 1921), 321–22.

7. Mitchell, *Righteous Propagation*, 105, 106.

8. Donald K. Pickens, *Eugenics and the Progressives* (Nashville, TN: Vanderbilt University Press, 1968), 163–81; Dorr, *Segregation's Science*, 1–19; John P. Jackson and Nadine Weidman, *Race, Racism, and Science: Social Impact and Interaction* (New Brunswick, NJ: Rutgers University Press, 2006), 97–127.

9. Charles Darwin, *The Descent of Man, and Selection in Relation to Sex* (1871; repr., London: Penguin Books, 2004), 207.

10. Ibid., 208.

11. Ibid., 207.

12. Ibid., 203. See also Nancy Stepan's discussion of Darwin's ambiguous stance on race in *The Idea of Race in Science* (Hamden, CT: Archon Books, 1982), 47–82.

13. George Stocking, "The Turn-of-the-Century Concept of Race," *Modernism/Modernity* 1, no. 1 (1994): 1, 11.

14. George Stocking, "The Persistence of Polygenist Thought in Post-Darwinian Anthropology," in *Race, Culture and Evolution: Essays in the History of Anthropology* (1968; repr., Chicago: University of Chicago Press, 1982), 42–68.

15. Stocking, "Turn-of-the-Century Concept of Race," 12.

16. Stocking, "Persistence of Polygenist Thought," 72–76.

17. Ronald Hamowy, *Government and Public Health in America* (Northampton, MA: Edward Elgar Press, 2007), 28–29.

18. Ibid., 28.

19. Susan M. Reverby, *Examining Tuskegee: The Infamous Syphilis Study and Its Legacy* (Chapel Hill: University of North Carolina Press, 2009), 22.

20. Hamowy, *Government and Public Health in America*, 364–65.

21. Allan Brandt, *No Magic Bullet: A Social History of Venereal Disease in the United States since 1880* (New York: Oxford University Press, 1987), 57; Hamowy, *Government and Public Health in America*, 29.

22. Hamowy, *Government and Public Health in America*, 29.

23. Brandt, *No Magic Bullet*, 115.

24. Hamowy, *Government and Public Health in America*, 29.

25. Christina Simmons, "African Americans and Sexual Victorianism in the Social Hygiene Movement, 1910–40," *Journal of the History of Sexuality* 4, no. 1 (1993): 58, 57.

26. Paul Lombardo and Gregory Dorr, "Eugenics, Medical Education, and the Public Health Service: Another Perspective on the Tuskegee Syphilis Experiment," *Bulletin of the History of Medicine* 80, no. 2 (2006): 291–316.

27. Ibid., 292.

28. Ibid., 294.

29. Francis Galton, "Eugenics: Its Definition, Scope, and Aims," *American Journal of Sociology* 10, no. 1 (1904): 1–25.

30. Madison Grant, *The Passing of the Great Race, or the Racial Basis of European History* (New York: Charles Scribner's Sons, 1916), 29.

31. Stepan, *The Idea of Race in Science*, 128–29.

32. Charles Davenport, "Effects of Race Intermingling," *Proceedings of the American Philosophical Society* 130 (1917): 364.

33. Josiah C. Nott, *Two Lectures on the Natural History of the Caucasian and Negro Races* (Mobile, AL: Dade and Thompson,1844), 17.

34. Ibid., 34.

35. Josiah C. Nott, "The Problem of the Black Races," *De Bow's Review* 1 (March 1866): 266–83.

36. Stepan, *The Idea of Race in Science*, 134.

37. Ibid., 35–46.

38. Stephen Jay Gould, *The Mismeasure of Man* (New York: W. W. Norton, 1996), 177–263; Daniel J. Kevles, *In the Name of Eugenics: Genetics and the Uses of Human Heredity* (Cambridge, MA: Harvard University Press, 1995); Jackson and Weidman, *Race, Racism, and Science*, 110.

39. Darwin, *The Descent of Man*, 203.

40. Peter J. Bowler, *Evolution: The History of an Idea* (Berkeley: University of California Press, 1989), 246.

41. Ibid.

42. Hoffmann, *Race Traits and Tendencies*, 94.

43. Ibid., 93.

44. Ibid., 94.

45. Ibid., 94–95.

46. Ibid., 95 (emphasis in original).

47. Ibid., v.

48. George M. Frederickson, *The Black Image in the White Mind: The Debate on Afro-American Character and Destiny, 1817–1914* (1971; repr., Middletown, CT: Wesleyan University Press, 1987), 249.

49. Ibid., 249–50; Lee D. Baker, *From Savage to Negro: Anthropology and the Construction of Race 1989–1954* (Berkeley: University of California Press, 1996), 79.

50. Frederickson, *Black Image*, 249.

51. Paul Barringer, *The American Negro: His Past and Future* (Raleigh, NC: Edwards and Broughton, 1900), 3.

52. Dorr, *Segregation's Science*, 41, 42.

53. Ibid., 42; Lombardo and Dorr, "Eugenics, Medical Education," 294.

54. Barringer, *The American Negro*, 2.

55. Ibid.

56. Frederickson, *Black Image*, 256–58.

57. Barringer, *The American Negro*, 3.

58. Ibid.

59. Ibid., 15.

60. Ibid., 8, 16.

61. Ibid., 8.

62. The articles referenced were read before the General Sessions of the American Public Health Association meeting that took place in Jacksonville, Florida, November 30–December 4, 1914. They were subsequently published in the March 1915 issue of the *American Journal of Public Health*.

63. For articles in this journal, see William F. Brunner, "The Negro Health Problem in Southern Cities"; L. C. Allen, "The Negro Health Problem"; and Lawrence Lee, "The Negro as a Problem in Public Health Charity," all in *American Journal of Public Health* 5, no. 3 (1915): 183–85; 194–200; 207.

64. Simmons, "African Americans and Sexual Victorianism," 57.

65. Brandt, *No Magic Bullet*, 13, 116.

66. For a discussion of other black leaders who also opposed the racial science of the Progressive Era, see Dorr, *Segregation's Science*, 98–106; Mitchell, *Righteous Propagation*, 76–108; Bay, *White Image in the Black Mind*, 187–218.

67. Linda C. Chandler, "C. V. Roman, Leader Worthy of His Namesake," *Dallas Medical Journal* 80, no. 12 (December 1994): 499.

68. Charles V. Roman, *Meharry Medical College: A History* (Nashville, TN: Sunday School Publishing Board of the National Baptist Convention, 1934).

69. Ibid., 51; Sheena M. Morrison and Elizabeth Fee, "Charles V. Roman: Physician, Writer, Educator," *American Journal of Public Health* 100, supplement 1 (2010): S69.

70. Morrison and Fee, "Charles V. Roman," S69.

71. Roman, *Meharry Medical College*, 45.

72. Morrison and Fee, "Charles V. Roman," S69.

73. Ibid.

74. Chandler, "C. V. Roman," 499.

75. Karen Morris, "The Founding of the National Medical Association" (PhD diss., Yale University School of Medicine, 2007), 75.

76. L. Hirschfeld and H. Hirschfeld, "History," National Medical Association, accessed April 12, 2012, http://www.nmanet.org/page/History.

77. Ibid.

78. Charles V. Roman, "The Deontological Orientation of Its Membership and the Chief Function of a Medical Society," *Journal of the National Medical Association* 1, no. 1 (1909): 20.

79. Simmons, "African Americans and Sexual Victorianism," 58.

80. Roman, *Meharry Medical College*, 45.

81. Ibid., 204–6.

82. Ibid., 205.

83. Charles V. Roman, "Fifty Years' Progress of the American Negro in Health and Sanitation: Delivered at Semi-centennial at Howard University," *Journal of the National Medical Association* 9, no. 2 (1917): 61–67.

84. On the secularization of medical and scientific knowledge, see Nancy Leys Stepan and Sander L. Gilman, "Appropriating the Idioms of Science: The Rejection of Scientific Racism," in *The "Racial" Economy of Science: Toward a Democratic Future*, ed. S. Harding (Bloomington: Indiana University Press, 1993), 171–72. For more on the shared religious discourse between black and white advocates of social hygiene, see Simmons, "African Americans and Sexual Victorianism"; and Amy Laura Hall, *Conceiving Parenthood: American Protestantism and the Spirit of Reproduction* (Grand Rapids, MI: Eerdmans Publishing, 2008).

85. Roman, *American Civilization and the Negro*.

86. Ibid., 9–21.

87. Ibid., 322.

88. Ibid., 321.

89. Ibid., 323–24.

90. Ibid., 324, 321.

91. Ibid., 322, 321.

92. Ibid., 321–22.

93. Ibid., 327.

94. Roman, "Fifty Years' Progress," 67.

95. Ibid., 61.

96. Ibid., 66.

97. Ibid.

98. Ibid., 62.

99. Ibid., 66.

100. Charles V. Roman, "Syllabus of Lecture to Colored Soldiers at Camps Grant, Stewart, Hill and Humphreys," *Journal of the National Medical Association* 10, no. 3 (1918): 104.

101. Ibid., 106.

102. Ibid.

103. Simmons, "African Americans and Sexual Victorianism," 58.

104. Ibid., 63–67.

105. Ibid., 63.

106. Roman, "Fifty Years' Progress," 62.

Chapter 4

1. Friedemann Schrenk and Stephanie Muller, *The Neanderthals* (New York: Routledge, 2009), 1.

2. Richard Green, Johannes Krause, Adrian Briggs, Tomislav Maricic, Udo Stenzel, and Martin Kircher, "A Draft Sequence of the Neanderthal Genome," *Science* 328 (May 2010): 717.

3. Ibid., 721.

4. Recently Dorothy Roberts has challenged claims about the emergence of a "paradigm shift" in modern scientific theories of race and the eventual decline of scientific racism, arguing instead that the concept of race was far from being universally rejected by scientists over the course of the twentieth century and has in fact yielded what she calls "the new racial science." See Dorothy Roberts, *Fatal Invention: How Science, Politics, and Big Business Re-create Race in the Twenty-First Century* (New York: New Press, 2012). Jenny Reardon has also contested the decline of the race thesis, showing how biologists have steadily retooled race within the life sciences since the UNESCO statements on race following World War II. See Jenny Reardon, *Race to the Finish: Identity and Governance in an Age of Genomics* (Princeton, NJ: Princeton University Press,

2005), 17–44. Both Roberts and Reardon offer compelling alternatives to the narrative of decline found in the work of Elazar Barkan, *The Retreat of Scientific Racism: Changing Concepts of Race in Britain and the United States between the World Wars* (Cambridge: Cambridge University Press, 1992).

5. John P. Jackson Jr. and Nadine M. Weidman, *Race, Racism and Science: Social Impact and Interaction* (New Brunswick, NJ: Rutgers University Press, 2006), 130–37.

6. Lee Baker, *From Savage to Negro: Anthropology and the Construction of Race, 1896–1954* (Berkeley: University of California Press, 1998), 110.

7. Michael Yudell, *Race Unmasked: Biology and Race in the 20th Century* (New York: Columbia University Press, 2014), 111–37. Barkan, *Retreat of Scientific Racism*; Jackson and Weidman, *Race, Racism and Science*, 153–59; Audrey Smedley, *Race in North America: Origin and Evolution of a Worldview* (Boulder, CO: Westview Press, 1999), 303–10.

8. Jonathan Marks, "Race: Past, Present, Future," in *Revisiting Race in a Genomic Age*, ed. Barbara Koenig, Sandra Soo-Jin Lee, and Sarah S. Richardson (New Brunswick, NJ: Rutgers University Press, 2008), 22.

9. Barkan, *Retreat of Scientific Racism*; Luigi Luca Cavalli-Sforza, *Genes, Peoples, and Languages* (Berkeley: University of California Press, 2001).

10. Jonathan Marks, *Human Biodiversity: Genes, Race, and History* (New Brunswick, NJ: Aldine Transaction, 1995), 89–92.

11. Ibid., 22–23.

12. Ashley Montagu, *A Statement on Race: An Extended Discussion in Plain Language of the UNESCO Statement by Experts on Race Problems* (New York: Henry Schuman, 1951).

13. Yudell, *Race Unmasked*, 139–65; Reardon, *Race to the Finish*, 23.

14. Reardon, *Race to the Finish*, 30–31.

15. Ibid.

16. Ibid., 34–35.

17. Ibid., 43.

18. Frank B. Livingstone, "On the Nonexistence of Human Races," *Current Anthropology* 3, no. 3 (1962): 279–81.

19. Veronika Lipphardt, "Isolates and Crosses in Human Population Genetics; or, A Contextualization of German Race Science," *Current Anthropology* 53, no. 5 (2012): S69–S82.

20. Duana Fullwiley, "The Molecularization of Race: U.S. Health Institutions, Pharmacogenetics Practice, and Public Science after the Genome," in Koenig, Lee, and Richardson, *Revisiting Race in a Genomic Age*, 150.

21. Craig Venter, "Statement on Decoding of Genome," *New York Times*, June 27, 2000, D8.

22. Jenny Reardon, "Race without Salvation: Beyond the Science/Society Divide in Genomic Studies of Human Diversity," in Koenig, Lee, and Richardson, *Revisiting Race in a Genomic Age*, 304.

23. Duana Fullwiley, "The Biologistical Construction of Race: 'Admixture' Technology and the New Genetic Medicine," *Social Studies of Science* 38, no. 5 (2008): 695–735;

Nadia El Haj, "The Reinscription of Race," *Annual Review of Anthropology* 36 (2000): 283–300; Jonathan Marks, "Race: Past, Present, Future," 22–25; Alexandra Shields, Michael Fortun, Evelynn Hammonds, Patricia King, Caryn Lerman, Rayna Rapp, and Patrick Sullivan, "The Use of Race Variables in Genetics Studies of Complex Traits and the Goal of Reducing Health Disparities: A Transdisciplinary Perspective," *American Psychologist* 60, no. 1 (2005): 104–14; Reardon, *Race to the Finish*.

24. Fullwiley, "Biologistical Construction of Race," 701–6.

25. Ibid., 701–2.

26. Ibid., 704–5.

27. Ibid., 701–6.

28. Henry T. Greely, "Genetic Genealogy: Genetics Meets the Marketplace," in Koenig, Lee, and Richardson, *Revisiting Race in a Genomic Age*, 215–23; Kimberly Tallbear, "Native-American-DNA.com: In Search of Native American Race and Tribe," in Koenig, Lee, and Richardson, *Revisiting Race in a Genomic Age*, 235–52.

29. Fullwiley, "Biologistical Construction of Race," 706.

30. Deborah Bolnick, "Individual Ancestry Inference and the Reification of Race as a Biological Phenomenon," in Koenig, Lee, and Richardson, *Revisiting Race in a Genomic Age*, 70–85.

31. Kenneth M. Weiss and Jeffrey C. Long, "Non-Darwinian Estimation: My Ancestors, My Genes' Ancestors," *Genome Research* 19 (2009): 703–10.

32. Fullwiley, "Biologistical Construction of Race," 698.

33. Peter J. Bowler, *Evolution: The History of an Idea* (Berkeley: University of California Press, 1989), 229–30.

34. Ibid., 230, 229.

35. Ibid., 230–31.

36. Schrenk and Muller, *The Neanderthals*, 6–7.

37. Thomas Huxley, *On the Negro Question* (London: Ladies' London Emancipation Society,1864), 7–8.

38. Schrenk and Muller, *The Neanderthals*, 6.

39. Ibid., 7.

40. Bowler, *Evolution*, 232.

41. Ibid., 233.

42. Ibid.

43. Ibid., 230.

44. Charles Darwin, "On the Races of Man," in *The Descent of Man and Selection in Relation to Sex* (1871; repr., London: Penguin Classics, 2004), 202–203.

45. Thomas Huxley, "On Some Fossil Remains of Man," in *Man's Place in Nature and Other Anthropological Essays* (1863; repr., New York: D. Appleton, 1896), 185.

46. Ibid., 186.

47. Ibid.

48. Hermann Schaaffhausen, "On the Crania of the Most Ancient Races of Man," trans. George Busk, *Natural History Review* 1 (April 1861): 162.

49. Ibid., 163.

50. Huxley, "On Some Fossil Remains of Man," 204.

51. Thomas Huxley, "The Aryan Question," in *Man's Place in Nature and Other Anthropological Essays* (New York: D. Appleton, 1896), 321.

52. Huxley, "On Some Fossil Remains of Man," 199.

53. Ibid., 205.

54. Green et al., "Draft Sequence," 717.

55. Interview with Professor "X" of the Neanderthal Genome Project, September 18, 2010.

56. Green et al., "Draft Sequence," 710.

57. Ibid.

58. Ibid., 720–21.

59. Interview with Professor "X" of the Neanderthal Genome Project, November 18, 2010.

60. Kenneth M. Weiss and Brian W. Lambert, "Does History Matter? Do the Facts of Human Variation Package Our Views or Do Our Views Package the Facts?," *Evolutionary Anthropology* 19, no. 3 (2010): 97.

61. Weiss and Long, "Non-Darwinian Estimation," 706; Weiss and Lambert, "Does History Matter?," 97; Bolnick, "Individual Ancestry Inference," 80–82.

62. Weiss and Long, "Non-Darwinian Estimation," 706; Weiss and Lambert, "Does History Matter?," 97.

63. Weiss and Long, "Does History Matter?," 95.

64. Weiss and Long, "Non-Darwinian Estimation," 705.

65. Ibid.

66. Ibid.

67. Ibid., 706; Weiss and Lambert, "Does History Matter?," 97; Bolnick, "Individual Ancestry Inference," 80–82.

68. Svante Paabo, *Neanderthal Man: In Search of Lost Genomes* (New York: Basic Books, 2014), 246–47.

Chapter 5

1. Mary A. Gerend and Manacy Pai, "Social Determinants of Black-White Disparities in Breast Cancer Mortality: A Review," *Cancer Epidemiology, Biomarkers, and Prevention* 17, no. 11 (2008): 2913–23.

2. Subhasree Basu, Thibaut Barnoud, Che-Pei Kung, Matthew Reiss, and Maureen E. Murphy, "The African-Specific S47 Polymorphism of p53 Alters Chemosensitivity," *Cell Cycle* 15, no. 19 (2016): 2557–60.

3. Ibid., 2557.

4. Ibid., 2557–58.

5. "Researchers Identify Gene Variant That May Contribute to Increased Cancer Risk in African Americans," Wistar Institute, March 31, 2016, https://www.wistar.org/news-and-media/press-releases/researchers-identify-gene-variant-may-contribute-increased-cancer-risk.

6. Jonathan Marks, "Race: Past, Present, and Future," in *Revisiting Race in a Ge-*

nomic Age, ed. Barbara Koenig, Sandra Soo-Jin Lee, and Sarah S. Richardson (New Brunswick, NJ: Rutgers University Press, 2008), 21–38.

7. Moumita Sinha, Emma Larkin, Robert Elston, and Susan Redline, "Self-Reported Race and Genetic Admixture," *New England Journal of Medicine* 354, no. 4 (2006): 421–22.

8. Ibid., 421.

9. See John Oliver L. DeLancey, Michael J. Thun, Ahmedin Jemal, and Elizabeth M. Ward, "Recent Trends in Black-White Disparities in Cancer Mortality," *Cancer Epidemiology, Biomarkers, and Prevention* 17, no. 11 (2008): 2908–12; Monica E. Peek, Judith V. Sayad, and Ronald Markwardt, "Fear, Fatalism and Breast Cancer Screening in Low-Income African-American Women: The Role of Clinicians and the Health Care System," *Journal of General Internal Medicine* 23, no. 11 (2008): 1847–53; Keith Wailoo, *How Cancer Crossed the Color Line* (Oxford: Oxford University Press, 2011); Angela Rose Black and Cheryl Woods-Giscombé, "Applying the Stress and 'Strength' Hypothesis to Black Women's Breast Cancer Screening Delays," *Stress and Health?: Journal of the International Society for the Investigation of Stress* 28, no. 5 (2012): 389–96.

10. Neha Vora, "Producing Diasporas and Globalization: Indian Middle Class Migrants in Dubai," *Anthropological Quarterly* 81, no. 2 (2008): 377–406.

11. Cary Funk and Becky A. Alper, "Religion and Science," Pew Research Center, October 22, 2015, http://www.pewinternet.org/2015/10/22/science-and-religion/.

12. Colin A. Russell, "The Conflict of Science and Religion," in *Science and Religion: A Historical Introduction*, ed. Gary Ferngren (Baltimore: Johns Hopkins University Press, 2002), 3–12.

13. David B. Wilson, "The Historiography of Science and Religion," in Ferngren, *Science and Religion*, 13–30.

14. David C. Lindberg and Ronald L. Numbers, "Beyond War and Peace: A Reappraisal of the Encounter between Christianity and Science," *Perspectives on Science and Christian Faith* 39 (1987): 140–45; John Hedley Brooke, *Science and Religion: Some Historical Perspectives* (Cambridge: Cambridge University Press, 1991), 16–51.

15. Jonathan Marks, *What It Means to Be 98% Chimpanzee: Apes, People, and Their Genes* (Berkeley: University of California Press, 2002), 22.

16. Ashley Montagu, *Statement on Race: An Extended Discussion in Plain Language of the UNESCO Statement by Experts on Race Problems* (New York: Henry Schuman, 1951), 57.

17. Immanuel Kant, "Preface," in *Critique of Pure Reason*, trans. Paul Guyer and Allen W. Wood (1781; repr., Cambridge: Cambridge University Press, 1998), Bxxvi–Bxxvii.

18. Montagu, *Statement on Race*, 56.

19. For Ronald L. Numbers's position, see "Science without God: Natural Laws and Christian Beliefs," in *When Science and Christianity Meet*, ed. David C. Lindberg and Ronald L. Numbers (Chicago: University of Chicago Press, 2003), 265–85.

20. Funk and Alper, "Religion and Science."

BIBLIOGRAPHY

Allen, L. C. "The Negro Health Problem." *American Journal of Public Health* 5, no. 3 (1915): 194–203.

Asad, Talal. *Formations of the Secular: Christianity, Islam, Modernity*. Stanford, CA: Stanford University Press, 2003.

Augstein, Hannah F. "From the Land of the Bible to the Caucasus and Beyond: The Shifting Ideas of the Geographical Origin of Humankind." In *Race, Science, and Medicine, 1700–1960*, edited by Waltraud Ernst and Bernard Harris, 58–79. New York: Routledge, 1999.

Bachman, John. *A Defense of Luther and the Reformation against the Charges of John Bellinger, M.D., and Others to Which Are Appended Various Communications of Other Protestant and Roman Catholic Writers Who Engaged in the Controversy*. Charleston, SC: William H. Paxton, 1853.

———. *The Doctrine of the Unity of the Human Race Examined on the Principles of Science*. Charleston, SC: C. Canning, 1850.

———. "An Examination of Professor Agassiz's Sketch of the Natural Provinces of the Animal World, and Their Relation to the Different Types of Man, with a Tableau Accompanying the Sketch." *Charleston Medical Journal and Review* 10, no. 4 (1855): 482–534.

———. *A Notice of the "Types of Mankind," with an Examination of the Charges Contained in the Biography of Dr. Morton, Published by Nott and Gliddon*. Charleston, SC: James, Williams, and Gitsinger, Steam Power Press, 1854.

Bailey, Richard A. *Race and Redemption in Puritan New England*. Oxford: Oxford University Press, 2011.

Baker, Lee D. *From Savage to Negro: Anthropology and the Construction of Race 1896–1954*. Berkeley: University of California Press, 1998.

Barkan, Elazar. *The Retreat of Scientific Racism: Changing Concepts of Race in Britain and the United States between the World Wars*. New York: Cambridge University Press, 1992.

Barr, James. "Pre-scientific Chronology: The Bible and the Origin of the World." *Proceedings of the American Philosophical Society* 143, no. 3 (1999): 379–87.

Barringer, Paul. *The American Negro: His Past and Future*. Raleigh, NC: Edwards and Broughton, 1900.

Basu, Subhasree, Thibaut Barnoud, Che-Pei Kung, Matthew Reiss, and Maureen E. Murphy. "The African-Specific S47 Polymorphism of p53 Alters Chemosensitivity." *Cell Cycle* 15, no. 19 (2016): 2557–60.

Baum, Bruce. *Rise and Fall of the Caucasian Race: A Political History of Racial Identity.* New York: New York University Press, 2006.

Bay, Mia. *The White Image in the Black Mind: African American Ideas about White People, 1830–1925.* Oxford: Oxford University Press, 2000.

Black, Angela Rose, and Cheryl Woods-Giscombé. "Applying the Stress and 'Strength' Hypothesis to Black Women's Breast Cancer Screening Delays." *Stress and Health: Journal of the International Society for the Investigation of Stress* 28, no. 5 (2012): 389–96.

Blackbourn, David. *History of Germany, 1780–1918: The Long Nineteenth Century.* Malden, MA: Blackwell Publishing, 2003.

Blumenbach, Johann Friedrich. *The Anthropological Treatises of Johann Friedrich Blumenbach.* Translated by Thomas Bendyshe. 1795. Reprint, London: Longman, Green, Longman, Roberts, and Green, 1865.

———. *Contributions to Natural History.* Translated by Thomas Bendyshe. 1790. Reprint, London: Longman, Green, Longman, Roberts, and Green, 1865.

———. *On the Natural Varieties of Mankind.* Translated by Thomas Bendyshe. 1795. Reprint, London: Longman, Green, Longman, Roberts, and Green, 1865.

———. "Uber den Bildungstrieb (Nisus formativus) und seinen Einfluss auf die Generation und Reproduction." *Gottingisches Magazin der Wissenschaften* 2 (1780).

———. *Uber den Bildungstrieb und das Zeugungsgeschaft.* Göttingen: Johann Christian Dieterich, 1781.

Blumenberg, Hans. *The Legitimacy of the Modern Age.* Translated by Robert Wallace. Cambridge, MA: MIT Press, 1981.

Boas, Franz. "Some Recent Criticisms of Physical Anthropology." *American Anthropologist* 1, no. 1 (1898): 98–106.

Bodemer, Charles. "Regeneration and the Decline of Preformationism in 18th-Century Embryology." *Bulletin of the History of Medicine* 38 (1964): 20–31.

Bolnick, Deborah. "Individual Ancestry Inference and the Reification of Race as a Biological Phenomenon." In *Revisiting Race in a Genomic Age*, edited by Barbara Koenig, Sandra Soo-Jin Lee, and Sarah S. Richardson, 70–85. New Brunswick, NJ: Rutgers University Press, 2008.

Bowler, Peter J. *The Eclipse of Darwinism: Anti-Darwinian Evolution Theories in the Decades around 1900.* Baltimore: Johns Hopkins University Press, 1983.

———. *Evolution: The History of an Idea.* Berkeley: University of California Press, 1989.

Boyarin, Jonathan. *The Unconverted Self: Jews, Indians, and the Identity of Christian Europe.* Chicago: University of Chicago Press, 2009.

Bozeman, Theodore D. *Protestants in an Age of Science: The Baconian Ideal and Antebellum American Religious Thought.* Chapel Hill: University of North Carolina Press, 1977.

Brace, C. Loring. *"Race" Is a Four-Letter Word: The Genesis of the Concept.* Oxford: Oxford University Press, 2005.

Brandt, Allan M. *No Magic Bullet: A Social History of Venereal Disease in the United States since 1880.* New York: Oxford University Press, 1987.

Brattain, Michelle. "Race, Racism, and Antiracism: UNESCO and the Politics of Presenting Science to the Postwar Public." *American Historical Review* 122, no. 5 (2007): 1386–1413.

Braude, Benjamin. "The Sons of Noah and the Construction of Ethnic and Geographical Identities in the Medieval and Early Modern Periods." *William and Mary Quarterly*, 3rd ser., 54, no. 1 (1994): 103–42.

Brigham, Charles. *A Study of American Intelligence.* Princeton, NJ: Princeton University Press, 1923.

Broca, Paul. *On the Phenomenon of Hybridity in the Genus* Homo. 1856. Reprint, London: Longman, Green, Longman, and Roberts, 1864.

Brooke, John Hedley. "Religious Belief and the Content of the Sciences." In *Science in Theistic Contexts: Cognitive Dimensions*, Osiris 16, edited by J. H. Brooke, M. J. Osler, and J. M. van der Meer, 3–28. Chicago: University of Chicago Press, 2001.

———. *Science and Religion: Some Historical Perspectives.* Cambridge: Cambridge University Press, 1991.

Brooke, John Hedley, and Geoffrey Cantor. *Reconstructing Nature: The Engagement of Science and Religion.* Edinburgh: T&T Clark, 1998.

Browne, Janet. *Charles Darwin: The Power of Place.* Princeton, NJ: Princeton University Press, 2002.

———. *Charles Darwin: Voyaging.* Princeton, NJ: Princeton University Press, 1996.

———. "Noah's Flood, the Ark, and the Shaping of Early Modern Natural History." In *When Science and Christianity Meet,* edited by David C. Lindberg and Ronald L. Numbers, 111–38. Chicago: University of Chicago Press, 2003.

Brunner, William F. "The Negro Health Problem in Southern Cities." *American Journal of Public Health* 5, no. 3 (1915): 183–90.

Buell, Denise Kimber. "Early Christian Universalism and Racism." In *The Origins of Racism in the West*, edited by Miriam Eliav-Feldon, Benjamin Isaac, and Joseph Ziegler, 109–31. Cambridge: Cambridge University Press, 2009.

———. *Why This New Race: Ethnic Reasoning in Early Christianity.* New York: Columbia University Press, 2005.

Byrd, W. Michael, and Linda Clayton. *The American Dilemma: Race, Medicine, and Health Care in the United States, 1900–2000.* New York: Routledge, 2002.

Carmichael, Emmett B. "Josiah Clark Nott." *Bulletin of the History of Medicine* 22 (1948): 250.

Carter, J. Kameron. *Race: A Theological Account.* Oxford: Oxford University Press, 2008.

Cavalli-Sforza, Luigi Luca. *Genes, Peoples, and Languages.* Berkeley: University of California Press, 2001.

Chakrabarty, Dipesh. *Provincializing Europe: Postcolonial Thought and Historical Difference.* Princeton, NJ: Princeton University Press, 2008.

Chandler, Linda C. "C. V. Roman, Leader Worthy of His Namesake." *Dallas Medical Journal* 80, no. 12 (1994): 499.

Curtis, Moses A. "Unity of the Races." *Southern Quarterly Review* 7 (1845): 372–448.

Darwin, Charles. *The Descent of Man, and Selection in Relation to Sex.* 1871. Reprint, London: Penguin Classics, 2004.

Davenport, Charles. "Effects of Race Intermingling." *Proceedings of the American Philosophical Society* 130 (1917): 364–68.

DeLancey, John Oliver L., Michael J. Thun, Ahmedin Jemal, and Elizabeth M. Ward. "Recent Trends in Black-White Disparities in Cancer Mortality." *Cancer Epidemiology, Biomarkers, and Prevention* 17, no. 11 (2008): 2908–12.

Dorr, M. *Segregation's Science: Eugenics and Society in Virginia.* Charlottesville: University of Virginia Press, 2008.

Douglass, Frederick. "The Claims of the Negro Ethnographically Considered." In *The Frederick Douglass Papers*, ser. 1, 2:506. New Haven, CT: Yale University Press, 1854.

———. "The Future of the Race." *A.M.E. Church Review* 6 (October 1889): 230–31.

El-Haj, N. "The Genetic Reinscription of Race." *Annual Review of Anthropology* 36 (2000): 283–300.

Epstein, Steven. *Inclusion: The Politics of Difference in Medical Research.* Chicago: University of Chicago Press, 2007.

Flourens, M. P. "Memoir of Blumenbach." In *The Anthropological Treatise of Johann Friedrich Blumenbach*, translated by Thomas Bendyshe, 141–47. 1847. Reprint, London: Longman, Green, Longman, Roberts, and Green, 1865.

Foucault, M. "Nietzsche, Genealogy, History." In *The Foucault Reader*, edited by Paul Rabinow, 76–100. New York: Pantheon, 1984.

Frederickson, George. *The Black Image in the White Mind: The Debate on Afro-American Character and Destiny, 1817–1914.* 1971. Reprint, Middletown, CT: Wesleyan University Press, 1987.

Fujimura, Joan. "Crafting Science: Standardized Packages, Boundary Objects and 'Translations.'" In *Science as Practice and Culture*, edited by A. Pickering, 168–214. Chicago: Chicago University Press, 1992.

Fullwiley, Duana. "The Biologistical Construction of Race: 'Admixture' Technology and the New Genetic Medicine." *Social Studies of Science* 38, no. 5 (2008): 695–735.

———. "The Molecularization of Race: U.S. Health Institutions, Pharmacogenetics Practice, and Public Science after the Genome." In *Revisiting Race in a Genomic Age*, edited by Barbara Koenig, Sandra Soo-Jin Lee, and Sarah S. Richardson, 149–71. New Brunswick, NJ: Rutgers University Press, 2008.

Funk, Cary, and Becky A. Alper. "Religion and Science." Pew Research Center, October 22, 2015. http://www.pewinternet.org/2015/10/22/science-and-religion/.

Füssel, Stephan. "The Book of Books." In *The Luther Bible of 1534: A Cultural-Historical Introduction.* Cologne: Taschen, 2002.

Galton, Francis. "Eugenics: Its Definition, Scope, and Aims." *American Journal of Sociology* 10, no. 1 (1904): 1–25.

Gerend, Mary A., and Manacy Pai. "Social Determinants of Black-White Disparities in Breast Cancer Mortality: A Review." *Cancer Epidemiology, Biomarkers, and Prevention* 17, no. 11 (2008): 2913–23.

Gillespie, Michael Allen. *The Theological Origins of Modernity*. Chicago: University of Chicago Press, 2008.

Goetz, Rebecca Anne. *The Baptism of Early Virginia: How Christianity Created Race*. Baltimore: Johns Hopkins University Press, 2012.

Goodman, Alan, and Evelynn Hammonds. "Reconciling Race and Human Adaptability: Carleton Coon and the Persistence of Race in Scientific Discourse." In *Krober Anthropological Society Papers*, edited by Jonathan Marks, 28–44. Berkeley: University of California Press, 2000.

Gossett, Thomas. *Race: The History of an Idea in America*. New York: Oxford University Press, 1963.

Gould, Stephen Jay. *The Mismeasure of Man*. New York: W. W. Norton, 1996.

Grant, Madison. *The Passing of the Great Race, or the Racial Basis of European History*. New York: Charles Scribner's Sons, 1916.

Greely, Henry T. "Genetic Genealogy: Genetics Meets the Marketplace." In *Revisiting Race in a Genomic Age*, edited by Barbara Koenig, Sandra Soo-Jin Lee, and Sarah S. Richardson, 215–23. New Brunswick, NJ: Rutgers University Press, 2008.

Green, Richard, Johannes Krause, Adrian Briggs, Tomislav Maricic, Udo Stenzel, and Martin Kircher. "A Draft Sequence of the Neanderthal Genome." *Science* 328 (May 2010): 710–22.

Greene, John C. *The Death of Adam: Evolution and Its Impact on Western Thought*. Ames: Iowa State University Press, 1959.

Greene, Mott T. "Genesis and Geology Revisited: The Order of Nature and the Nature of Order in Nineteenth-Century Britain." In *When Science and Christianity Meet*, edited by David C. Lindberg and Ronald L. Numbers, 139–60. Chicago: University of Chicago Press, 2003.

Hale, Matthew. *The Primitive Origination of Mankind: Considered and Examined according to the Light of Nature*. London: Printed by W. Godbid, for W. Shrowsbery, 1677.

Hall, Amy Laura. *Conceiving Parenthood: American Protestantism and the Spirit of Reproduction*. Grand Rapids, MI: Eerdmans Publishing, 2008.

Hammonds, Evelynn, and Rebecca Herzig. *The Nature of Difference: Sciences of Race in the United States from Jefferson to Genomics*. Cambridge, MA: MIT Press, 2008.

Hamowy, Ronald. *Government and Public Health in America*. Northampton, MA: Edward Elgar Press, 2007.

Harrison, Peter. *The Territories of Science and Religion*. Chicago: University of Chicago Press, 2015.

Hess, Jonathan M. *Germans, Jews and the Claims of Modernity*. New Haven, CT: Yale University Press, 2002.

———. "Johann David Michaelis and the Colonial Imaginary: Orientalism and the Emergence of Racial Antisemitism in Eighteenth-Century Germany." *Jewish Social Studies* 6, no. 2 (2000): 56–101.

Hirschfeld, Ludwig, and Hannah Hirschfeld. "Serological Differences between the Blood of Different Races." *Lancet* 194, no. 5016 (1919): 675–79.

Hoffmann, Frederick L. *Race Traits and Tendencies of the American Negro.* New York: Macmillan, 1896.

Horsman, Reginald. *Josiah Nott of Mobile: Southerner, Physician, and Racial Theorist.* Baton Rouge: Louisiana State University Press, 1987.

———. *Race and Manifest Destiny: The Origins of American Racial Anglo-Saxonism.* Cambridge, MA: Harvard University Press, 1981.

Hudson, N. Charles. "From 'Nation' to 'Race': The Origin of Racial Classification in Eighteenth-Century Thought." *Eighteenth-Century Studies* 29, no. 3 (1996): 247–64.

Hull, David. *The Metaphysics of Evolution.* Albany: State University of New York Press, 1989.

———. *Science as a Process: An Evolutionary Account of the Social and Conceptual Development of Science.* Chicago: University of Chicago Press, 1993.

Huxley, Thomas. "The Aryan Question." In *Man's Place in Nature and Other Anthropological Essays,* 271–328. New York: D. Appleton, 1896.

———. "On Some Fossil Remains of Man." In *Man's Place in Nature and Other Anthropological Essays,* 157–208. 1863. Reprint, New York: D. Appleton, 1897.

———. *On the Negro Question.* London: Ladies' London Emancipation Society, 1864.

Jackson, John P., Jr., and Nadine Weidman. *Race, Racism and Science: Social Impact and Interaction.* New Brunswick, NJ: Rutgers University Press, 2006.

Jennings, Willie James. *The Christian Imagination: Theology and the Origins of Race.* New Haven, CT: Yale University Press, 2011.

Johnson, Sylvester. *The Myth of Ham in Nineteenth-Century American Christianity: Race, Heathens, and the People of God.* New York: Palgrave Macmillan, 2004.

Kant, Immanuel. *Critique of Pure Reason.* Translated by Paul Guyer and Allen W. Wood. 1781. Reprint, Cambridge: Cambridge University Press, 1998.

Katz, Jacob. *Out of the Ghetto: The Social Background of Jewish Emancipation, 1770–1870.* Cambridge, MA: Harvard University Press, 1973.

Kaufman, Jay S. "Ethical Dilemmas in Statistical Practice: The Problem of Race in Biomedicine." In *Mapping "Race": Critical Approaches to Health Disparities Research,* edited by L. Gomez and N. Lopez, 53–66. New Brunswick, NJ: Rutgers University Press, 2013.

Kevles, David J. *In the Name of Eugenics: Genetics and the Uses of Human Heredity.* Cambridge, MA: Harvard University Press, 1995.

Kidd, Colin. *The Forging of the Races: Race and Scripture in the Protestant Atlantic World, 1600–2000.* Cambridge: Cambridge University Press, 2006.

Kolb, Robert. "The Lutheran Doctrine of Original Sin." In *Adam, the Fall, and Original Sin: Theological, Biblical, and Scientific Perspectives,* edited by Hans Madueme and Michael Reeves, 109–28. Grand Rapids, MI: Baker Press, 2014.

Krieger, Nancy. *Epidemiology and the People's Health: Theory and Context.* Oxford: Oxford University Press, 2011.

———. "The Science and Epidemiology of Racism and Health: Racial/Ethnic Categories, Biological Expressions of Racism, and the Embodiment of Inequality—an Ecosocial Perspective." In *What's the Use of Race? Modern Governance and the Biology of Difference*, edited by I. Whitmarsh and D. Jones, 225–58. Cambridge, MA: MIT Press, 2010.

———. "Theories for Social Epidemiology in the 21st Century: An Ecosocial Perspective." *International Journal of Epidemiology* 30 (2001): 668–77.

Kupperman, Karen Ordahl. "Fear of Hot Climates in the Anglo-American Colonial Experience." *William and Mary Quarterly* 41, no. 2 (1984): 213–40.

Latour, Bruno. *We Have Never Been Modern*. Cambridge, MA: Harvard University Press, 1993.

Lee, Lawrence. "The Negro as a Problem in Public Health Charity." *American Journal of Public Health* 5, no. 3 (1915): 207–11.

Lee, Sandra Soo-Jin, J. Mountain, and Barbara Koenig. "The Meanings of Race in the New Genomics: Implications for Health Disparity Research." *Yale Journal of Health Policy, Law and Ethics* 1 (2001): 33–75.

Legaspi, Michael C. *The Death of Scripture and the Rise of Biblical Studies*. Oxford: Oxford University Press, 2010.

Lindberg, David C. *The Beginnings of Western Science: The European Scientific Tradition in Philosophical, Religious, and Institutional Context, Prehistory to A.D. 1450*. 2nd ed. Chicago: University of Chicago Press, 2007.

Lindberg, David C., and Ronald L. Numbers. "Beyond War and Peace: A Reappraisal of the Encounter between Christianity and Science." *Perspectives on Science and Christian Faith* 39 (1987): 140–49.

Lipphardt, Veronika. "Isolates and Crosses in Human Population Genetics; or, A Contextualization of German Race Science." *Current Anthropology* 53, no. 5 (2012): S69–S82.

Livingstone, David. *Adam's Ancestors: Race, Religion, and the Politics of Human Origins*. Baltimore: Johns Hopkins University Press, 2008.

Livingstone, Frank B. "On the Nonexistence of Human Races." *Current Anthropology* 3, no. 3 (1962): 279–81.

Lombardo, Paul, and Gregory Dorr. "Eugenics, Medical Education, and the Public Health Service: Another Perspective on the Tuskegee Syphilis Experiment." *Bulletin of the History of Medicine* 80, no. 2 (2006): 291–316.

Luther, Martin. *Luther's Works*. Vol. 1, *Lectures on Genesis Ch. 1–5*. Translated by George V. Schick. 1535–45. Reprint, St. Louis, MO: Concordia Publishing House, 1958.

Marks, Jonathan. *Human Biodiversity: Genes, Race, and History*. New Brunswick, NJ: Aldine Transaction, 1995.

———. "Race: Past, Present, Future." In *Revisiting Race in a Genomic Age*, edited by Barbara Koenig, Sandra Soo-Jin Lee, and Sarah S. Richardson, 21–38. New Brunswick, NJ: Rutgers University Press, 2008.

———. *What It Means to Be 98% Chimpanzee: Apes, People, and Their Genes*. Berkeley: University of California Press, 2002.

Martyr, Justin. *Dialogue with Trypho*. In *The Ante-Nicene Fathers*, vol. 1, *The Apostolic Fathers with Justin Martyr and Irenaeus*, edited by A. Roberts, J. Donaldson, and A. C. Coxe. New York: Cosimo Classics, 2007.

Marx, Karl Friedrich Heinrich. "Memoir of J. F. Blumenbach." Translated by Thomas Bendyshe. In *The Anthropological Treatises of Johann Friedrich Blumenbach*, 3–45. London: Longman, Green, Roberts, and Green, 1865.

Masci, David. "Public Opinion on Religion and Science in the United States." Pew Research Center, November 6, 2009. http://pewforum.org/Science-and-Bioethics/ Public-Opinion-on-Religion-and-Science-in-the-United-States.aspx.

Merrens, H. Roy, and George D. Terry. "Dying in Paradise: Malaria, Mortality, and the Perceptual Environment in Colonial South Carolina." *Journal of Southern History* 50, no. 4 (1984): 533–50.

Michaelis, Johann D. *Commentaries on the Laws of Moses*. Translated by A. Smith. London: F. C. and J. Rivington, 1814.

Mitchell, Michele. *Righteous Propagation: African Americans and the Politics of Racial Destiny after Reconstruction*. Chapel Hill: University of North Carolina Press, 2004.

Montagu, Ashley. *Statement on Race: An Extended Discussion in Plain Language of the UNESCO Statement by Experts on Race Problems*. New York: Henry Schuman, 1951.

Moore, James R. "Geologists and Interpreters of Genesis in the Nineteenth Century." In *God and Nature: Historical Essays on the Encounter between Christianity and Science*, edited by David C. Lindberg and Ronald L. Numbers, 322–50. Berkeley: University of California Press, 1986.

Morris, Karen. "The Founding of the National Medical Association." PhD diss., Yale University School of Medicine, 2007.

Morrison, Sheena M., and Elizabeth Fee. "Charles V. Roman: Physician, Writer, Educator." *American Journal of Public Health* 100, supplement 1 (2010): S69.

Morton, Samuel G. *Crania Aegyptiaca; or, Observations on Egyptian Ethnography derived from Anatomy, History and the Monument*. Philadelphia: John Penington, 1844.

———. *Crania Americana; or, A Comparative View of the Skulls of Various Aboriginal Nations of North and South America*. Philadelphia: J. Dobson, 1839.

Mosse, Werner. "From 'Schutzjuden' to 'Deutsche Staatsbürger Jüdischen Glaubens.'" In *Paths of Emancipation: Jews, States, and Citizenship*, edited by P. Birnbaum and I. Katznelson, 59–93. Princeton, NJ: Princeton University Press, 1995.

Murrell, Thomas. W. "Syphilis and the Negro." *Journal of the American Medical Association* 34, no. 11 (1910): 846–49.

Nelson, G. Blair. "'Men before Adam!': American Debates over the Unity and Antiquity of Humanity." In *When Science and Christianity Meet*, edited by David C. Lindberg and Ronald L. Numbers, 111–38. Chicago: University of Chicago Press, 2003.

Nobles, Melissa. *Shades of Citizenship: Race and the Census in Modern Politics*. Stanford, CA: Stanford University Press, 2000.

Nott, Josiah Clark. "Diversity of the Human Races." *De Bow's Review* 10 (February 1851): 113–32.

———. "The Instincts of the Races." *New Orleans Medical and Surgical Journal* 19 (1866): 1–16, 145–56.

———. "The Problem of the Black Races." *De Bow's Review* 1 (March 1866): 266–83.

———. "Statistics of Southern Slave Population." *Commercial Review* 4, no. 3 (1847): 275–87.

———. *Two Lectures on the Connection between the Biblical and Physical History of Man.* New York: Bartlett and Welford, 1849.

———. *Two Lectures on the Natural History of the Caucasian and Negro Races.* Mobile, AL: Dade and Thompson, 1844.

Nott, Josiah Clark, and George Robbins Gliddon. *Types of Mankind.* Philadelphia: Lippincott, Grambo, 1854.

Numbers, Ronald L. "'The Most Important Biblical Discovery of Our Time': William Henry Green and the Demise of Ussher's Chronology." *American Society of Church History* 69, no. 2 (2000): 257–76.

———. "Science without God: Natural Laws and Christian Beliefs." In *When Science and Christianity Meet,* edited by David C. Lindberg and Ronald L. Numbers, 258–86. Chicago: University of Chicago Press, 2003.

O'Brien, Michael. *Intellectual Life in the American South, 1810–1860.* Chapel Hill: University of North Carolina Press, 2010.

Oleson, Alexandra, and John Voss. *The Organization of Knowledge in Modern America, 1860–1920.* Baltimore: Johns Hopkins University Press, 1979.

Ossorio, Pilar, and Duster, Troy. "Race and Genetics: Controversies in Biomedical, Behavioral, and Forensic Sciences." *American Psychologist* 60, no. 1 (2005): 115–28.

Outram, Simon, and George Ellison. "Arguments against the Use of Racialized Categories as Genetic Variables in Biomedical Research: What Are They, and Why Are They Being Ignored?" In *What's The Use of Race? Modern Governance and the Biology of Difference,* edited by I. Whitmarsh and D. Jones, 91–124. Cambridge, MA: MIT Press, 2010.

Paabo, Svante. *Neanderthal Man: In Search of Lost Genomes.* New York: Basic Books, 2014.

Peek, Monica E., Judith V. Sayad, and Ronald Markwardt. "Fear, Fatalism and Breast Cancer Screening in Low-Income African-American Women: The Role of Clinicians and the Health Care System." *Journal of General Internal Medicine* 23, no. 11 (2008): 1847–53.

Pickens, Donald K. *Eugenics and the Progressives.* Nashville, TN: Vanderbilt University Press, 1968.

Pinkard, Terry. *German Philosophy, 1760–1860: The Legacy of Idealism.* Cambridge: Cambridge University Press, 2002.

Po-chia Hsia, Ronnie. "Religion and Race: Protestant and Catholic Discourses on Jewish Conversion in the Sixteenth and Seventeenth Centuries." In *The Origins of Racism in the West,* edited by Miriam Eliav-Feldon, Benjamin Isaac, and Joseph Ziegler, 265–75. Cambridge: Cambridge University Press, 2009.

Prichard, James Cowles. *Researches into the Physical History of Man.* London: Printed for John and Arthur Arch, 1813.

Ray, John. *The Wisdom of God Manifested in the Works of Creation.* 1691. Reprint, London: William Inney and Richard Manby for the Royal Society of London, 1735.

Reardon, Jenny. *Race to the Finish: Identity and Governance in an Age of Genomics.* Princeton, NJ: Princeton University Press, 2005.

———. "Race without Salvation: Beyond the Science/Society Divide in Genomic Studies of Human Diversity." In *Revisiting Race in a Genomic Age*, edited by Barbara Koenig, Sandra Soo-Jin Lee, and Sarah S. Richardson, 304–19. New Brunswick, NJ: Rutgers University Press, 2008.

Reill, Peter H. *Vitalizing Nature in the Enlightenment.* Berkeley: University of California Press, 2005.

Reverby, Susan M. *Examining Tuskegee: The Infamous Syphilis Study and Its Legacy.* Chapel Hill: University of North Carolina Press, 2009.

Richards, Robert J. *The Romantic Conception of Life: Science and Philosophy in the Age of Goethe.* Chicago: University of Chicago Press, 2002.

Ritterbush, Philip C. *Overtures to Biology: The Speculations of Eighteenth-Century Naturalists.* New Haven, CT: Yale University Press, 1964.

Roberts, Dorothy. *Fatal Invention: How Science, Politics, and Big Business Re-create Race in the Twenty-First Century.* New York: New Press, 2012.

Roger, Jacques. "The Mechanistic Conception of Life." In *God and Nature: Historical Essays on the Encounter between Science and Religion*, edited by David C. Lindberg and Ronald L. Numbers, 277–95. Berkeley: University of California Press, 1986.

Roman, Charles V. "A College Education Is a Requisite Preparation for the Study of Medicine." *Journal of the National Medical Negro Association* 9, no. 1 (1917): 6–8.

———. *American Civilization and the Negro: The Afro-American in Relation to National Progress.* Philadelphia: F. A. Davis, 1921.

———. "Constitution and By-Laws of the National Medical Association." *Journal of the National Medical Association* 45, no. 4 (1953): 308–18.

———. "The Deontological Orientation of Its Membership and the Chief Function of a Medical Society." *Journal of the National Medical Association* 1, no. 1 (1909): 19–23.

———. "Fifty Years' Progress of the American Negro in Health and Sanitation: Delivered at Semi-centennial at Howard University." *Journal of the National Medical Association* 9, no. 2 (1917): 61–67.

———. *Meharry Medical College: A History.* Nashville, TN: Sunday School Publishing Board of the National Baptist Convention, 1934.

———. "Syllabus of Lecture to Colored Soldiers at Camps Grant, Stewart, Hill and Humphreys." *Journal of the National Medical Association* 10, no. 3 (1918): 104–8.

Rosen, Christine. *Preaching Eugenics: Religious Leaders and the American Eugenics Movement.* New York: Oxford University Press, 2004.

Rossi, Paolo. *The Dark Abyss of Time: The History of the Earth and the History of Nations from Hooke to Vico.* Translated by L. G. Cochrane. Chicago: University of Chicago Press, 1984.

Rudwick, Martin J. S. "The Shape and Meaning of Earth History." In *God and Nature: Historical Essays on the Encounter between Christianity and Science*, edited by David C. Lindberg and Ronald L. Numbers, 296–321. Berkeley: University of California Press, 1989.

Rürup, Reinhard. "The Tortuous and Thorny Path to Legal Equality: 'Jew Laws' and

Emancipatory Legislation in Germany from the Late Eighteenth Century." *Leo Baeck Institute Yearbook* 31 (1986): 3–33.

Russell, Colin A. "The Conflict of Science and Religion." In *Science and Religion: A Historical Introduction*, edited by G. Ferngren, 3–12. Baltimore: Johns Hopkins University Press, 2002.

Sanlon, Peter. "Original Sin in Patristic Theology." In *Adam, the Fall, and Original Sin: Theological, Biblical, and Scientific Perspectives*, edited by Hans Madueme and Michael Reeves, 85–108. Grand Rapids, MI: Baker Press, 2014.

Schaaffhausen, Hermann. "On the Crania of the Most Ancient Races of Man." Translated by George Busk. *Natural History Review* 1 (April 1861): 155–80.

Schneider, William H. "Blood Transfusions between the Wars." *Journal of the History of Medicine and Allied Sciences* 58, no. 2 (2003): 187–224.

Schrenk, Friedemann, and Stephanie Muller. *The Neanderthals*. New York: Routledge, 2009.

Sheehan, James. *German History*. Oxford: Oxford University Press, 1994.

Sheenan, Jonathan. *The Enlightenment Bible: Translation, Scholarship, Culture*. Princeton, NJ: Princeton University Press, 2005.

Shields, Alexandra, Michael Fortun, Evelynn Hammonds, Patricia King, Caryn Lerman, Rayna Rapp, and Patrick Sullivan. "The Use of Race Variables in Genetics Studies of Complex Traits and the Goal of Reducing Health Disparities: A Transdisciplinary Perspective." *American Psychologist* 60, no. 1 (2005):104–14.

Simmons, Christina. "African Americans and Sexual Victorianism in the Social Hygiene Movement, 1910–40." *Journal of the History of Sexuality* 4, no. 1 (1993): 51–75.

Sinha, Moumita, Emma Larkin, Robert Elston, and Susan Redline. "Self-Reported Race and Genetic Admixture." *New England Journal of Medicine* 354, no. 4 (2006): 421–22.

Smedley, Audrey. *Race in North America: Origin and Evolution of a Worldview*. 2nd ed. Boulder, CO: Westview Press, 1999.

Smith, Charles Hamilton. *The Natural History of the Human Species: Its Typical Forms, Primeval Distribution, Filiations, and Migrations*. Boston: Gould and Lincoln, 1851.

Smith, Jonathan Z. "Religion, Religions, Religious." In *Critical Terms for Religious Studies*, edited by M. C. Taylor, 269–84. Chicago: University of Chicago Press, 1998.

Stanton, William R. *The Leopard's Spots: Scientific Attitudes toward Race in America 1815–1859*. Chicago: University of Chicago Press, 1960.

Stepan, Nancy. *The Idea of Race in Science*. Hamden, CT: Archon Books, 1982.

Stepan, Nancy L., and Sanders Leas Gilman. "Appropriating the Idioms of Science: The Rejection of Scientific Racism." In *The "Racial" Economy of Science: Toward a Democratic Future*, edited by S. Harding, 175–77. Bloomington: Indiana University Press, 1993.

Stocking, George. "The Persistence of Polygenist Thought in Post-Darwinian Anthropology." In *Race, Culture and Evolution: Essays in the History of Anthropology*, by George Stocking, 42–68. 1968. Reprint, Chicago: University of Chicago Press, 1982.

———. "The Turn-of-the-Century Concept of Race." *Modernism/Modernity* 1, no. 1 (1994): 4–16.

Tallbear, Kimberly. "Native-American-DNA.com: In Search of Native American Race and Tribe." In *Revisiting Race in a Genomic Age*, edited by Barbara Koenig, Sandra Soo-Jin

Lee, and Sarah S. Richardson, 235–52. New Brunswick, NJ: Rutgers University Press, 2008.

———. *Native American DNA: Tribal Belonging and the False Promise of Genetic Science*. Minneapolis: University of Minnesota Press, 2013.

Tapper, Melbourne. "An 'Anthropathology' of the 'American Negro': Anthropology, Genetics, and the New Racial Science, 1940–1952." *Society of the Social History of Medicine* 10, no. 2 (1997): 263–89.

Taylor, Charles. *A Secular Age*. Cambridge, MA: Harvard University Press, 2007.

Tomes, Nancy. "The Private Side of Public Health: Sanitary Science, Domestic Hygiene, and Germ Theory." *Bulletin of the History of Medicine* 64, no. 4 (1990): 509–39.

Venter, Craig. "Statement on Decoding of Genome." *New York Times*, June 27, 2000, D8.

Vogt, Karl. *Lectures on Man: His Place in Creation and in the History of the Earth*. Edited by J. Hunt. London: Longman, Green, Longman, and Roberts, 1864.

Voltaire, François-Marie Arouet. "Of the Different Races of Men," from *The Philosophy of History*. In *The Idea of Race*, edited by R. Bernasconi and L. Lott, 5–7. 1766. Reprint, Indianapolis, IN: Hackett Publishing, 2000.

Vora, Neha. "Producing Diasporas and Globalization: Indian Middle Class Migrants in Dubai." *Anthropological Quarterly* 81, no. 2 (2008): 377–406.

Wailoo, Keith. *Drawing Blood: Technology and Disease Identity in Twentieth-Century America*. Baltimore: Johns Hopkins University Press, 1999.

———. *Dying in the City of Blues: Sickle Cell Anemia and the Politics of Race and Health*. Chapel Hill: University of North Carolina Press, 2000.

———. *How Cancer Crossed the Color Line*. New York: Oxford University Press, 2011.

Washington, Harriet A. *Medical Apartheid: The Dark History of Medical Experimentation on Black Americans from Colonial Times to the Present*. New York: Anchor Books, 2006.

Weber, Max. *The Protestant Ethic and the Spirit of Capitalism*. 1905. Reprint, New York: Routledge, 1995.

———. "Science as Vocation." In *From Max Weber: Essays in Sociology*, edited by Hans Gerth and C. Wright Mills, 129–58. 1919. Reprint, New York: Routledge, 2007.

Weiss, Kenneth M., and Brian W. Lambert. "Does History Matter? Do the Facts of Human Variation Package Our Views or Do Our Views Package the Facts?" *Evolutionary Anthropology* 19, no. 3 (2010): 92–97.

Weiss, Kenneth M., and Jeffrey C. Long. "Non-Darwinian Estimation: My Ancestors, My Genes' Ancestors." *Genome Research* 19 (2009): 703–10.

Wells, Spencer. *The Journey of Man: A Genetic Odyssey*. Princeton, NJ: Princeton University Press, 2003.

———. *Journey of Man: The Story of the Human Species*. DVD. Directed by Clive Maltby. Arlington, VA: Public Broadcasting Station, 2005.

Wilson, David B. "The Historiography of Science and Religion." In *Science and Religion: A Historical Introduction*, edited by Gary Ferngren, 13–30. Baltimore: Johns Hopkins University Press.

Yudell, Michael. *Race Unmasked: Biology and Race in the 20th Century*. New York: Columbia University Press, 2014.

INDEX

Rudwick, Martin, 41, 60

savages, 99, 124. *See also* primitive
Scaliger, Joseph Justus, 67
Schaaffhausen, Hermann, 113–14, 126–27
Schutzgeld, 44
science: Christianity and, 15, 82, 122,
    140–41, 143–44, 149n21; race and, 6–11,
    30–31, 42, 93, 117–18, 139, 145, 148n11,
    165n4; religion and, 5–6, 21, 140, 143
*Science as a Process: An Evolutionary
    Account of the Social and Conceptual
    Development of Science* (Hull), 14
secular 11,14, 15, 17, 18, 21, 23–26, 28
secular creationism, 13–14, 17, 20, 86, 114,
    116, 121, 133. *See also* Christianity
sex (hygiene and morality of), 84–85, 91,
    99–100, 103, 107–9
Sheehan, Jonathan, 35, 45
Shem, Ham, and Japeth (Sons of Noah),
    20, 61–62, 67, 73
Singh, Greg Inibia Goobye, 2
single-nucleotide polymorphisms (SNP),
    19–20, 120–21, 132–33
skulls, 29, 63–70, 113, 116, 127–28
slavery, 74–75, 78, 109
social Darwinism, 85, 98, 117
soldiers, 90–91, 99, 108–9. *See also* the
    military
the South, 78–79, 97–99
Southern Quarterly Review, 76
Spingarn, Arthur B., 109
Stanton, William, 157n47, 158n50
"Statement on Race" (UNESCO), 118
"Statement on the Nature of Race
    and Race Difference by Physical
    Anthropologists and Geneticists"
    (UNESCO), 118–19
Stepan, Nancy, 92–93
Stocking, George, 88
supersessionism, 9–11, 48, 81–82. *See also*
    Christianity
Swammerdam, Jan, 25

Tallbear, Kim, 148n11
Taney, Roger B., 74
teleology, 24, 34, 94, 160n103
The Theological Origins of Modernity
    (Gillespie), 13
Thirty Years' War, 43
T-O maps, 61–62, 158n74
Topinard, Paul, 88
Tri-State Medical Association, 97
*Two Lectures on the Natural History of the
    Caucasian and Negro Races* (Nott), 55,
    66, 76, 158n50
2015 Pew Research Study Poll, 140, 144
Types of Mankind, 158n50

Uncle Tom's Cabin (Stowe), 97
Underwood, Joseph, 75
United Nations Educational, Scientific,
    and Cultural Organization
    (UNESCO), 118–19, 141
US Public Health Service (PHS), 83, 85,
    89–91, 93, 97, 102–3, 108–9
Ussher, James, 32, 59–60, 67

Venter, Craig, 120
Vogt, Karl, 88
Voltaire, 40

Wallace, Alfred Russell, 122, 125
Walther, Christoph, 39
Weiss, Kenneth M., 132–34
Wells, Spencer, 1–6, 11, 17, 147n3, 148n11
West, Benjamin, 51
White, Andrew Dixon, 140
whites and whiteness (people), 33, 39–40,
    51, 71, 83–84, 96, 138
Wilson, Woodrow, 89–90
*The Wisdom of God Manifested in the
    Works of Creation* (Ray), 71
Wistar Institute, 136
World War I, 90, 99
World War II, 118
Wright, Sewall, 117

CPSIA information can be obtained
at www.ICGtesting.com
Printed in the USA
LVHW040458081221
705585LV00005B/582

9 781503 610095